THE AERIAL WAR
1939-1945

THE AERIAL WAR

1939-1945

THE ROLE OF AVIATION IN WORLD WAR II

DAVID BAKER

This edition published in 2020 by Arcturus Publishing Limited
26/27 Bickels Yard, 151–153 Bermondsey Street,
London SE1 3HA

AD007934UK

Printed in the UK

CONTENTS

INTRODUCTION

THIS BOOK tells the story of aerial warfare during the 1939–45 conflict – a period in which the belligerent powers built more than 780,000 aircraft and developed new ways of waging war from the air. It saw the origin and evolution of entirely new types of aircraft, including jet and rocket-powered interceptors and means by which countries could be brought down. It is also the story of heroic deeds of survival – on both a personal and a national level – and of the stoicism and determination that empowered ordinary people to do extraordinary things.

From the outset, Hitler's Germany built its military around a blitzkrieg concept, supporting ground forces by massive air power, disregarding the need for a strategic bomber force until it was too late. The British focused, perhaps illogically, on the ability of the bomber to bring an enemy to its knees (which it never did) while using fighters to defend the country during the Battle of Britain. Russia prioritized massive ground forces to roll back the Nazi intruder, while the Americans bequeathed to future strategists the aircraft carrier, which ousted the battleship as the Navy's primary warship.

World War II was unique in that it saw the greatest expansion of conflict in the last 200 years, applying technology unheard of in preceding decades. Such innovation itself was nothing new: in the American Civil War of 1861– 65, the technologies of barbed wire, balloons for aerial reconnaissance and primitive submarines were first used; and the 1914–18 war saw the introduction of aeroplanes to warfare on a limited scale, as well as the first use of powered flight to bomb strategic targets, albeit on an experimental basis. The 1939–45 conflict, however, greatly expanded aerial warfare, introducing the mass bombing of urban and industrial areas, the inauguration of jet fighters, the introduction of the ballistic missile, and the first use of the atomic bomb. During this conflict, approximately 2 million civilians died as a result of bombing. Although this represented less than 4 per cent of the total 55 million killed, the mass bombing of civilians undoubtedly introduced a new chapter in the history of warfare.

Transcending the primitive technologies of earlier conflicts, this period also saw the application of science – through radio, radar and electronic devices – to enhance the war-fighting potential of relatively conventional systems. What began as a war of conquest and ideological confrontation turned quickly into an experimental proving ground for radical new ways of waging war, as well as for globalizing conflict at an unprecedented level.

The story of aerial warfare from 1939–45, then, is a tale of transformational scaling which evolved as it progressed, science and its application in technology forging new and increasingly sophisticated designs and devices. These would underpin the post-war expansion of military capabilities and launch new and increasingly capable weapons systems on the world – weapons of such terrifying magnitude in their use that they would, on several occasions, bring the world close to a third global conflict.

All these factors converge to justify an examination of how this came about – a reminder of the extraordinary expansion of science and engineering in those six turbulent years that framed the world of today. In a quite extraordinary way, the development of aerial warfare defined the future pattern of conflict resolution. By creating weapons of such unimaginable destructiveness, it became possible for nuclear-equipped nations to justify their possession as a means of deterring conflict.

This book is written from an apolitical stance, one in which the morality of aerial warfare is left to the judgement of the reader. It has been the purpose here merely to state the facts – in a loosely chronological order, starting with the formation and development of the Luftwaffe, the Polish Air Force and the RAF and moving on to the respective air forces and actions of France, Russia, the USA and Japan – and to explain how the belligerent powers came to use the aeroplane for their own political and military purposes. It has been written after consultation with pilots, air crews, strategists and war planners over several decades, in the UK, the USA, Germany, Russia and Japan, in the hope that it can throw fresh light on what was, to this date, the greatest clash of arms in modern times.

David Baker

CHAPTER 1
The Start of the Aerial War

At precisely 4.45 am local time on 1 September 1939, the aged German battleship *Schleswig-Holstein* fired its guns on a Polish transit depot near the Free City of Danzig on the Baltic coast – the opening shots of World War II. By this hour, clandestine German forces had already begun moving quietly on to Polish territory. Shortly afterwards, the Luftwaffe began attacking Polish airfields, towns, the capital Warsaw and defending ground units. So began the conflict that would, within days, sink the entire European continent into a war that would engulf the world and cause the deaths of more than 50 million people before it ended just over six years later.

At first, it was not a global war. Russia had just days earlier signed a pact with Nazi Germany pledging support for its offensive and agreeing to advance on Poland from the east less than three weeks into the invasion. To secure this partnership, Germany acquiesced to Soviet claims on the Baltic states of Estonia, Latvia and Lithuania and to Russia's desire to invade Finland, expanding its territorial claim to the border with Sweden. Not until June 1941 would Germany turn against Russia and make it an ally of Great Britain. Then, little more than five months later, on 7 December 1941, Japan joined the fray as it pushed its forces south while simultaneously attacking the US naval base at Pearl Harbor in the Pacific Ocean, bringing the USA into the conflict. From that date on it really was a world at war.

From the beginning, air power was a dominant factor in the outcome of land battles and would eventually be the means used to deploy the ultimate weapon – the atomic bomb. By the end of World War II, more bomb tonnage had been dropped by air than all the munitions detonated in every conflict since medieval times, killing more civilians than had died in every war since records began.

Aviation itself had come of age during World War I. Out of what in 1914 and 1915 began as a limited use of aeroplanes to spot artillery and conduct reconnaissance grew an increasing application during 1916 of one-on-one aerial combat – dogfighting – and, from 1917, the use of large aircraft for strategic bombing. Together, the fighter and the bomber gradually defined the application of aircraft for defensive and offensive requirements, the latter undermining the immunity granted to civilian populations of enemy states by the Hague Convention on the rules of war.

It was the use of Zeppelin and Schütte-Lanz airships in 1915 that opened the door to attacks on civilians. Initially, the Kaiser banned attacks on London except for the financial and business sector in the City, and then only after hours when the employees had left for home. However, this restriction did not last long and the bombing of towns and cities by airships across the UK increased, especially after June 1917, when the airships were joined by multi-engine bombers. It was in that year, too, that the British set up the Independent Force, which was equipped with four-engine Handley Page bombers. These were set the specific task of bombing strategic targets in Germany and on German-occupied marshalling yards and military stores elsewhere. As a result of these actions, the concepts of 'strategic bombing' (the destruction of infrastructure empowering an enemy to continue to fight) and 'tactical bombing' (the use of air power to inhibit an army in the field or during an assault) were first defined.

However, these developments were as nothing compared to the ferocity of the aerial warfare that characterized the 1939–45 conflict. The Germans were the first to closely integrate air power with lightning strikes in what quickly became known as blitzkrieg, a concept of 'lightning war' introduced by the nascent Luftwaffe when it was officially reformed in 1935, two years after Hitler came to power. The purpose of blitzkrieg was to win the war through massive use of land and air power to pulverize defending forces and completely annihilate the enemy as quickly as possible. To this end, air power was focused on providing tactical support, which saw the establishment of short- and medium-range air units, and there was a reduced emphasis on strategic warfare.

Blitzkrieg followed the Prussian concept of *Schwerpunkt* – sudden, massive and total destructive assault – which envisaged a frontal attack punching through defensive lines and battering the enemy into submission without taking prisoners. After spearing through enemy lines, the attacker would split into two encircling loops to trap the enemy either side of the gap, opening access to fresh troops from the rear to pour through and push forwards, pressing hard on the heels of the retreating forces. The initial assault troops would hold the trapped enemy forces in a siege grip (boxed 'killing zones') so that colossal use of air power could destroy everything in those areas.

Air power was key to this blitzkrieg doctrine, pioneered by Gen Heinz Guderian, who both oversaw the development of the tank for rapid armoured warfare and also embraced the use of air power to both support the forward edge of the battle area and destroy the enemy's capacity for defence. The notion of blitzkrieg was also envisaged as a terror weapon in itself, helped in no small part by the sirens attached to the forward undercarriage spats of dive-bombers, which sent chilling screams through the air as the aircraft dived down on their targets. This instilled fear in those under attack and proved to be an effective form of psychological warfare that brought terror and panic to civilians on the ground.

In 1939, the German armed forces were utilized in a war defined by political ideals and by a deep-seated resolve to put Germany back at the top table of international nations, to restore pride in the country and its citizens, and to substantiate a sense of superiority proclaimed by its national leadership. Told that they had been betrayed by the German High Command in 1918, the vast mass of the population believed the distortions of truth and the unachievable promises of the Nazi leadership and followed its political overlords to war in the false belief that wrongs would be righted and that the unjust dictates of the Allied victors could be overturned.

GRAND STRATEGY

The German assault on Poland in September 1939 was part of a larger plan to expand its influence east, eventually absorbing large parts of the Soviet Union and most territories west of the Ural Mountains. The grand scheme envisaged the use of Slavic people as slave labour on farms and settlements occupied and run by Germans, who would be given these lands to depopulate the industrial cities of the Fatherland. Hitler recoiled at the urbanization of Germany and overcrowding in megacities, and set down major government plans for expanding east to achieve *lebensraum* – 'living space' – even defining a limit on the number of people who could inhabit a certain urban area. From the early days of the regime, after Hitler had been appointed chancellor in January 1933, all Nazi planning had focused on that one directive.

Aggrieved by what was considered by the Germans to be an illegal adjustment of national boundaries and land prescribed by the Treaty of Versailles of 28 June

1919, the Nazis planned to take back areas occupied by beneficiaries from the peace talks that had ended World War I. In that regard, they had some legitimacy; the Treaty of Versailles had never been ratified by the US Senate, a fact that technically undermined its authority. Thus, when Allied troops occupied the Rhineland from 1920 to 1930, discontent was fuelled among Germans across the country – something that ultimately brought Hitler additional votes at the democratic elections held between 1928 and 1933.

Nevertheless, the Nazis' strategic plans were self-evident to only a few astute politicians across Europe and in the USA. The moral justification for the heavy reparations imposed upon post-war Germany were legitimized by the universal judgement that Imperial Germany had been responsible for the catastrophe of 1914. Support for the Treaty of Versailles was therefore based on this aspect and not the legal nuances of protocols and codicils. Thus Germany, under Hitler's Nazi Party, was effectively isolated from world opinion – ostracism that only empowered the extremists to undo what they saw as injustice and to right the wrongs inflicted upon their country by their opponents.

The long-term goal of the Nazis was not very different from that of the Republic that took over when the Kaiser abdicated and fled to the Netherlands for safety in 1918. Taking its name from the city in which the post-imperial government was constituted, the Weimar Republic attempted to hold together the fractured country. This was no mean feat, since the 1920s saw a prolonged civil war between the extreme right-wing nationalists – represented by the veteran organization Stahlhelm, Bund der Frontsoldaten ('Steel Helmet, League of Front Soldiers', or SBF for short) – and the Communist ideology initially exported from the Soviet Union in 1919 by Rosa Luxemburg and the Spartacists.

To this central focus on righting 'wrongs' and putting Germany back at the forefront of European politics with a strident nationalist ideology came clandestine re-armament, which began long before Hitler came to power. This is an important part of the story of the air war and has been underestimated in much that has been written about the rise of the Luftwaffe. Far from being a construct of the Nazis after they achieved power in 1933, for more than a decade the re-armament of Germany had been under way, through secret deals with the Italians and, paradoxically, with the Russians.

In this way, the supreme capabilities of the Luftwaffe, which unleashed such military might on Poland in 1939, had been in gestation for at least 17 years – the product of a determination to make Germany ready for any eventuality that might provide it with the chance to raise its stature once again. Following the immediate collapse of order with the end of World War I, Germany thus

Hitler poses for a propaganda shot as his troops move in to Poland, September 1939, shortly to be met by Soviet troops invading from the east. David Baker Archive

began to rebuild the air power that it had used to such effect in that conflict. This was not the case in other countries. As we shall see, in Britain there had been a clamour to disband the Royal Air Force as an unnecessary burden on government expenditure, and it was saved only by the persuasive powers of Winston Churchill and others. In Germany, by contrast, air power was recognized as an essential element in deterrence, defence and offensive action by land forces.

So it was that the desire to retain a capacity for aerial warfare pushed both the Weimar Republic and the Soviet Union into a co-operative agreement that saw the future USSR provide sanctuary for military training elites in specialized warfare. In exchange, Russia received large stocks of machine tools, jigs and manufacturing plants from Germany at a time when such exports were banned. The magnitude of that exchange was still in evidence in the 1980s in several Russian machine factories, where there remained noted aged machine tools and die presses bearing the name Krupp – the German armaments giant – which had been delivered to Russia in the 1920s and early 1930s.

The civil unrest in Germany helped to veil these export and exchange movements and in return the Germans sent land and air warfare specialists to the Soviet Union to develop their crafts and to train for what many Germans quietly believed would be the just restitution of their national place in the world.

Successive German governments either turned a blind eye to these activities, which were in flagrant contravention of the Treaty of Versailles, or tacitly condoned this activity. In Russia, Tomsk became the centre for tank and gas warfare and Lipetsk was the home for training the next generation of German combat pilots.

COVERT PREPARATIONS

Situated less than 240 miles south of Moscow, Lipetsk was an ideal location for the covert training of German pilots. The agreement to use it for this purpose was signed on 15 April 1923. For the Soviets, it was an opportunity to gain experience from the Germans; for the Germans, it was an opportunity to preserve the skills of the pilots, observers and gunners who had made such a major contribution to World War I. Over time, the inventory would grow to include several dozen aircraft, mostly trainers but some fighters and light bombers, with a growing emphasis on weapons – both their development and integration into airborne capabilities.

Prohibited from operating an offensive air force, the much-reduced German Army, the Reichswehr, was also prevented from supporting the development of offensive aircraft. Those conditions were relaxed in 1922 when the country was allowed to produce civilian aircraft – transport planes, airliners and training aircraft for commercial pilots. Thus began a culture of designing aircraft that could be readily converted for military purposes and for sending pilots to Russia for training. Moreover, Russia negotiated exports of these 'civilian' types of aircraft and set up factories to produce them in the USSR.

In several respects, Germany shared with Russia a sense of alienation from the rest of the world. Germany was an outcast that was blamed for the recent conflict, and Russia was in turmoil following the overthrow of the Tsar in favour of Bolshevism. As a result, both countries were penalized: Germany was denied advanced military projects and Russia was politically isolated and excluded from global markets.

But there was more to the relationship than that. The German plane maker Junkers began producing aircraft in Russia as early as 1922 from a factory at Fili, western Moscow, and, later in the decade, Heinkel exported many types of aircraft from its production plant at Warnemünde, north-east Germany, sending them to Sevastopol and elsewhere in the USSR. All of this would later provide Germany with a strong start in the more open and formal development of the Luftwaffe under Hitler, and it also provided a base from which the manufacturers would go on to develop a new generation of combat aircraft.

When Italy embraced Fascism under Benito Mussolini from 1924, pilots trained to fly for German airline Luft-Hansa were sent to Italy for conversion to fighters before being returned to Germany to resume their jobs as airline pilots. It should be noted, however, that this practice only really accelerated in the period after Hitler came to power in 1933 and before the Luftwaffe was officially formed two years later. Prominent among the group of pilots who underwent this training was Adolf Galland, who eventually went on to become General der Jagdflieger ('General of Fighter Pilots') during the war.

At Lipetsk, as restrictions on German aviation, industry and even on military capability was relaxed, the Weimar government began to retire its interest in funding the facility. By the time Hitler came to power, the training centre was devoid of Germans. However, lessons had been learned, which, when combined with progress in aircraft design and engineering at home, gave Germany a capability at least as technically advanced as that of other European countries and Britain.

Just as training and exchange with Russia benefited the sustained availability of personnel and training methods, so manufacturers gained an advantage from dispersal, away from the restrictions on what was allowed within Germany itself. This was crucial, since many of the old aircraft builders of the 1914–18 war had disappeared or been resurrected under different names. Gone were Albatros, Aviatik, Gotha, LFG Roland, LVG and Siemens-Schuckert. In their place came Junkers (formed in 1915), with plants in Sweden, Russia, Turkey and Denmark; Dornier, with facilities in Switzerland, Italy, Japan and Holland; and Heinkel, with a plant in Travemünde, northern Germany, fulfilling orders from the USA, Sweden and Japan.

Other manufacturers emerged from the design teams and owners of companies that were rendered defunct by the end of hostilities in 1918. Notable among them was arguably the most famous of all German aero-manufacturers, Bayerische Flugzeugwerke (BFW). This company was formed in Augsburg in 1926 and a year later employed Willy Messerschmitt, the designer who gave his name to a range of fighter aircraft that would form the mainstay of the Luftwaffe throughout World War II.

Brilliant in their own fields of aircraft design and engineering, these German aero-manufacturers, like their foreign counterparts (such as Avro, Bristol, Handley Page, Hawker and Supermarine in the UK, and Boeing, Curtiss, Consolidated and North American in the USA) each pursued specialized applications. Junkers and Heinkel, for example, concentrated on medium and large transport aircraft that could be readily adapted as bombers, whereas Dornier developed light and medium bombers and Messerschmitt built training aircraft and used their skill in that sector to develop powerful fighters shortly after Hitler came to power. However, no amount of money injected into development and production could compensate for a lack of infrastructure because essential resources were vital for production and delivery. That became a top priority for the Nazi government when it came to effective power on 5 March 1933 after Hitler persuaded President Hindenburg to dissolve parliament, a decision from which all subsequent events flowed. Providing industry with the wherewithal to re-arm Germany came after the stabilization of the economy and this became a pre-condition from that date.

In preceding years, the German economy had failed its population, brought to destitution by a succession of economic crises. Industrial production was about half that of the pre-crisis 1928 level and unemployment reached six million, with one in three people of working age out of a job. By 1937, however, that number of workers had been reintegrated into manufacturing and production as industrial output rose. By contrast, unemployment in Britain in 1937 was 10 per cent (70 per cent in some areas of the north-east) and in the USA almost 20 per cent. The Nazis poured more than five billion Reichsmarks into job creation, although military projects remained secondary to civilian ones until the end of 1934, largely because the Reichswehr could not see a quick way of obtaining the same return to the economy compared to investment in non-military projects.

From 1935, re-armament became a top priority but here too Hitler insisted that expenditure should extend to employment and not just to machines for war. After all, it had been the jobs programme of the preceding two years that had stimulated the economy and grown the coffers to pay for new weapons programmes. By 1935, industrial production had gone back to 1928 levels and a shortage of skilled labour was one of the limiting factors in expanding the armed forces, not money or material resources. Indeed, the share of spending on armaments grew disproportionately, increasing from 4 per cent of domestic spending in 1933 to 18 per cent in 1934 and 39 per cent in 1936. By 1938 it would be in excess of 50 per cent.

However, this shift towards deficit spending had an effect on long-term national policy, as the country began to outspend its ability for self-sustained growth. The civil service had already been indoctrinated in new ways of econometrics (employees were given three-month 'retraining' courses in special schools) and the government moved towards planning for territorial expansion so as to acquire the resources of foreign lands. From 1937, the effort to re-arm Germany became not only another jobs programme but also a factor that was vital to the long-term objective of Hitler's Third Reich.

You may ask, how is all of this relevant to the massive use of air power from 1939? For decades, economists and military historians have attempted to explain how Germany was able to rise to such heights of expenditure and relatively full employment in so short a period of time – a topic that has fuelled some controversy. In brief, the short-termism of Nazi monetary policy paid for the outstanding growth in land, sea and air power, at the price of a potentially bankrupt economy. Had Germany not gone to war when it did the economy would have collapsed by 1942. This was anticipated and it is why there was renewed urgency from 1937 to develop unassailable capabilities for land, sea and air warfare and the acquisition of resources by force from elsewhere.

BUILDING AN AIR FORCE

Under the Nazi government, development of the German aviation industry grew significantly, the number of employees in aircraft manufacturing increasing from fewer than 4,200 in 1933 to almost 54,000 in 1935, of whom 70 per cent were building aircraft, the rest making engines. It was a force that started from very low levels. A 1928 plan anticipated 15 Staffeln – the German equivalent of a squadron – with a total of 102 aircraft. When Hermann Göring formally announced the official existence of the new Luftwaffe on 1 March 1935, Germany had 34 Staffeln, of which 13 were equipped with bombers and four with fighters. Universal military service was introduced on 16 March and by 1 October 1936 there were 89 training facilities and flying schools across the country.

German youth was ready for the call to arms. Since the end of the war in 1918, young men had been drawn to a variety of energetic pursuits. In a country where outdoor activities such as hiking, gymnastics and team games became a key part of boys' clubs and youth organizations, a significant number had taken up gliding as the only unconstrained 'flying' activity allowed by the Treaty of Versailles. Unusually among all the belligerent powers of the 1914–18 war, Germany had raised its airmen to heroic status, the individual German states awarding their own medals. Each pilot would invariably adorn his aircraft with artistic embellishments – painting highly colourful geometric shapes as well as characters from Grimm's fairy tales along the fuselage, for example.

Brought up on tales of derring-do, many fighter pilots of the new Luftwaffe took as role models their flamboyant predecessors from the previous war. A great sense of national pride imbued the new generation, who were treated very well. For instance, the fighter aces of the first war equipped the new air force with high-quality accommodation, splendid architectural structures at headquarters in Berlin, and all the dazzle of a new heraldry with tailored uniforms and colourful embellishments on unit badges. While a few newcomers were politicized, attracted to the grand parades and ceremony of flag-waving Nazi rallies, the majority of Luftwaffe personnel were apolitical by nature and bestowed their pride on nation rather than an extreme ideology.

LEADERSHIP OF THE LUFTWAFFE

Hitler signed the order authorizing the official inauguration of the Reich Luftwaffe on 26 February 1935, with Herman Göring as General der Luftwaffe and ultimately responsible for its organization, equipment and operation. Born in 1893, Hermann Göring had himself been an air ace in World War I, with 20 victories to his credit (although three are contested).

The air group (Jagdgeschwader 1) and its four Jagdstaffel (fighter squadrons) Göring inherited had previously been organized and commanded by Manfred von Richthofen – the famous 'Red Baron', who was killed in April 1918 after becoming the highest-scoring pilot of that war with 80 verified victories. Also key to the establishment of the Luftwaffe and implicit in many of the decisions regarding equipment was another World War I ace, Ernest Udet, born in 1896. Udet had achieved the second-highest victory log of 62 kills, and during the interwar period had made a name for himself as a pilot, performing public displays, aerobatics at air shows and operating as a stunt pilot for many films. Later, he was blamed by Göring for the failure of the Luftwaffe in the Battle of Britain in 1940 and a year later he shot himself.

Yet another former World War I aviator, Erhard Milch (born in 1896), played an important role in the leadership of the Luftwaffe, becoming State Secretary of the Ministry of Aviation or Reichsluftfahrtministerium (RLM) in 1933 and orchestrating the establishment of the Luftwaffe.

Thus, under Göring, Udet made equipment decisions and Milch was in charge of aircraft production. In this position of power, Milch used politics to settle old scores with manufacturers and meddle in the selection of certain designers, notably being opposed to Willy Messerschmitt until he himself was outmanoeuvred. Tried as a war criminal in 1947 and sentenced to life imprisonment, Milch was released in 1954 and died at home in 1970.

To satisfy requirements for flying units, a number of *Lieferpläne* ('delivery schedules') directives anticipated a timetable of delivery for airframes and engines based on costing and the availability of support resources such as personnel, flying crew, airfields, armaments and machinery for maintenance and supply. These were continuously adjusted to take account of the production capacity of the factories. To support expansion, the government poured money into branch factories, sometimes with the opposition of the parent company, which feared a loss of independence. The government imperative overrode these concerns since the selection and production of appropriate aircraft designs was crucial to the requirements of the Wehrmacht – the combined land, sea and air forces.

The Luftwaffe was managed by the RLM, which made choices about the type and quantity of aircraft it ordered into production. As such, it had a close relationship with industry and decided the procurement strategy for different types of aircraft. Because the Nazi concept of blitzkrieg envisaged lightning strikes without protracted or entrenched warfare, there was little emphasis on transport aircraft to supply troops engaged on extended conflict.

Such was the case with the type of bombers required. Specific emphasis was placed on dive-bombing to pulverize enemy territory ahead of fast-moving ground troops, a role conducted by planes such as the Junkers Ju-87 Stuka. There was some opposition to this obsession with blitzkrieg. For example, Gen Walther Wever propounded the benefits of a long-range strategic bomber before his death in an air crash in 1936. Thereafter, advocates of smaller, shorter-range bombers led by former World War I air ace Ernst Udet, prevailed, partly on the basis of the quantity of resources required to build a very large aircraft versus those for lighter aircraft – hardly the premise on which to design an effective air fleet. Nevertheless, the design competition that began before Gen Wever's death did produce the sole long-range strategic bomber employed by the Luftwaffe later in the war: the Heinkel He-177.

Overall, there was a preoccupation with fighters, to protect the bombers and to suppress enemy attacks, with light and medium bombers to support ground operations. Insofar as tactics were debated, there was overwhelming influence from the senior leadership of the new Luftwaffe – men who were planning the next war as though they were fighting the previous conflict. Many of the younger pilots and certainly the intake of recruits shortly before World War II began were schooled in new and very different methods of aerial warfare and this would conflict with the edicts of senior leaders. We will see later how that played into the defeat of the Luftwaffe in 1940 during the Battle of Britain. However, there were exceptions and some, such as the World War I pilot Theo Osterkamp, strongly supported new ideas about air combat.

Coincidentally, this was a time of great technical change. For the rapidly evolving Luftwaffe, a new range of capabilities – from advances in aircraft engineering to technology applications – became available. These were developments that would influence aircraft design in other countries and serve as a stimulus to new and innovative possibilities. In particular, the 1930s saw the switch from biplanes made of wood, metal and canvas to stressed-skin, all-metal monoplane construction with closed cockpits and retractable undercarriages replacing open cockpits and fixed landing gear. New and increasingly complex hydraulic, pneumatic and electrical systems were also introduced, and engine power increased greatly.

At the end of World War I, power output for rotary, radial and in-line engines was typically 150–400 hp, with aircraft capable of maximum speeds of 150–200 mph. Within 15 years, engines of 750–1,000 hp were being developed and the new generation of monoplane fighters could achieve speeds of more than 350 mph. However, new concepts and advanced engineering design brought delays as flaws were ironed out and continuous development led to rapid redundancy. As a case in point, the soon-to-be-famous Messerschmitt Bf-109 – an exemplar of the new generation – made its first flight in 1935 but had to fly with a British Rolls-Royce Kestrel engine because the designated Junkers Jumo 210 engine was not ready. The type reached operational units in 1936 with its Jumo engine in situ, but that was soon changed to a Daimler Benz DB 605 with fuel injection and a power output of 1,450 hp.

GERMAN PLANE MARKINGS

The German national insignia was the Balkenkreuz, a straight-sided cross that was presented in various forms on different aircraft, with either solid bars or an open interior. The national political symbol of the Nazi Party, the Hakenkreuz, or swastika, was carried only on the vertical tail surfaces. In addition, each aircraft bore unit markings to identify its consignment and would also bear the flash markings of its commander.

Camouflage schemes varied widely and reflected the different temperate or tropical operating environments and the principal time of dark or light that the type was assigned to for day or night duties.

The new generation of German combat and support aircraft was to receive an evaluation during the Spanish Civil War when Luftwaffe units were deployed under the legendary Condor Legion. For this conflict, German national and unit markings on planes were replaced with a white cross formed of diagonal bars on a black field. The Nationalists under Gen Franco requested help from Fascist Italy and Nazi Germany shortly after the military coup of 17 July 1936. In plain sight, the ostensibly covert contribution made by these countries introduced the world to the new horror of mechanized air power. It brought international condemnation when carpet-bombing of Guernica by German Heinkel He-111 bombers and adapted Junkers Ju-52 transport aircraft on 26 April killed several hundred civilians, including women and children.

Many Luftwaffe airmen were appalled by the wanton destruction at Guernica and the carnage inflicted on innocent civilians. As Oberleutnant Harro Harder recalled:

'Today we flew to Guernica. It has been totally destroyed, and not by the Reds, as all the local newspapers report, but by German and Italian bombers. It is the opinion of all of us that it was a rotten trick to destroy such a militarily unimportant city... There are certainly thousands more dead beneath the rubble, unnecessary victims. Everywhere is smoking, rubble, bomb craters and empty facades.'

Air-to-air combat, including bombing, had a more nuanced detachment from the ugliness of the ground war; aerial successors to knights from a bygone heraldic age, fighter pilots engaged each other as willing volunteers sent into the fray and were distanced from the grim horrors of bloody hand-to-hand combat. These young men conducted their aerial jousts with deep respect for each other as fellow combatants, sharing exposure to the harshness of modern combat but bearing on their shoulders the mantle of a timeless code. It would be one of the fascinating products of aerial warfare that they were spared the guilt of genocide while bringing death and destruction to countless civilians. After the war, former antagonists expressed common cause and deep respect for their opponents – sentiments that were harder to find among ground troops.

For the Germans, participation in the Spanish Civil War provided little in the way of development of tactics and appropriate strategies for these new and more capable aircraft when it came to engaging opponents. It did, however, bring universal revulsion at the indiscriminate use of force and the consequences of aerial warfare in the 'modern' era. When the events of Guernica were reported in newspapers around the world, this event more than any other served as a recruiting poster for volunteers to fight on the side of the Republicans. These political opponents of Franco were openly supported by aircraft from the Soviet Union, which were relatively ineffective compared to the latest German equipment. Going up against German planes did, however, serve to give Joseph Stalin a measure of German capabilities.

On the German side, the events in Spain may not have added much of value to the development of operational tactics, but they did spur the development of the Bf-109 into a fully fledged fighting machine, which was subsequently used against the Polish Air Force in 1939. This, and the experience of real war gained by the new generation of German fighter pilots, provided an advantage for the Luftwaffe over the other air fleets they would face in the coming months.

Among the German airmen, a handful of pilots began to accrue victories over their Republican and Russian opponents. Johannes Trautloft, for instance, gained five air victories and exploited to the full the potential of the Bf-109. He recalled:

'At last the 109 is ready. However there is no instructor or expert to check me out... The take-off certainly is unusual, but as soon as I am in the air I feel at home in the new bird. Its flight characteristics are fantastic. When I am airborne I find an Italian Fiat fighter above the airfield. So far the Fiat has been reckoned to be the fastest of all Franco's fighters, but I get behind it and [have] overtaken it in a moment, leaving it far behind.'

Other pilots, too, would begin their meteoric rise to fame on the back of achievements in Spain. These included Werner Mölders, who claimed 15 victories, and Adolph Galland, who acquired valuable information on tactics and the requirements of a mobile fighter unit, which he would campaign for back in Berlin before the attack on Poland. What's more, participation in the Spanish Civil War provided the young pilots with practical examples of how *not* to conduct aerial warfare.

So it was that when Germany attacked Poland on 1 September it had a well-equipped air force comprising skilled pilots, and trained technicians and ground crew, together with unique experience in how to operate modern combat aircraft in a combat situation.

CHAPTER 2
Blitzkrieg Unleashed

AS A country, Poland had ceased to exist in 1793 when the territory that had previously been under the Polish-Lithuanian state had been absorbed by the Austro-Hungarian Empire. Nevertheless, its people had a proud legacy and held firm to the belief that they would once again be a recognized country. Meanwhile, various areas of Polish land were under the control of Germany, Austria-Hungary and Russia. When World War I broke out, as an inducement to loyalty to the Triple Alliance, both Germany and Austria pledged to resurrect the defunct country as an independent state. This happened in 1916, although the land was fought over by both Germany and Russia, and the Treaty of Versailles reinstated the country as an independent state.

During this readjustment of territories after World War I, Poland acquired significant areas of former German land, including a region that had previously been under Prussian rule. After the Treaty of Versailles, East Prussia was cut off by a sliver of land gifted to Poland and known as the Polish Corridor, isolating the Free City of Danzig. This land allowed Poland to have a port on the Baltic but separated Danzig from Germany, despite Germans forming the majority of its population. The Germans demanded that Danzig be incorporated back into the Reich and that direct land access be afforded to East Prussia, which the Poles refused to accept. In a series of staged provocations, Hitler orchestrated a charade in which it attacked Poland on the pretext of defending the interests of the majority in Danzig.

In reality, Hitler had pledged to erase Poland as an independent state, remove all forms of national identity and divide its land between Germany and Russia, agreement with the latter being a temporary expedient to remove any sense of threat and to minimize the risk of the USSR attacking Germany. Under *Fall Weiss* ('Case White'), Hitler took a drastic gamble and deployed 60 divisions – the bulk of the German Army – to the Polish frontier, leaving the borders with France and the Low Countries relatively unprotected.

PREPARING FOR ATTACK

Despite having left it late to make preparations, Poland was prepared for the attack, mobilizing 30 divisions as well as its military air arm (Lotnictwo Wojskowe). The latter included a Fighter Brigade and a Bomber Brigade under the command of the General Staff and the Army Air Force, which consisted of individual wings and squadrons assigned to seven separate Polish Army commands. The Fighter Brigade boasted 53 aircraft in five squadrons, which were assigned to protect Warsaw from attack. The Bomber Brigade had 36 medium and light bombers.

In all, Poland was able to muster 404 frontline aircraft, of which only 308 had any operational value. About 128 fighters were less than five years old and were sturdy, reliable and possessed good handling qualities, but the overriding concern was their limited performance compared to that of the German air units, and the lack of experience and general preparedness of the crew. Together with 114 reconnaissance and light bomber types, hardly capable of adequate performance, the equipment was well below the level required to match the Luftwaffe.

The Polish aviation industry that had emerged after World War I had been slow to produce results, although Polish designs were technically capable of meeting the requirements of an industry that was unable to obtain sufficient resources. Nevertheless, the industry was energetic and prolific, producing a total of 4,100 aircraft between 1918 and 1939. Unfortunately for domestic needs, however, a large number of these were sold to foreign users, leaving the military with lower numbers than desired. Worse, by the late 1930s, the aviation industry employed fewer than 13,000 people.

On the German side, the Luftwaffe order of battle comprised Luftflotten (air fleets) 1 and 4. In all, there were 1,538 combat aircraft, including 339 Bf-109 fighters, 82 Bf-110 twin-engine fighters and 258 Ju-87 Stuka dive-bombers. The rest was made up of Heinkel He-111 and Dornier Do-17 bombers and a single Staffel (squadron) of Henschel Hs-123 ground attack aircraft. Backing these up were 102 additional Bf-109s, previously assigned to home defence, with 202 aircraft assigned to army units in ground support roles. In all, there were 1,942 aircraft with more than 100 replenishments brought in before the campaign was over.

ORGANIZATION OF THE GERMAN AIR FORCE

The Luftwaffe went through several structural changes in terms of how the various units were organized in the run-up to the outbreak of war in 1939. Its eventual form in 1939 was four Luftflotten (air fleets): No. 1 in north-east Germany; No. 2 in north-west Germany; No. 3 in south-west Germany; No. 4 in south-east Germany and Austria. More were added later in the war: No. 5 (Norway, Finland and northern Russia) from 1940; No. 6 (central Russia) in 1943; Luftflotte Reich (home air defence) from 1944; No. 10 (replacement and training) in 1944.

At the core of this organization were the Staffeln (squadrons), each of which contained up to 12 aircraft identified by Arabic numerals (1, 2, 3, 4, etc). Gruppen (groups) were initially made up of three Staffeln and a total of 30–40 aircraft, identified with Roman numerals (I, II, III, etc). Gruppen were organized into Geschwader (wings) carrying Arabic numerals but prefixed by a word indicating fighter (Jagd), bomber (Kampf), transport (Transport), or night fighter (Nacht), etc. Thus, a fighter Geschwader was called Jagdgeschwader and would be identified with the abbreviated prefix JG, and a bomber unit was a Kampfgeschwader, abbreviated to KG.

The organizational structure and complement of each grouping would grow as the war progressed. While the Gruppe remained the single most basic and autonomous unit in the Luftwaffe, as events unfolded individual Staffeln would be sequestered or could be assigned to other Gruppen on a different war front.

WARSAW UNDER ATTACK

The first air-to-air engagement occurred just after 7.00 am local time on 1 September 1939, when three Stukas encountered three Polish fighters taking off from the secret airfield at Balice near Kraków. Captain (Capt) Medwecki, commanding the Kraków Army Fighter Wing, became the first aerial victim of the attack on Poland. The other two Polish fighters climbed to attack two Do-17 bombers returning from a bombing raid on Kraków, and one scored several hits before losing contact and returning to his airfield, not knowing that the two bombers had collided and crashed near the village of Żurada.

Elsewhere, despite bad weather hampering operations and keeping some German fighters on the ground for a time, Warsaw was the main focus of attack. Heinkels duly bombed the capital city before they turned to Polish airfields, factories and rail junctions. Some Stukas attacked pillboxes and cleared roads for ground troops, while other planes turned to strafing civilians to clear the routes for German tanks.

In all, on this first day, some 30 operational Gruppen operations were completed as the focus of air attack concentrated on Warsaw. Well-organized observation networks provided the Poles with advance warning as fleets of bombers made for the capital, which meant that they could be intercepted by the full force of 52 defending fighter aircraft. This proved effective. Six Heinkels were shot down at the expense of one Polish fighter, the stoic determination of the pilots coming as a surprise to the Germans, who turned away from the target to escape retribution. Also during this engagement, Second Lieutenant (2nd Lt) Borowski shot down a stray Bf-109, the first of this type lost during the attack on Poland.

On the afternoon of the first day, heavy fighting focused around the second air raid on Warsaw when Bf-110 and Bf-109 fighters escorted Heinkel bombers and came under attack from the Fighter Brigade, which was able to get to the bombers before they reached their targets. Four Polish fighters were shot down in the skirmish, the first Luftwaffe strikes of the war.

The primary fighter operated by the Polish Air Force was the PZL P.11c, a high-wing monoplane with a fixed undercarriage and open cockpit designed in the early 1930s that had two or four machine guns. With a maximum speed of 240 mph, it was no match for the sleek new Bf-109, although this performance deficiency was to some extent compensated for by the fighting resolve of the Polish pilots. Seemingly fearless and with an intensity that frequently overwhelmed the confident Luftwaffe fighter pilots, these men showed an unexpected determination to resist the aggressor. Less than a year later, this mettle was once more tested, the Polish pilots going on to play a key role during the Battle of Britain over the countryside of south-east England.

On the ground in Warsaw, though, civilians were enduring the horrors of aerial bombardment that had already been experienced by the citizens of Guernica. In the Polish capital, the ferocity of the aerial assault was backed up by an intense ground campaign developed by Gen Franz Halder and directed by Gen Walther von Brauchitsch. The main assault was commanded by Colonel-General (Col-Gen) Gerd von Rundstedt, with a second incursion led by Col-Gen Fedor von

Bock and supported by a tertiary attack from Slovak units of Army Group South's Allied land forces. The plan was that all three were to converge on Warsaw and take the capital. But that took some time.

Over the next few days, the Luftwaffe changed tactics and used small concentrations of fast aircraft to criss-cross the front from several directions. This worked to an extent, although Polish fighters managed to shoot down 47 enemy aircraft by 6 September. What's more, while Polish communication lines were disrupted or destroyed by Luftwaffe aircraft, the rapid movement of German ground units under this first demonstration of blitzkrieg made it difficult to distinguish friend from foe – a lesson that would be carried forward to the following spring in western Europe.

Action by the Poles in defence of their country was also compromised by the declaration of war against Germany made by the British government on 3 September, two days after Germany had launched its unannounced attack. Britain's involvement was inevitable given that it had signed an agreement on 31 March 1939 pledging to 'lend the Polish government all support in their power' should Germany attack, but actually providing that 'support' would prove troublesome. The geographic location of Poland prohibited military support on land, and from the air required Britain to attack Germany in the west. This was fine in principle – Germany was only 30 minutes' flying time away from RAF bases in England – and there were some discussions at the Air Ministry in London about bombing targets in north-east Germany, west of the industrial Ruhr. However, although these raids did take place, they didn't make sufficient impression to influence German actions in the east.

Concern at Germany's response to what was now a declaration of war from Britain and France led to requests that Poland desist bombing German territory, even in defence. Instead, the Polish bombers were turned against the invading troops, but to little effect. The progress of some tanks near Radomsko, central Poland, was stunted by the Polish raids, but the aircraft fell foul of the roaming Bf-109s and were quickly dispatched. By 17 September, only 17 out of 86 bombers remained on the inventory of Polish Bomber Brigade. Then, six days later, 420 German aircraft attacked Warsaw and dropped 650 tonnes of high explosive and incendiary bombs in three raids.

The Russians began their own invasion of eastern Poland on 17 September, sending massive forces on a wide front, supported by aviation units that were still being re-formed following the major purges of the late 1930s. Widely regarded as having decimated the Soviet military potential, these purges had also removed an entire generation of seasoned military leaders, many of whom had helped the Communist cause and fought defiantly to resist foreign interventions intent on reversing the revolution. Numerically, Russia had a total strength of 3,300 combat aircraft available for the invasion of eastern Poland but lacked quality in their technical capabilities and an absence of experience among the air crew. This would change; by the time Hitler attacked Russia in June 1941, the situation had improved somewhat.

Warsaw surrendered to German forces on 27 September 1939 and to Russian forces on 7 October. Losses to all sides had been heavy, particularly to the Germans and the Poles. Poland had lost 333 aircraft, of which 260 were as a result of enemy action, with 100 of those on combat operations and the balance damaged beyond repair. As a measure of the bravery of the air crew who threw themselves into the fray, only 25 aircraft were destroyed on the ground, the rest repeatedly taking to the air under almost impossible circumstances. What's more, in addition to these losses, a great many training aircraft and civilian planes were also destroyed.

Of the 2,000 or so aircraft used against Poland, the Luftwaffe lost around 258 planes – 230 of which were destroyed in action by the Polish Air Force or through ground fire. A further 263 were damaged, of which only 100 or so could be repaired and returned to service. The Luftwaffe also lost some 400 air crew and a further 120 were wounded. On the ground, 217 German tanks were destroyed and 457 were damaged beyond repair, the majority taken out by Polish Bomber Brigade. The Poles had acquitted themselves well.

Resolved to avenge the destruction of their country, Polish airmen fled to neighbouring states, eventually finding their way to France and then to England, where they made a disproportionately successful contribution in the Royal Air Force. Their story is told in the next chapter.

Poland itself was subsequently fought over by Germany and Russia until the beginning of 1945. It was occupied first by both Germany and the Soviet Union, then by Nazi forces in 1941, and then by Soviet forces in 1944. It remained under the Soviet sphere of influence for the next 45 years. The Polish people suffered terribly under these regimes during a conflict that saw several million people killed on Polish territory in death camps.

CHAPTER 3
The Island of Last Hope

WHILE HISTORY records that Britain went to war with Germany over Hitler's invasion of Poland because it had a pact with that country, in reality the situation was more nuanced and could have taken a very different turn. Deeply concerned at the military build-up in Germany, in August 1939 Soviet premier Joseph Stalin approved an offer to Britain and France whereby 120 Soviet divisions, 9,500 tanks and 5,500 combat aircraft would be sent to Germany's eastern border as a deterrent to German aggression if the Allies presented an equally strong force on Germany's western flank.

This would have required Russian forces to move across Poland. It was widely known that the Soviets had harried the Poles since the revolution and relations between the two countries were too poor to allow that, for fear that it would mean permanent occupation. In the event, Russia got half of Poland anyway, through the pact with Germany signed when all other options had been exhausted.

Bizarrely, fearing an assault from the west, Hitler made a vain attempt to prevent action from Britain and France by pledging the use of the German armed forces to protect the British Empire! In the diplomatic words of a notice delivered to the Americans: '[Hitler] accepts the British Empire and is ready to pledge himself personally for its continued existence and to place power of [the] German Reich at its disposal if his colonial demands, which are limited … can be fulfilled.'

None of this worked, however, and Britain found itself at war with Germany when a notice from the British government to Hitler demanding a response by 11.00 am on 3 September 1939 failed to arrive in time. Consequently, in the words of Prime Minister Neville Chamberlain, 'this country is at war with

Germany'. Reaction was mixed and immediate. An erroneous report that enemy bombers were on their way triggered air raid sirens to be sounded across London, their operators called to action by a false alarm. In the country at large, there was a greater state of readiness than many realized, or indeed is recognized in many accounts of that period today. This despite the fact that in 1939 there was profound uncertainty about what Germany's response would be or the actions the British government would take.

THE EARLY DAYS OF AERIAL WARFARE IN BRITAIN

By the outbreak of World War II, Britain already had a long and proud history of military aviation that had begun during the Boer War at the end of the 19th century, when hot air balloons were used by the Royal Engineers for reconnaissance and intelligence gathering. Then, on 13 April 1912, the Royal Flying Corps (RFC) was formed by Royal Warrant after deliberations by the Committee of Imperial Defence. It operated aircraft to support the British Army on reconnaissance, gun-laying and spotting operations at a time when the country saw its land forces as expeditionary rather than as field armies equipped for set-piece battles.

Two years later, on 1 July 1914, the Royal Naval Air Service (RNAS) was formed in order to support naval operations, including spotting, reconnaissance and light bombing duties from an inventory of aircraft and airships. The planes used for bombing had a greater range and were able to stay aloft a lot longer than the conventional aircraft of the day. This superior air capability matched Britain's naval prowess, which reached its global zenith shortly before World War I, when Dreadnought-class battleships were a threat to every other nation in possession of maritime forces.

This arms race in the sea lanes was important to the history of aircraft since it prompted the use of aircraft and airships to protect maritime traffic and enforce international law regarding the passage of free trade on the world's oceans. Because of this, it is perhaps not surprising, then, that when Britain went to war in 1914, the RNAS was larger than the RFC.

At the beginning of 1914, the RNAS had more than 100 qualified pilots and had conducted significant work on the development of armament for aircraft, including guns, bombs and the dropping of torpedoes. By the outbreak of war later that year, the RNAS had 93 aircraft, of which 12 were airships and two were balloons, all supported with some 727 personnel.

The RFC, meanwhile, had five squadrons with a sixth forming – a total of about 75 aircraft. Four RFC squadrons took the field on the Continent in August

1914 with 66 aircraft, 95 transport vehicles and 109 officers. Expansion of the RFC was rapid; within two years, orders were in hand for 11,345 aircraft and 14,755 engines and the figures would continue to grow until the Armistice two years after that.

Recognizing the seminal role the RFC and the RNAS had played so far during World War I, in 1917 debate focused on amalgamating these two branches of the land and naval forces into the world's first independent air service. The Royal Air Force formally came into existence on 1 April 1918. When hostilities ceased on 11 November 1918, the RAF boasted 280 operational squadrons with numerous training units at home and abroad supporting activities on several fronts in western Europe, the Middle East and elsewhere.

AN INTERNATIONAL PLANE-BUILDING BOOM

Supported by a growth in manufacturing, a significant improvement in production and a surge in technical development, the British aircraft industry produced just over 55,000 airframes and 41,000 aero-engines during the course of World War I, and spawned companies that were to become household names, such as Hawker, Shorts, Sopwith, Supermarine, Bristol and Handley Page.

During the same period, France produced 68,000 aircraft and more than 85,000 engines; Germany produced almost 48,000 airframes and more than 40,000 engines; and Italy's totals were 20,000 and 38,000, respectively. The USA entered the war in April 1917 ill prepared to contribute any aircraft of her own design for use in combat but its industry delivered 15,000 aircraft and 41,000 engines, almost all from British and French types.

BOOM AND BUST

The rapid increase in production demands affected work trends, too. In particular, there was a major influx of women and boys into the workforce, accounting for almost half of the 347,112 workers who built aircraft, engines, accessories and spares in 1918. Skilled in sewing and stitching from working in clothing, drapery and furnishing industries, women were an important part of the labour force and not, as almost contemptuously quoted in more recent history (inferring they had no intrinsic value), just because the men had gone to fight. Women had a long tradition of skilled employment in areas requiring detailed, precise and accurate work and the preparation of canvas, the finishing of stitched wings with waterproofing and appropriate varnishing, and the attachment of canvas and fabric to wood were tasks they were well primed to perform.

Placed in perspective, the number of people employed building aircraft, engines and accessories at the end of World War I was three times that of the total employment figures for the British aerospace industry in 2019. However, this remarkable skill base was subsequently greatly diminished and disrupted as a result of the Armistice and, without the protection clauses in contracts that would later safeguard aircraft manufacturing at the end of World War II, in 1919 many companies were driven to bankruptcy by the abrupt termination of orders. With no compensation available to recompense the outlay made on now-redundant long-lead items such as wood from abroad, all forms of metal fixtures and fittings, and rigging equipment – orders for which had to be placed with ancillary suppliers – many major firms were left without any financial buffer.

These companies included arguably the most famous name in aircraft design and manufacturing of the day, Sopwith, which was forced into voluntary liquidation in September 1920 after it was presented by the government with an enormous bill for duty on 'war taxes'. The assets of what was left of the company were eventually reconstituted under the name Hawker. This company went on to produce fine aircraft and provided the RAF with a successful line of light bombers and fighters, including one of the most famous aircraft in the Battle of Britain two decades later.

INTERWAR MALAISE

Industry was not the only thing to suffer at the end of World War I. Amid the uncertainty about Britain's future role in the world and a general feeling of war weariness and emotional fatigue – despite the temporarily reassuring formation of the League of Nations – plans were formulated to disband the RAF and discharge its personnel. What followed next is of vital concern to any student of aerial warfare and of the build-up to World War II since it provides the reason why Britain was more prepared than most when the time came to re-arm and make preparations for defending the country and its broader global interests during the late 1930s.

By 1918, the RAF had become the most powerful air force in the world. It had also supported through scientific research a broad body of knowledge regarding the mechanics of flight, the development of military aircraft and the production and deployment requirements of a modern fighting force. Despite this, few Members of Parliament fully appreciated the importance and accomplishments of the RAF.

Indeed, many refused to attempt to understand why an air force was necessary at all, and there was no stomach for continued public expenditure on preparations for war. As a consequence, by March 1921 only 28 squadrons remained: four in Britain (of which three were with the Navy), three in Ireland and 21 abroad. What's more, in addition to the negative view held by most government officials, for partisan reasons the admirals and generals were dismissive of the need for an independent RAF, believing instead that air capabilities should be allied to the Navy and Army.

What post-war plans there were harked back to the Air Minister, Lord Weir, who as early as mid-1918 summarized the view of the Air Staff that if Britain were to retain her lead in the air it must be as a result of an amalgamation between civil aviation and a government-funded research and development body for pushing forward the technical and scientific capabilities of flight and flying. However, in 1918 Lord Weir left government for industry and the concept was lost with him. His successor was Secretary of State for War Winston Churchill, who was given Weir's position on 14 January 1919.

Churchill was an advocate of flying and the development of aviation, and was a stalwart supporter of an independent air force. In his prime position, he therefore took the opportunity to return the RAF to its former position. He was aided in this by Hugh Trenchard, a former commander of the Royal Flying Corps in France and then Chief of the Air Staff, who had been key to creating the RAF and eventually to the establishment in 1916 of its prime training facility, RAF Cranwell in Lincolnshire. This combination of Churchill and Trenchard managed to deflect a call for the abolition of the service. What's more, in his capacity as Chief of the Royal Air Force from 31 March 1919, Trenchard went on to preside over a restoration of faith in the viability of the RAF as an effective peacekeeping force in foreign territories, principally in the Middle East, where British interests were strong.

Paradoxically, Trenchard, who had orchestrated the inception of the Independent Air Force in France in 1918 as a strategic bombing wing of the RAF, could never convince the government of the need for expanded capabilities in this sector. Perhaps this was due in part, in fairness to his opponents, to the fact that Trenchard himself admitted to relying more on the morale and calibre of his air crew than the technical capabilities of the aircraft. Either way, this lack of support for bombers reflected the ever-enlarging debate during the interwar years about whether it was best to provide defensive fighters or offensive bombers. This question would haunt British air policy throughout the period.

Mocked in later years for having been party to naivety, in a Cabinet meeting on 5 August 1919 Churchill suggested that all estimates of international threats should be based on the assumption that no significant European conflict would break out for the next five to ten years – a theory that became known as the Ten Year Rule. Thus it would be possible, claimed Churchill, to recognize the warning signs early enough to re-arm. This may have been true in 1919, when the ramifications of the Treaty of Versailles had yet to play out, but the same argument became less plausible as time passed and the threat from abroad increased, notably when Benito Mussolini came to power in 1923 and Adolf Hitler became Chancellor in 1933. For now, though, all of that lay in the future.

PART-TIME PILOTS

One great achievement of Hugh Trenchard was the establishment on 9 October 1924 of the Royal Auxiliary Air Force (RAuxAF). This consisted of weekend aviators who had learned to fly and who could attend annual training for 15 days, put in several hours' flying every three months, and sign on for five years. This helped to relieve the service budget and produced a cadre of volunteer enthusiasts who could, in times of emergency, be called upon to serve their country.

These young men came primarily from relatively wealthy families, or had independent financial means; the cost of learning to fly was considerable and far beyond the budget of the working classes. There were some pilots from other walks of life, however, and in the RAuxAF, as elsewhere during World War II, class barriers were broken as never before, the mentality of being 'all in it together' helping to bond the men.

By early 1939, when international political tensions were reaching a peak, the RAuxAF had 21 squadrons, 20 of which were automatically incorporated into the regular RAF. Flyers whose five-year terms had expired before the war were required to sign up to the Royal Air Force Volunteer Reserve (RAFVR) and in a time of war to join operational units.

From the day war broke out, these squadrons performed with honour and merit. In so doing, the service helped to bolster the strength of the full-time RAF and to provide a level of proficiency that would otherwise have been costly both in terms of money and time. In the Battle of Britain, RAuxAF squadrons provided 14 of the 62 squadrons in Fighter Command.

THE QUESTION OF OFFENCE VS DEFENCE

On 20 June 1923, during his first term as prime minister, Stanley Baldwin approved an expansion plan to equip the RAF with 52 squadrons, emphasis going on home defence and the provision of fighters. However, Trenchard was a bomber man at heart and he therefore interpreted the mission for 'home defence' to mean offensive operations with bombers that could pulverize the enemy before they could mobilize their aircraft. As a result, the RAF expansion plan envisaged 35 bomber and 17 fighter squadrons. During high-level meetings later that year Trenchard dominated proceedings and brooked no opposition to his proposition: to first calculate how many squadrons were required to achieve an effective strike force and then to allocate fighters to what was left! Reverting to his prime mantra regarding the stoic determination and stout resolve of the British people, he expressed the view that the 'nation that would stand being bombed longest would win in the end'.

Trenchard's authority was helped by the fact that he held almost mythical status in the RAF and among the members of the Committee for Imperial Defence. For instance, Sir Samuel Hoare, Air Minister from 1922 to 1929, was clearly in awe of the man when he wrote in his memoirs: 'Whilst Trenchard spoke, I felt myself in the presence of a major prophet. My mission was to be the prophet's interpreter to a world that did not always understand his dark sayings. Thenceforth for nearly seven continuous years, I was destined to play the interpreter's part.'

Unfortunately, Trenchard's view was flawed, based in large measure on the misplaced assumption that offensive operations would prove supreme (Bomber Command would operate throughout the war on this premise) and that his experience in the 1914–18 war would be a template for the next conflict – an error made by so many old soldiers on too many occasions in too many wars.

Then there was the debate about whether the bombers should operate by day or by night – the requirements for each being quite unique in regard to operational performance and aiming devices. Some opinions suggested that area bombing should be performed during night operations, with specific targets being addressed during daylight. The options, given the limited capabilities of the technical devices of the day, appeared logical. The counter view, that offensive fire from the ground would be so intense during daylight hours that the bombers would be forced to fly so high that it would be impossible for them to hit targets with any precision, was also expressed. Nobody had a conclusive answer to this conundrum. Trenchard eventually brokered an agreement to divide the first 24 bomber squadrons equally for day and night roles, although he opined that the definitive breakdown ultimately striven for should be 22:13 respectively.

Amid all the conjecture and convoluted explanations, a clear line of thinking was expressed by Squadron Leader (Sqn Ldr) J.C. Slessor by way of an article he wrote for the journal of the Royal United Services Institute, which they published in May 1931:

'Purely passive self-protection, that is to say waiting for an enemy's attack and then attempting to repel it, has never been the British conception of national defence, and it is peculiarly ineffective in the three-dimensional battlefields of the air... It must therefore be apparent that to afford us any sort of protection against air forces that could now be directed against us, we should require a force of fighters immeasurably greater than we can afford in peace. And even then we should not be secure. So the policy is to provide the essential minimum of fighters for close defence in co-operation with the ground anti-aircraft defences, and to concentrate the bulk of our resources on the maintenance of a formidable striking force of bombers, the positive proportion of the defences, to enable us to launch a counter-offensive if we are attacked.'

And therein lay a flaw. The bomber offensive envisaged by Trenchard, and indeed by Slessor, had the RAF conduct long-range strategic bombing operations across the Continent. The type of fighter that was envisaged was in reality an interceptor – one that could fly fast and shoot down enemy bombers if they threatened Britain. They were not imagined as dogfighting aircraft engaging in close combat with other fighters. The limited range of the fighter designs of the day meant that they were incapable of playing the role of bomber escort. This capability would be increasingly important during the war to come but was not deemed technically possible when the bombers would be flying deep into enemy territory on the Continent.

Thus, it was assumed that RAF fighters would not be engaging other fighters (which would not have the range to get to British skies), rather that they would be intercepting bombers in order to shoot them down. This assumed role for the fighter had dire consequences for tactics, in that massed formations of fighters attacking bombers in a pack would expose the single-seaters to threats from an enemy who would prove to have a better understanding of the way modern aerial warfare was conducted.

CIVILIAN PREPARATION FOR RAIDS

As a practical reaction to growing fears about air raid casualties if enemy bombers reached Britain, the government formed an Air Raid Precautions Committee (ARPC) in 1924, chaired by Sir John Anderson. In 1939, Anderson became Home Secretary and undertook a nationwide programme equipping every home with an 'Anderson shelter', the small air raid shelter so familiar to wartime families. Some 5,000 lives were saved by this simple design – an inverted U-shaped corrugated form with vertical end closures and a single door that was readily assembled by civilians.

However, there was a whiff of naivety about relying on the terror it was presumed British bombing of enemy targets would bring about, and the number of casualties at home, which would be judged by 'the strength and efficiency of the counter-offensive of our bombing aircraft'. The myth that civilians will simply cave in if they are subject to sufficient attack has never been realized in any conflict, yet the notion persists to this day, usually propounded by staunch advocates of outstanding military force and the use of a disproportionate and overwhelming response to aggression. However, the ARPC itself, on hearing testimony from Trenchard, concluded in a report that: 'In our opinion the most effective reply to an attack from the air is the provision of a strong attacking force wherewith to carry the war to the enemy's country.'

That this view was challenged is evidenced by the official documents of the period, the Chiefs of Staff Committee (CSC) being particularly sceptical. Two individuals in particular – Sir Charles Madden (Navy) and Sir George Mile (Army), Chief of the Imperial General Staff – expressed opposition. Milne objected not only on empirical grounds – that Trenchard's assertions were unproven – but also on moral grounds, claiming 'that we are advocating what might be termed the indiscriminate bombing of undefended towns and of their unarmed inhabitants'. This is an argument that was never fully resolved and exists to this day.

EXPANSION OF THE RAF

Financial woes and other priorities prevented the RAF from getting the 52-squadron programme it was promised, the target date for that goal shifting first from 1928 to 1935 and then to 1938. A series of world monetary crises and economic depression would starve the armed services of the cash to fulfil their expectations. Chancellor of the Exchequer from 1924 to 1929, Churchill was a staunch advocate of government fiscal constraint and from July 1928 decreed that the Ten Year Rule should advance by one day, every day. It remained Treasury doctrine until 1931.

THE RAF OVERSEAS

One aspect of the history of British air power that is frequently missed is the degree to which the RAF was actively engaged in supporting political aspirations and requirements across what was still considered the British Empire. Territories in the Middle East were policed by the RAF from bases extending from North Africa to Mesopotamia and from Palestine to India. There was not a single day between the wars when the RAF was not on active duty, either in passive deployment on airfields overseas or engaged in suppressing revolt or uprisings in places associated with British interests. The pressures and responsibilities placed on RAF squadrons and their personnel in far-flung places were therefore no less than those undertaken by the RFC and the RNAS during the 1914–18 war.

Across Europe, the spectre of further aggression leading to another war haunted the corridors of power. In February 1932, with a Fascist government in power in Italy and the Nazi Party gaining widespread support in Germany, Geneva played host to the Disarmament Conference as a means of bringing guarantees against conflict through a limitation on arms. Bombers came up as the primary concern. However, when Britain seemed poised to support a ban on such aircraft, the Air Staff strongly objected and claimed that it would be impossible to enforce such a policy. In defence of their position, the Air Staff could have drawn evidence from the emerging development of airliners in Germany, which clearly had dual roles. Later, both the Heinkel He-111 and the Dornier Do-17 were developed from civilian aircraft to become the mainstay of the Luftwaffe's bombing capability from the outbreak of war in 1939.

Disarmament talks went on until March 1933, when the increasing takeover of power by the Nazi Party after Hitler became Chancellor rendered them pointless. Germany was in no mood to talk down its military potential. The hinge point at which RAF expansion was inevitable had been reached.

In Britain, contrary to clear signs across Europe that uncompromising extremes of National Socialism and Fascism were taking hold, public expectation was that the talks would bring a universal assurance of disarmament and pacification. In response to and reinforcing this assumption, the newspapers were full of disarmament talk – an erroneous position that the government was ill-placed to reverse, being mired in internal conflict.

Lord Londonderry, Air Minister at the time, summarized the contradictions: 'There was ill-disguised discontent in the Air Ministry. Everybody was dissatisfied and many were positively apprehensive of the future. It was felt that the government was prepared to sacrifice the Air Force without even examining the pros and cons of the case. This, of course, was not actually correct...'

Real change finally occurred in 1935, when the technical capabilities of the RAF were weak. At this stage, of the 35 anticipated bomber squadrons, 28 had been formed. Of these, 20 were equipped with day bombers, only half of which were regular squadrons. And of those ten, two were carrying out experimental and technical development work and two were assigned to a 'paper' Expeditionary Force – which was unmanned and did not have any equipment – on standby for dispatch overseas in the event of war. Thus, only six bomber squadrons were ready for immediate assignment. The other ten squadrons were with the RAuxAF and the Special Reserve squadrons and were far from being frontline ready. The night bomber squadrons were better equipped, five being regular units, but were such a small percentage of the total force that they were of lesser significance. It had been hoped to have 15 night and 20 day bomber squadrons in the full 35-squadron force but as of March 1933 there were only five and six respectively.

What was more alarming was the low level of technical capability. Industry was vocal about the ineffectiveness of government planning, a view articulated by C.R. Fairey of Fairey Aviation: 'The technical knowledge of building aircraft during the war had grown largely because the designers were allowed to produce the best kind of aircraft which the service required. After the war, specifications were laid down too rigidly by the Air Ministry and this led to less careful design of the aircraft as a whole.' While tremendous strides were made between 1914 and 1918, the post-war RAF made do for a decade with aircraft no better than those types developed by industry during World War I. This was not the fault of the industry or the RAF, rather the convergence of circumstances that prevented the government from supplying the necessary resources. The situation was also due in large part to the continual insistence on quality of personnel rather than quality and quantity of the aircraft procured, as proselytized by Trenchard.

It was also a legacy from the RFC that the Air Staff placed priority on light bombers such as the Hawker Hart, which had a capacity to carry four 112 lb bombs to a maximum range of 230 miles. Aircraft like this did much work policing across the Empire. And the emphasis on bombers produced aircraft that were faster than the fighters that were supposed to shoot them down. A dismissive attitude toward the latter did little to redress the balance. Yet despite this prevailing preference for bombers, there were dissident voices warning of the danger of relegating the role of the fighter merely to the defence of London (as had been asserted in some analyses, which believed that the fighter would eventually become extinct). Writing in the Royal United Services Institute (RUSI) journal on November 1931, Sqn Ldr J.O. Andrews challenged the underestimation of defence:

'We must bear in mind that the doctrines of the use of air power are at present, and until proved by war, speculative. Resting largely on a theoretical basis, the doctrine that air forces must be used primarily in an offensive role has had much influential support and appears well on the way to becoming sacrosanct. Consequently the approved policy is one of aggression, with the development of the maximum strength of bombing aircraft. As a corollary, defensive commitments tend to be regarded with disfavour, and air forces allocated to play a strategically defensive role are reduced to the minimum.'

He pointed out that while the maximum speed of the bomber had increased by only 25 per cent, the rate of climb of fighters had risen by 40 per cent, and that on this basis alone it was premature to dismiss the defensive role over the offensive use of air power; he could not conceive of heavy losses to such an attacking force if the fighters persisted in their role. It was just this prediction that would prove correct in 1940 when the Luftwaffe suffered unsustainable losses and withdrew from their attacks during the Battle of Britain, only to lose the attack on the cities.

This debate about the role of aircraft in future conflicts took place at a time when the aviation industry was on the cusp of technological change. It also came at the onset of a stronger determination on the part of the British government to fully fund a major expansion of military power, if only to serve as a deterrent to potential aggression from a resurgent Germany.

Italy, too, was making expansionist moves and on 3 October 1935 it invaded Abyssinia (now Ethiopia), creating the first real challenge to the authority of the League of Nations. However, nobody was ready for war. So, the British gritted their teeth and let Italian ships through the Suez Canal to replenish their forces while the RAF sent supplies to bases in Egypt, Aden and Palestine. The only positive outcome from an increasingly tense situation was the rehearsal it allowed for rapid mobilization and a simulation of preparations for war.

CHAPTER 4
Deterrence

THE INCREASE in expenditure for the Army, the Navy and the Air Force provided Britain with four years in which to prepare for war. The period is much misunderstood, in that consolidation and improvement of equipment for the armed forces is incorrectly associated with political appeasement at the end of the 1930s and interpreted as being a time when the country rested in sublime isolation from an increasingly dangerous threat. The two are completely separate, and the frequent misrepresentation of this hides the fact that between 1935 and 1939 Britain increased its defence expenditure at a rate greater than at any other peacetime period in its history.

EXPENDITURE ON UK ARMAMENTS BY YEAR 1924–33 IN £ MILLIONS:

Year ending 31 March	Navy	Army	RAF
1924	11.8	2.6	4.9
1925	13.0	2.6	6.9
1926	14.1	2.2	7.6
1927	16.0	1.8	7.4
1928	16.3	1.8	7.6
1929	15.0	2.0	7.1
1930	14.4	2.2	7.9
1931	10.7	1.5	8.9
1932	10.3	1.8	8.7
1933	10.7	1.6	7.8

EXPENDITURE ON UK ARMAMENTS BY YEAR 1934–39 IN £ MILLIONS:

Year ending 31 March	Navy	Army	RAF
1934	20.9	6.9	9.4
1935	24.2	8.5	9.9
1936	29.6	12.5	18.6
1937	42.0	21.4	39.3
1938	65.3	44.3	66.0
1939	82.9	67.6	109.9

Far from being unprepared and inadequately equipped, great steps towards re-armament had been taken. This came on the cusp of a change in administration, the Labour Prime Minister Ramsay MacDonald's five-year term giving way in June 1935 to the Conservative Stanley Baldwin, who served until 28 May 1937, when he was replaced by Neville Chamberlain. Over this period, a universal agreement had been concluded in what was essentially a government of national unity: Britain's defences were woefully inadequate and a major injection of cash was necessary, a recommendation passed by Parliament.

Specifically, in general response to emerging Continental threats, total defence spending increased from £37.2 million in 1934 to £42.6 million the following year, and from £104.2 million in 1937 to £273.1 million in 1939. Manpower preparations saw the total rise from 383,000 at the beginning of 1938 to 1.273 million in September 1939, increasing to 1.559 million by the end of that year. Expenditure on the RAF increased more than 11-fold in five years. Not since the Napoleonic Wars of the late 18th century had such a spending boost on arms been passed by a British government.

The formal structure of the various expansion schemes would progress from 1935 through to the start of the war with Germany. Each laid down a plan for how many aircraft and squadrons the RAF would have by a given year and each bore a letter of the alphabet as they were instituted. Scheme A anticipated a force of 84 squadrons, which was to be completed by 31 March 1939 (the end of the financial year), divided into 43 bomber and 28 fighter squadrons with 500 and 336 aircraft respectively. Included within the total were eight coastal squadrons and five Army co-operation squadrons, a total force of 960 aircraft.

Scheme C, implemented after Foreign Secretary Anthony Eden met Hitler in Berlin on 26 March 1935, was the first designed to enable the RAF to reach parity with the Luftwaffe. It envisaged an accelerated complement of 123 squadrons to be up and ready by 31 March 1937, with a total of 1,512 aircraft, of which 840 were to be bombers and 162 fighters. However, over the next few months, as estimates of German force levels increased, so too did the ambitions for a larger RAF. Approved on 25 February 1936, Scheme F laid down a force level of 124 squadrons and 1,736 aircraft but Scheme H grew this still further, with the final Scheme M predicting a force of 163 squadrons and 2,549 aircraft by 31 March 1942.

Of interest is the high priority given to bombers, from 52 per cent of the total force for Scheme A to 67 per cent for Scheme H and back down to 53 per cent for Scheme M. Fighters accounted for 35 per cent in Scheme A, just 19.6 per cent in Scheme H but were back up to 31.4 per cent by Scheme M.

Almost imperceptibly, a shift in priorities for defence against incoming bombers had occurred. This was reflected not only in the numbers but also in the direction of scientific research and development with regard to the defence of the country.

THE EMERGENCE OF NUCLEAR AND RADAR TECHNOLOGIES

By the mid-1930s, great progress was being made by British scientists at Oxford and Cambridge into the physics of atomic structures, and the nucleus of the atom in particular. It became apparent that similar work on Radio Direction Finding (RDF), known as radar from 1941, by Robert Watson-Watt could provide Britain with a world first in the detection of approaching aircraft by measuring reflected radio signals. This work greatly expanded in 1936 when Watson-Watt set up a research team at Bawdsey Manor near Felixstowe on the Suffolk coast. Following several experimental tests involving aircraft fitted with primitive equipment it quickly became apparent that such a system was not only feasible but also potentially critical to the defence of Britain.

The government now had to balance the unknowns regarding the potential use and efficacy of atomic bombs – and the vast amount of money and resources it would take to produce such a weapon – and the relatively inexpensive development of RDF. The logical choice was to give full development approval to the latter defensive system and stations, codenamed Chain Home (CH), were therefore constructed all around the southern, south-eastern and eastern coastline of the UK. These were fully integrated with the RAF as an early warning screen against attack – a system that provided a more positive means of detecting approaching bombers than parabolic acoustic mirrors, which worked by focusing the sound waves from the engines of approaching aircraft.

As a result of these developments, early warning was developed to a sophisticated level in Britain. It involved RDF detecting aircraft as they left the

Continent, followed by observers along the coast picking up and plotting the visually tracked course of the aircraft and reporting these to a series of sector control stations. These in turn were tied in with RAF stations, which were able to put up defensive fighters as and where needed and thereby maximize the amount of flying time they could use to intercept the oncoming bombers.

Paradoxically, Britain had been late in realizing the potential of RDF. It had in fact been invented by a German before World War I but had been rejected by Britain as being of little practical use. Many other countries, too, were working hard on experimental systems of this type. In fact, the Germans had thrown a lot of resources into the concept and were ahead of Britain when war broke out. However, their work was purely experimental and was not linked to a fully operational alert network, such as that deployed by the British. It was a long time before they finally realized how sophisticated the British system was.

THE NEW ORDER

While expansion schemes took control of the structural size and cost of evolving plans for the RAF, the complete administration and operational organization of the RAF was restructured in 1936. This was in part because the existing command system of the Air Defence of Great Britain (ADGB) was unfit for expansion and had become increasingly unwieldy. On 1 May, the first of the new organizational elements, RAF Training Command, was formed with headquarters at Bentley Priory, Middlesex. This was followed on 14 July by the formation of Bomber Command (Hillingdon House, Uxbridge), Fighter Command (Bentley Priory) and Coastal Command (Lee-on-the-Solent, Hampshire). These commands would exist throughout the war and form the operational elements of the RAF, with their own squadrons, wings and groups organized according to operational requirements.

Equally important to the air war of 1939–45 were the aircraft of the Royal Navy, formerly of the RNAS, which had been amalgamated into the Royal Air Force in 1918. As occurred in the RAF, by 1919 the naval component had shrunk considerably and consisted of one reconnaissance squadron, one fighter flight (about three aircraft) and half a torpedo squadron, together with one seaplane flight and a flying boat flight. Over the next two decades, the Admiralty strove hard to regain control of its aviation and only incremental steps were made to accommodate demands from the Royal Navy for new and improved equipment and a larger force. To mark this delineation between the RAF and the naval component, officers were given naval rank and up to 70 per cent of pilots held dual RAF and naval rank. Then, in April 1924 the Fleet Air Arm (FAA) was formed, further consolidating the distinction. In 1937, control of the FAA was handed over directly to the Royal Navy. The Admiralty would now have shore stations, as the RNAS had before 1918.

Away from the squabbling and the paper shuffling, the expansion of the Fleet Air Arm grew ponderously slowly. When war broke out there were only 20 squadrons with a total of 340 aircraft, of which 225 were in aircraft carriers and the rest in catapult flights. To accommodate them, five new carriers were commissioned: *Eagle* in 1922; *Hermes* in 1923; *Glorious* and *Courageous* in 1928; and *Ark Royal* in 1938. For all the lack of planes, however, while most major powers had naval aviation and several operated carriers, progress made by the Royal Navy in the techniques of operating aircraft at sea was seminal, both in terms of effectiveness and in implementation by navies all over the world. The cutting-edge technologies included a deck landing system with arrestor wires and a hydro-pneumatic catapult system.

CRAFT OF THE FLEET AIR ARM

While new operational techniques were being pioneered, such as the numerical establishment of the FAA itself, the technical performance of its aircraft lagged far behind that of the RAF. The interwar years had seen a stalling of British naval aviation development. This was in part because it was difficult for manufacturers to meet the demand to produce aircraft that were capable of operating from carriers. Thus, when war broke out, the FAA's planes were far from being state of the art. For instance, while the RAF was equipping its pilots with fast monoplane fighters, the best the FAA could put up was the Gloster Sea Gladiator, a navalized variant of the ageing RAF biplane with fixed undercarriage and a top speed of 245 mph, supporting four machine guns mounted in the fuselage.

Also in service was the Fairey Swordfish, a torpedo-spotter reconnaissance aircraft affectionately known as the 'Stringbag' because of its ageing appearance; it was effectively a biplane held together with struts and wire. Despite bearing all the design conventions of a mid-interwar design (open cockpit, fixed undercarriage), however, its precarious appearance belied its potential. In fact, the Swordfish went on to serve the Navy throughout the war years and achieved fame for being instrumental in sinking the *Bismarck*, Hitler's flagship battleship which, along with the *Tirpitz*, was the largest warship built for the German Navy.

With a top speed barely reaching 135 mph and flown mostly at little more than 100 mph, the Swordfish carried a crew of three in open cockpits and had two machine guns for defence. There was provision for one torpedo under the fuselage or up to 1,500 lb of bombs. Despite its shortcomings, the 'Stringbag' was a remarkable aircraft to fly and a great survivor under fire.

The Swordfish was found everywhere, from the mid-Atlantic on the heaving decks of a carrier to Mediterranean shore bases, and from attacking the Italian Navy at Taranto to escorting convoys across Arctic waters north of Norway. Despite this, what this aircraft and others in the FAA achieved was usually out of sight and because of that the service and the aircraft they flew never quite caught the imagination of the public. This was perhaps not surprising since civilians were understandably distracted by dogfights going on in the skies overhead and were being terrorized by endless nights of bombing. Yet it was aerial warfare just the same.

Lesser-known Navy aircraft included the Albacore, another product from Fairey, which entered service in 1940 as a potential replacement for the Swordfish, but which failed to outlast the plane it was meant to succeed. Then there was the Navy's first all-metal torpedo-bomber and dive-bomber, the Fairey Barracuda, which entered service in 1943 and acquitted itself with honour, as well as the Blackburn Baffin, which replaced the Ripon from the same stable.

The unique requirements of the naval aviation meant that few land aircraft could be adapted to a life aboard carriers, although the Hurricane and the Spitfire were 'navalized' in some variants, with mixed results. This was because a good landing on a carrier brought higher vertical forces and loads, which would propagate through the entire structure of the aircraft, requiring them to be designed with much stronger airframes as well as resilience to salt water and spray. Very few land aircraft were therefore capable of being adapted for carrier use. For different reasons, the obverse was also true: naval aircraft had greater structural mass, which affected to some degree the warload they could carry.

LAND PLANES

On land, progress was being made by the RAF and the technical capability of operational aircraft was raised as new technologies and engines improved. During the second half of the 1930s, a period of general expenditure and industrial resources, several new types made their first flight. These proved to be aircraft that equalled the capabilities of the best the Luftwaffe could put in the air and provided a defensive bulwark against German aggression.

Principal among these new planes were the Hurricane and the Spitfire. These fighters were built to replace ageing biplanes, which had open cockpits and fixed landing gear. The Hurricane came from a long line of successful RAF types from the drawing board of a team led by Sir Sydney Camm. These early aircraft included the Hart, Hind, Audax, Fury I and Demon, all of which were biplanes of the early to mid-1930s and represented an era of obsolete and outclassed designs. Each was powered by a Rolls-Royce Kestrel engine, one of the finest of its day with a power output variously in the range of 500–600 hp. Possessing a top speed of less than 180 mph, however, these types were no match for the latest German Bf-109 monoplanes. Indeed, even the Fury II of 1936, with its 640 hp Kestrel VI, had a top speed of only 223 mph.

The Hawker Hurricane, however, represented a quantum leap in terms of performance. A redefined Fury II, it had a monoplane wing, closed cockpit and retractable undercarriage – advantages that meant it was much faster and more manoeuvrable. It was also powered by a 1,030 hp Rolls-Royce Merlin engine, which gave it a top speed of 316 mph and a service ceiling of 33,000 ft – a great improvement on previous models. Better still, it followed the traditional Hawker convention of fabric-covered, tubular steel construction, which meant that it could be built quickly and easily, with minimal manpower and maximum yield. Having made its first flight in November 1935, it appeared in service in 1937, just a year after the Fury II biplane.

Equally quick off the stocks, the Supermarine Spitfire had a completely different pedigree. While Hawker built for mass production, Supermarine had a tradition of hand-built seaplanes and flying boats, small production runs and high-performance racing aircraft built to compete for the Schneider Trophy. The design team working these seaplanes had secured a close relationship with Rolls-Royce and that provided a pathway for the development of the Spitfire, using similarly refined aeronautical design concepts married to a powerful engine.

However, despite this association, the oft-made claim that the Spitfire came right out of the Schneider Trophy seaplanes is a myth. Aspects of the design introduced by chief designer Reginald Mitchell were in fact similar to German types, particularly the Heinkel He-70 mail plane, whose elliptical wing inspired that of the Spitfire. That said, while the thin, low-drag elliptical wing of the Spitfire possessed approximately the same geometric shape as the wing of the He-70, it had completely different characteristics. A key feature was the degree of washout, or twist, between the root of the wing and the tip, the angle of incidence (angle to the airflow in level flight) transitioning from 2 degrees where it joined the root at the fuselage to 0.5 degrees at the tip. This gave it the advantage of higher aerodynamic performance across a wide speed and altitude range. The He-70 had none of those technically sophisticated characteristics.

True to form, Supermarine designed a thoroughbred but with no consideration of its potential for mass production. With a smooth stressed skin,

Pilots of No 310 (Czechoslovak) Squadron pose in front of their Hawker Hurricane at RAF Duxford on 7 September 1940. David Baker Archive

semi-monocoque fuselage and that characteristic elliptical wing, the Spitfire was a complex structure featuring compound curves and advanced structural elements. It was therefore an altogether different design to the Hurricane, but one that had enormous potential.

The first significant challenge after its first flight on 5 March 1936 was to get the aircraft into production. This required Supermarine to work with the Air Ministry to change the way the component elements were broken down, for ease of manufacture – a change that resulted in delays. The Ministry ordered 310 Spitfire aircraft on 3 June 1936 but it was not until May 1938 that the first production aircraft rolled off the assembly line.

What both these new aircraft had was greatly improved armament – the result of an Air Ministry conference held on 19 July 1934 that advocated an eight-gun formula. Capt F.W. Hill, the senior ballistics officer at the Aircraft and Armament Experimental Establishment (A&AEE), Martlesham Heath, had provided evidence that this number of guns, discharging at 1,000 rounds per minute, would be required in order for a pilot to shoot down a bomber in a two-second burst, which might be all the time he had in close combat. The Spitfire had been designed from the outset with eight guns, whereas the Hurricane was designed with four. However, Sydney Camm subsequently modified the design of his fighter to incorporate eight guns also. These were buried within the wing, four on each side. Consideration regarding the armament was not made, as some have asserted, in relation to what the Germans were doing; they had a different configuration of machine guns and cannon. The requirement for eight guns was quite a revolution and proved essential in the high-speed era of combat introduced by the new generation of single-seat monoplane fighters. These included the first production Hurricane Mk 1 (L1695), which was singled out for trials and as a result was fitted with armour plate and a bulletproof windscreen. Some Hurricanes, however, were produced with just four 0.5-in Browning guns, specifically the ones ordered by the Belgians.

ARMAMENT ARRANGEMENTS

Both the Hurricane and the Spitfire had eight machine guns, which were smaller-calibre weapons than the cannon carried by the Bf-109. The reason for this lies in a rather bizarre story. In 1868, the St Petersburg convention on arms and the rules of war had prohibited the use of explosive shells below 37 mm calibre. In the 19th century, there had been concern over the horrific wounds caused by such weapons and the Air Ministry was therefore worried that it would contravene the rules of war should it proceed with such armament. Eventually, however, the decision was made that as the guns were firing at machines and not directly at people, 20 mm cannon would not contravene the rules of the convention. This meant that a twin-engine fighter, the Westland Whirlwind, could carry a battery of four cannon grouped in the nose. Developed as a closely guarded secret, it would make its inaugural flight on 11 October 1938 and first entered operational service at the end of 1940.

The RAF's Boulton Paul Defiant night fighter, meanwhile, carried four machine guns, in a turret manned by a gunner situated just aft of the cockpit. Since World War I there had been a conviction that there was a need for a stable gun platform equipped with armament that could be brought to bear on an enemy. The first such type had been the Bristol F.2B of 1917. Ineffective when flown straight and level, leaving the rear gunner to lay his guns on the enemy, it only worked when the pilot flew the aircraft like a fighter. The legacy of the F.2B was the Defiant, which made its first flight on 11 August 1937 and was in service in time to see action during the Battle of Britain three years later. While it achieved limited success over Dunkirk, it was unable to survive against the German Bf-109. It turned out to be a flawed concept and only 1,064 were ever built.

For all their benefits, there were some design problems associated with fitting eight guns in the wings, as well as a significant change in operational utility. Previously, gun breeches had been within reach of the pilot. This meant that jammed guns could be addressed by the pilot, who could either reach forwards or outside the open cockpit. With the guns and their magazines isolated from access during flight, though, any mechanical problem could only be addressed after landing.

Moreover, with the Spitfire, which had a narrow undercarriage track with landing legs that folded outwards (unlike the Hurricane, whose wheels folded inwards) the outer pair of guns in each wing was staggered further outboard to accommodate the wheels in the thin wing. All of this was quite radical and brought new procedures for ground crew and armaments technicians. To complicate matters further, because of the performance of the aircraft the guns had to be heated from ducts routing hot air from the engine, to prevent them from freezing.

There were other changes, too. To supplement the conventional ring-and-bead sight used by the pilot to align his aircraft, adopting a technique not dissimilar to that of a marksman with a rifle, a new reflector gun sight was installed. For this, the illuminated image of a ring sight was projected on to an oval mirror situated in front of the pilot's eyes and immediately behind the armoured windscreen. This meant that if the pilot knew the wingspan of the adversary he could adjust the sight to fit the size and know immediately when he was within range. The conventional, old-style sight was retained, in case of an electrical failure.

Cine cameras were also fitted, which would record shots in 16 mm film for the period the guns were firing. The ports of these cameras were covered with red-painted square fabric patches until they were blown through by the first shots. This helped to provide evidence, or at least an indication, of whether the target had been shot down. This was vital intelligence information that could be used to assess the strength of the enemy force returning home after a raid – data that would feed back into an assessment of the attrition rate of enemy forces.

PREPARATIONS FOR WAR

With war clouds gathering it was apparent that parent airframe manufacturers were not geared for large-scale production. The Air Ministry therefore entered talks with Morris Motors at Cowley to sound out the prospect of them building Spitfires. In the end, however, the government built a bespoke facility at Castle Bromwich, close to the airfield, which could function as a top-class assembly plant for volume production.

In fact, the prospect of manufacturing the Spitfire had initially proved so difficult that the government had considered cancelling the type after the initial production run. Supermarine stuck to their guns, though, and worked with government teams and transformed the way it could be broken down into sections to be sympathetic to rapid assembly. This worked very well; the Spitfire was the only aircraft in full production on every day of the war. Some 20,351 were built, of which 4,533 were lost. In addition, around 2,646 Seafires were built – navalized versions of the Spitfire that were used by the Fleet Air Arm off carriers and shore installations abroad.

The decision to order the production of both the Spitfire and the Hurricane had been a wise one. The mass production of Hurricanes would see 497 delivered by the outbreak of war, equipping 18 squadrons, compared to only nine squadrons of Spitfires. Yet the Spitfire was engineered for progressive development. During its evolution, this fighter went through more than two dozen variants and achieved unprecedented performance capabilities through the application of more powerful Merlin engines and, in 1942, the Griffon engine, which had twice the power output of the Merlin used in the Mk 1. Indeed, the Spitfire was the first in a new generation of planes that, structurally at least, would lead directly into the jet-powered fighters that followed. By contrast, the Hurricane represented the end of the line in terms of design, with little further development other than variants adapted for specific theatres of operation, such as the Middle East and the Far East.

As mentioned earlier, the RAF had a preoccupation with bombers. Four types ushered in the monoplane era, replacing biplanes such as the Vickers Virginia and the Handley Page Heyford, which had been stalwarts over many years. Two medium bombers, the Bristol Blenheim and the Fairey Battle, were in service before World War II began, the former making its first flight on 25 June 1936 and creating a great impression with its speed and overall performance. With a bomb load of 1,000 lb and powered by two 840 hp Bristol Mercury engines, the Blenheim had a top speed of 260 mph. It entered service in 1937. The Battle, which was powered by a single Merlin engine, had a similar bomb load and performance to the Blenheim, but was not quite as fast. Together, these planes provided an early opportunity for the RAF to hit targets on the Continent. Despite this, they were soon replaced.

Three other bombers provided opportunities for hitting Germany: the Armstrong Whitworth Whitley with squadrons from March 1937; the Handley Page Hampden in service from late 1938; and the Vickers Wellington, also operational from 1938. The Whitley was a heavy night bomber with a capacity to carry 7,000 lb of bombs and defensive armament in its nose and tail turrets. It had a cruising speed of only 160 mph. Almost all RAF bombers had gunners placed in nose, tail, mid-upper or mid-lower positions, isolated from the flying crew, but the Hampden broke that tradition with defensive gun positions in ventral and dorsal positions closer to the flight crew. This was the universally preferred configuration for German bombers but was unusual for British aircraft. The Hampden had a bomb capacity of 4,000 lb and was delivered to the RAF in August 1938. Both the Whitley and the Hampden, along with the Battle and the Blenheim, would represent the first generation of British monoplane bombers and would be redundant by 1942.

The brainchild of Barnes Wallis, inventor of the 'bouncing bomb' used by the Dam Busters, the Wellington was designed with a geodetic construction, which provided a robust lattice-like fuselage capable of absorbing immense amounts of damage. Carrying a maximum bomb load of 4,500 lb and with defensive nose and tail positions, each equipped with two 0.303 machine guns, the 'Wimpey' as it was nicknamed saw service throughout the war in a wide variety of roles. Not only was it the mainstay of the RAF's bombing capability until 1942, but it also served as a maritime reconnaissance aircraft, a training aircraft for navigators and a converted transport aircraft.

CHAPTER 5
The Gathering Storm

PREPARATIONS FOR air defences against enemy bombers got under way during early 1939. By 28 July, the first 500 barrage balloons were ready to protect London from dive-bombers, such as the Ju-87 Stuka. Tethered at a height of 2,000 ft by wires through which aircraft could not fly, the balloons were reeled out to a height of up to 30,000 ft during night-time raids. By the time war broke out there were several hundred more, and suburban gardens were commandeered to serve as tethering stations for giant balloons nicknamed 'Jumbos' by residents. Roads and open spaces were also quickly reserved as tethering places for these unlikely defenders.

On 8 August 1939, Biggin Hill airfield in Kent was used for a mass test of London's air defences. Involving 500 barrage balloons, 1,300 aircraft and 1,400 anti-aircraft artillery (AAA, or 'triple A'), this was the most comprehensive air exercise ever carried out in Britain. Elsewhere, air raid precautions had been under way for much of that year, the first Anderson shelters being delivered by lorry to residents on 25 February. Civilians were then required to assemble the curved sheets of corrugated iron, bolt them together and place them in their gardens, covered as much as possible with soil.

Preparations were extraordinarily complete: notices and leaflets were distributed to homes telling inhabitants what to do when the air raid sirens were heard, where to go for safety and the quickest way to get help after a raid, especially if their home had been destroyed. The government also manufactured and distributed 38 million gas masks, making it an offence not to carry one at all times. Despite this edict, however, large quantities turned up at lost property offices. Education even extended to children's toys being equipped with little gas masks to make them more familiar for youngsters. Mothers of babies were issued with gas tents into which the infant could be placed, as though in a cradle. However, the rubber smell often created more panic than the tent itself!

All of these measures reflected the uncertainty about just what the effects of a bombing raid would be, and revealed that the impact of the German raid on Guernica in Spain had caused considerable alarm. Fearing the worst from raids, on 1 September trains were mobilized for the mass evacuation of children. Rail lines across Britain were subsequently criss-crossed with people being redistributed from cities to villages and communities in the countryside. A lot of this was premature, but it did have the effect of generating a feeling throughout the country that the nation was well prepared for the worst and that the general public had been adequately informed of measures.

Meanwhile, the armed forces also had several months in which to prepare for what many realized was an inevitable clash with German forces. Then, once an ultimatum had been sent to Germany on 2 September 1939, a day after the Wehrmacht crashed into Poland, all aircraft of the RAF Advanced Air Striking Force (AASF) began deploying to France, in expectation of the Germans mounting a lightning strike in western Europe. There was, however, some breathing space. Intelligence provided by the French and the British, together with clandestine outlets in Germany, indicated that there were insufficient German forces on the French border for an attack in the west to take place immediately.

THE PHONEY WAR

The first units to fly across to France were Fairey Battles of No. 1 Group Bomber Command. This left five bomber groups back in the UK, one of which was for training pooled squadrons. Fighter Command, meanwhile, having recently assimilated the Auxiliary Air Force squadrons into the RAF on full-time service, now had 39 squadrons and just over 700 aircraft. Two squadrons of fighters flew Gauntlet and Hind biplanes, and 30 squadrons flew single-engine fighters – Hurricanes, Spitfires and Defiants. At the outbreak of war, Fighter Command sent an expeditionary force of four squadrons of Hurricanes to assist the French patrolling the border with Germany. They also took the opportunity to generally familiarize themselves with French culture.

DISPERSAL OF BOMBER SQUADRONS AT THE OUTSET OF WAR

Bomber Command lost some of its strength on home soil with the movement of No. 1 Group to France. All that remained were: No. 3 Group with six operational Wellington squadrons and two non-operational squadrons; No. 4 Group with five Whitley squadrons and one non-operational squadron; and No. 5 Group with six Hampden squadrons and two non-operational squadrons.

With all of the action taking place in Poland, it was literally 'all quiet on the Western Front' during the first few months of the war, with only spasmodic activity suggesting that the Germans had any intention of invading France, Belgium or the Netherlands. The RAF was only there in order to fulfil a commitment made by the British to go to the assistance of France, and indeed there was strong opposition to the British contribution from those who thought that the defence of Britain should come first. These voices of dissent included senior officials. For instance, when six additional squadrons were deployed to France, Fighter Command Commander-in-Chief (C-in-C) Sir Hugh Dowding wrote to the Air Ministry protesting in strong terms against the dilution of home forces.

Even as the RAF was deploying in a defensive mode, the fighter squadrons were in the process of switching from ageing aircraft to the latest Hurricanes and Spitfire types. For the French Air Force, which was equipped with older aircraft, available in smaller numbers and with less operational capability, the British contribution was a reassuring support. Although the stoicism of their pilots and air crew was without question, the French Armée de l'Air was the product of a less-than-enthusiastic approach to re-armament, many believing that the Maginot Line – an array of defensive forts parallel to the German border – would be sufficient to keep the country secure. It would prove not to be so, and in dramatic fashion.

For all the public face of shoulder-to-shoulder support for France, at government and military levels there were severe disagreements about how to put up a consolidated front against further German aggression. What there was consensus on was that it could only be a matter of time before this aggression occurred. On 23 October, Air Vice-Marshal (Air V-Mshl) Douglas Evill went by air to France to discuss these matters with Gen Gamelin, the Supreme Commander, and Gen Vuillemin, who represented the view of the Armée de l'Air. The purpose of the meeting was to outline a policy approved by the War Cabinet in London that 'the initiative is with Germany' and that 'we should conserve and develop our resources until the gap in numerical strength is narrowed'. It was fortunate that the major expansion programmes of Britain's air capabilities had already been implemented, but with production programmes still under way, each week that passed meant that the RAF was getting stronger.

The view of the RAF, endorsed by Cabinet, was that Britain should not launch an immediate assault on the Ruhr by air. Indeed, it could not have done, given the parlous state of the equipment at this time. However, in the event of German hostility in the west, that move should be made. The French were not impressed by this and stressed their view that strategy should be driven by a defensive approach, not an offensive one. The two approaches were in fact poles apart: the French were terrified of a mighty onslaught induced through provocation; the British believed that at the first sign of attack, an offensive bomber strategy should begin immediately. With France still viewing the heavy bomber as support for ground operations, they interpreted the British approach as implying that a major land attack on Germany would be mobilized – an attack that they felt they were uncertain of winning.

Yet nobody could be sure about the defences in the Ruhr – Germany's industrial heartland. This was important, since an effective offensive there was in several respects the key to bringing the Nazi regime to its knees. Writing to Dowding, C-in-C of Bomber Command Edgar Ludlow-Hewitt warned that a pre-emptive attack on the Ruhr might result in such damage to attacking forces that a large number of his bombers could be lost. What's more, the resources and time required to replenish a force of large aircraft would open a gap for opportunistic German assault.

It is clear, then, that in the opening weeks and months of war there was widespread uncertainty over what to do, how to respond to different levels of German aggression and when to mobilize a response. What was apparent, though, was that is was impossible to provide direct air support for Poland, situated as it was some 700 miles from the RAF bomber stations in England.

BOMBER ACTION

For Fighter Command, the war in 1939 was a waiting game but for Bomber Command there was action from day one, with Blenheim, Wellington and Hampden aircraft conducting reconnaissance sorties searching for German shipping north of Wilhelmshaven. Indeed, the first RAF aircraft to cross the coast of Germany during World War II was Blenheim N6215. Following in their wake,

Whitleys flew over the industrial heartland of Germany dropping propaganda leaflets – an action that was the prime focus of Bomber Command during the opening weeks of the war.

Back in Britain, meanwhile, exercises were held to fine-tune tactics and to simulate dummy runs on a phantom enemy, using some 60 bombers from Nos 3 and 5 Groups as 'targets' around Belfast, Northern Ireland.

So, for all that this period was dubbed the 'Phoney War' – in that it was no war at all but just a bunch of young men testing each other's mettle – offensive operations *did* take place, although neither side engaged fully in sizeable combat. What's more, it was a time when some serious probing of the enemy and testing of equipment occurred. For instance, the first RAF aircraft to fly over Berlin accomplished a 1,000-mile round-trip flight on the night of 1/2 October. Then, on 3 December, some 24 Wellingtons attacked a force of enemy warships in the vicinity of Heligoland, dropping a total of 63 500 lb armour-piercing bombs on at least one cruiser. Twenty Luftwaffe fighters rose to the occasion, some of which were attacked, but despite suffering some limited damage, all of the British bombers returned.

More raids followed, specifically on naval targets since the RAF was forbidden to attack land targets for fear of provoking the enemy to 'unreasonable action', particularly reprisal raids on British towns. For the time being, then, for the Allies it was a war of the machines – aircraft against warships – and the reality of all-out conflict had yet to explode upon western Europe.

THE SITUATION IN GERMANY

For the Germans, it was a different matter. With the conflict now over in Poland and the country occupied by both German and Russian troops, the Luftwaffe moved Luftflotten 1 and 4 to western Germany, consolidating Luftflotten 2 and 3, which had been stationed near the border throughout the action so far.

Reciprocally, the Luftwaffe flew raids against British ships, but these too were exploratory rather than part of a specific plan. Hitler still retained hope for a settlement with Britain, a prospect that evaporated rapidly after the government refused a 'peace feeler' from Berlin on 6 October. Seeing how France was unprepared for war and the British growing stronger every day, with new men and equipment flowing into the military arsenal, Hitler pressed for an early occupation of France in order to isolate Britain and bring the country to its knees. Furthermore, Hitler recognized that if the British turned their bomber force against the Ruhr it would decapitate the ability of the German war machine to replenish itself. For all of these reasons, it was, therefore, important to attack in the west as quickly as possible.

Accordingly, plans were laid for the consolidation of forces for a major campaign to occupy the rest of mainland Europe, all the way to the English Channel. However, there was strong opposition to this plan from senior Nazi figures and even from the German military leadership. Set against the certainties of military planners and experienced strategists, Hitler presented a nervous disposition that belied the strident and bellicose self-confidence with which he strode the public stage. Uncertain about the consequences and anxious about overextending his opportunistic use of quick action, Hitler was unsure about teasing Britain into a premature response. In fact, he was every bit as cautious as the British were about antagonizing him into a pre-emptory strike.

The Wehrmacht leadership, too, were very worried about an offensive in the west. In his talk to them on 23 November, Hitler therefore tried to allay fears, even to seek approval for what he himself realized was an ambitious undertaking. This would be the third invasion of France in a lifetime – 70 years since the Franco-Prussian War of 1870–1 and just over 25 years since the attack in 1914. He lectured the military elites on 'the nation's very existence' and on 29 November issued a directive to 'deal an annihilating blow to the English economy' by encircling the British coast with mines so as to deny it the ability to resist pressure from Germany for a settlement. He went on to define a way to put a stranglehold on Britain by forcing a confrontation on the battlefield of France to erode what was, realistically, only an expeditionary force – the British had never prepared for a great Continental war and had come to rely on naval and, latterly, air power to protect the Empire.

As head of the Luftwaffe, on 7 December 1939, Göring issued his own directive for a war in the west: to defeat the French Army as completely as possible in Belgium and France before turning on the Royal Navy in the Channel and in the North Sea. Luftflotten 2 and 3 were assigned to support the Army, much as air support had been mobilized for the attack on Poland. The Luftwaffe High Command wanted to start as quickly as possible so as to gain the optimum advantage, citing 1 January 1940 as the preferable date. However, carrying the bombing raids to British soil was to be handled with care. Only Göring could give permission for air raids on conurbations with more than 5,000 inhabitants and even then only those that were home to military targets.

The German policy as it was articulated by the most senior leadership of the Nazi hierarchy was to attempt at all costs to retain the British Empire but to bring the country to its knees so that it would not be a military threat to German ambitions in territories the Germans judged to be outside British interests. For its part, the Wehrmacht High Command was highly dubious about a premature start to the air war, citing that 'unleashing a full air war against Britain before we have acquired a favourable starting position and have strong forces suitable for that purpose is incompatible with our overall strategy'.

There was considerable doubt, not least from Göring himself, about the ability of Germany to wage such a conflict with Britain. First-hand sources later told of the deep concerns prevalent in late 1939 about the capability of the Luftwaffe to wage war on three fronts: the military war zone; the productivity of the armaments industry; and the German public's support for such a war. None of these were secure. Göring also complained that exemptions from military service for industry workers would prevent there being sufficient replacements for personnel lost in combat; the losses in the attack on Poland had been sufficiently severe to raise such a spectre.

Furthermore, concerns were expressed about the ability of the German war machine to provide for itself while leaving relatively untouched the domestic lives and living standards of the majority of the German population. It required a radical solution: the occupation and use of foreign industrial plants and sequestered (slave) workers to supplement losses. This was deemed the only way to maintain popular support for the Party while preserving its course of action in foreign policy and military activities. That this was at the core of integrated planning is frequently missed, but it played a major role in shaping air policy as it related to the war as a whole. Indeed, it is the sole reason why orders restricted the bombing of industrial towns without compelling reason. Working plants, intact factories and able workers would be crucial to the econometric balance of German society at home.

Of course, the British and French knew nothing of this internal strife. On 14 April 1940, when Air Chief Marshal (Air Chf Mshl) Arthur Barratt, liaison officer to the French, failed to reach a compromise over how to address attacks on German targets, the French again resisted any provocative action. Plans to attack the Freiburg and Basel railway lines had already been dropped, and the French declined to allow the launch of attacks on German industrial targets on the Ruhr from their soil, again for fear of reprisal. A compromise was eventually reached nine days later when the French agreed to RAF raids on selected targets in the Ruhr if the Germans attacked Belgium and Holland, but on no other industrial plant.

This degree of tip-toeing is all the more remarkable given the pace of aerial activity that would quickly unleash itself on France and the Low Countries after this period of dithering ended. What it reveals is the extent of the uncertainty on both sides about how to proceed and the optimum course of action. In reality, it was impossible for the Wehrmacht to mount an offensive in the west before spring 1940. Of critical importance, this lull before the storm enabled the Luftwaffe to reconsolidate its forces and the RAF to grow stronger – outcomes that would only excite the potential for unconstrained war in the air when Germany finally did make its move in the west.

OPERATION *WESERÜBUNG*

All attempts by some elements in the Wehrmacht to prevent Hitler from attacking in the west were confounded on 24 February when the High Command worked out a strategy for preventing British and French consolidation in the Low Countries to precede a general assault across the northern territories of France itself. Opposition, however, was still voiced by several senior commanders, though only regarding the minutiae of the plan rather than the logic of the strategy. A prime objective, as viewed by the High Command, was to secure Holland early on and to lock out an Allied initiative in this area.

The Luftwaffe was eager to press on with attacking the RAF at its airfields and command centres, essentially preparing the way for future options regarding invasion by ground and seaborne forces. However, it was against Britain's maritime supply routes that most of the offensive was said to be required, since this action would starve Britain of merchant fleets that were critical for supplies. To some degree, the Luftwaffe saw itself as an alternative to the pre-eminence of attack by ground forces, which had worked so well in Poland, recognizing that both geographically and geopolitically Britain was in a very different place and that neutralizing it as a threat was not just about physically occupying it.

This view was adapted to some extent by another plan, which preferred to see the subjugation of the RAF prior to an attack on France and the Low Countries, thus preventing Britain's air power from supporting France in the coming conflict. The Germans knew that while the British were weak in 'army co-operation' through lack of suitable aircraft for blitzkrieg, the RAF was investing more than they were in a strategic potential that could grind away at the industrial heart of Germany in a protracted war; they knew that the material and production assets of the British Empire could outgun Germany in the long term and that if defeat was to be ensured, it would have to be quick and decisive.

Concerns over the potential threat from Luftwaffe aircraft that were able to strike at UK targets from bases closer to Britain than those within Germany anticipated the potential for a German occupation of Norway. Should Germany make a move to occupy Scandinavia, the British would implement Plan R4 and occupy neutral Norway and Sweden. Strategic considerations focused Germany's attention on the need for material resources, particularly iron ore, which was available in abundance from Sweden through the Norwegian ice-free port of Narvik when the Swedish port of Luleå on the Gulf of Bothnia was frozen over. The other main source of supplies for Germany was France, but that was closed at the outbreak of war.

For Britain, directly facing Scandinavia, German occupation of Norway would threaten the entire north-eastern side of the UK with air attacks from a location far closer than existing Luftwaffe bases. And, as would later prove to be the case, German attacks on Arctic convoys sending aid to Russia after the German invasion in June 1941 were remorseless and incessant. Of course, none of this was known in early 1940, but time would certainly show how valuable a staging base for Luftwaffe operations Norway would be.

Unaware of British plans, but convinced that it was only a matter of time before the Allies occupied Norway and cut off German access, Operation *Weserübung* ('Exercise on the Weser') was authorized on 27 January 1940. It was to be mounted by XXI Army Corps, the 3rd Mountain Division, which was composed of troops who were experienced in Arctic warfare. It was supported by approximately 1,000 aircraft, which dropped paratroopers, and other aircraft, which conducted bombing operations and attacks on coastal and naval targets. Concerned that the British could invade territory further to the south if given time, on 1 March the invasion of Denmark was added to the plan, supplanting an earlier decision to negotiate access only after the occupation of Norway had been accomplished.

The Germans weren't the only ones to target Scandinavia. When the Russians entered Poland in late September 1939, they also began an offensive against Finland. By early March 1940, despite fierce resistance, the Finns were all but defeated under the sheer weight of numbers. On 3 March, Hitler urged that the invasion of Denmark and Norway continue apace. Nine days later, Finland capitulated.

There was some relief in London, where the government had pledged to help Finland and then reneged on its promise. This was a deceit that brought a challenge to Chamberlain's government, not least from Harold Macmillan, who had returned, wounded, from a fact-finding trip to Finland only to learn that despite promises, none of the weapons pledged by the British had been delivered. This is of note only insofar as it added further calls for Chamberlain to stand down, which happened less than two months later, significantly altering the course of the war.

On returning to his former job at the Admiralty when war broke out, Winston Churchill had pushed a plan, Operation *Catherine*, to force into the Baltic a flotilla of large warships fitted out with armoured protection and anti-aircraft guns. However, this did not happen, its adoption being deemed too risky and likely to leave isolated naval units overexposed far from British territory.

By early April, there was widespread concern in Britain that it was being left to the Germans to decide where the next initiative would be staged. There were calls in the national press to do something, to take the fight to Hitler and not wait for him to choose the next battlefield. But there were enough uncertainties to raise caution; while aircraft production was increasing, poor production levels for anti-aircraft guns raised concerns about the effective defence of urban areas should Germany decide on an all-out air war.

Then there were reports that the Germans had clustered 147 divisions in western Germany, more than 100 of which were close to the border with France. The Joint Intelligence Committee noted, too, that Germany had 1,200 troop-carrying aircraft, supported by fighter units in northern Germany, ready to conduct a snap invasion of Sweden, maybe even Norway, and that a reduction of access to iron ore was of equal concern. This heightened uncertainty affected both sides in this stand-off, with time running out to reach a decision on how to spring a trap. The Germans alone knew where their next target was going to be and the British only had R4 – the plan to occupy neutral Norway and Sweden – and that was a reactive proposition.

The direction of travel became clear on the afternoon of 7 April when HMS *Glowworm*, operating on mine-laying escort duties, announced that it was engaging a German destroyer off Trondheim and that a German naval force appeared to be heading in the direction of Narvik. The transmission from *Glowworm* faded, disappeared and nothing more was heard of her. It later transpired that, running into gunfire from the German heavy cruiser *Admiral Hipper*, *Glowworm* had turned about, rammed the German warship and ripped off 120 ft of her armour plate. However, *Glowworm* had lost her bow in the process and sank shortly thereafter.

The first news of what amounted to a massive assault by German forces was brought to the British government during the morning of 9 April. As Major General (Maj Gen) Hastings Ismay, Deputy Secretary of the Cabinet Office, recalled:

'In the very early hours … I was awakened out of a deep sleep by the telephone bell. It was the duty officer at the War Cabinet Office. I could not make head or tail of what he was saying, in spite of frequent requests for repetition ... so I suggested that he should draw the blackout curtains, switch on the lights, find his false teeth and say it all over again... His report was brutal in its simplicity. The Germans had seized Copenhagen, Oslo, and all the main ports of Norway... As I hurried into my clothes I realised for the first time in my life, the devastating and demoralising effect of surprise.'

That there had been several reports during the preceding two days of German naval activity in the North Sea was certain; what that implied was less clear. The British Home Fleet had sailed from Scapa Flow, Scotland, prepared to engage what they perceived to be a major breakout of elements of the German naval forces, including the battleships *Scharnhorst* and *Gneisenau*, to attack British merchant ships in the North Atlantic. The Germans had conducted a masterstroke in that they teased the British into believing this so that the Royal Navy would steam full speed west in pursuit, while the bulk of the invasion force headed for the Norwegian coast.

The successful occupation of Denmark and Norway by the Germans demanded that speed was of the essence. This involved close co-ordination between the Kriegsmarine (Navy) and the Luftwaffe, specifically the Kampfgeschwader zur besonderen Verwendung (bomber Geschwader for special use), which were essentially the air transport formations. Commanding X Fliegerkorps (10th Air Corps), Lieutenant General (LT Gen) Hans Geisler was charged with subduing the Danish and Norwegian air forces while suppressing Allied operations coming ashore. The massive transport task was assigned to seven transport Gruppen, which had been formed for this operation in support of the one existing transport Geschwader in the Luftwaffe. These units had Junkers Ju-52/3m transport aircraft together with a mixture of landplanes and seaplanes.

The transport aircraft loaded with paratroopers took off from airfields in Schleswig-Holstein on the morning of 9 April, dropping on airfields at Aalborg in Denmark and Oslo-Fornebu and Stavanger-Sola in Norway so that they could be taken under German control. The air drops were instantly followed by infantry units to secure the area for German control of all air operations. Twin-engine Bf-110 heavy fighters protected the lumbering transports and flew patrols to retain control of the skies.

Information about the exact level of activity came only slowly. RAF reconnaissance flights were dispatched and a Short Sunderland flying boat of No. 228 Squadron confirmed on the afternoon of 10 April that there were enemy ships in Trondheim, triggering a strike by Swordfish aircraft from HMS *Furious* the following day in what was the first aerial torpedo attack of the war. Unfortunately, by this time the ships had gone. So, redirecting their efforts to a nearby fjord, the Swordfish attacked a German destroyer at anchor. They failed to hit it and returned disconsolate.

Recognizing that destruction of Norwegian airfields was paramount, Blenheim bombers were sent to deny their use to the Luftwaffe and some strafing operations were carried out. However, the Luftwaffe had brought in Stukas, fighters, transport aircraft and anti-aircraft guns and rapidly consolidated their positions. Bomber Command suffered major losses when nine Hampdens and Wellingtons were shot down and, with unacceptable losses, on 12 April the RAF abandoned its prewar policy of self-defending daylight attacks. The Blenheims of No. 2 Group soldiered on in a tactical role, which also brought heavy losses.

Targets for these aircraft were in direct or at the very least peripheral support for naval and commando operations as the R4 plan unfolded and British forces began to deploy on what turned out to be a fiasco, with no chance of reversing the German invasion. As for Fighter Command, two squadrons were deployed to Norway. These included Gladiators of No. 263 Squadron from Filton, which were transported to Lake Lesjaskog aboard the carrier HMS *Glorious*. *Glorious* again carried out a ferry operation, moving 18 Hurricanes of No. 46 Squadron, deployed from RAF Digby to Skånland on 26 May. Ironically, they were told not to intercept enemy aircraft unless the airfield itself came under attack. Problems at Skånland prompted a move to Bardufoss and on 28 May a Ju-88 was shot down, followed by another six enemy aircraft for the loss of three Hurricanes the following day.

The outcome was inevitable, the British experiencing their first withdrawal. At another time it would have been called a retreat, perhaps even a defeat. The only serious opposition to the German onslaught was fielded by the Hurricanes. Over the course of 13 days, the squadron flew 389 sorties with 72 combat engagements and the shooting down of 26 Luftwaffe aircraft. Both squadrons were taken out of the country by HMS *Glorious* on 8 June but with the enemy in virtual control of the skies, the carrier was sunk the following day. Ten aircraft of No. 46 Squadron, its commanding officer and seven of its pilots were lost. The campaign in Norway had been problematic from the outset, yet there had been just a few voices in Britain casting doubt on the merits of risking lives on a fruitless endeavour. Some senior military advisers were loath to identify themselves but kept up a quiet insistence that it would be wrong to intervene militarily. They were ignored.

At the time, there were a few significant enclaves of people both in Denmark and Norway who expressed pro-German sentiment. They had a shared bond of

Nordic peoples that had given credence to some political support for the Nazi movement, as witnessed by the rise of Vidkun Quisling and his National Union Party of Fascists in 1933. However, the vast majority of Norwegians were horrified at the prospect of their freedom being suppressed under the Nazi jackboot. Indeed, the partisan movement that emerged after the German occupation is far more representative of Norwegian attitudes than any of the extreme views of Quisling, whose name is now forever linked to collaborators and traitors wherever they emerge.

Over the next four years, Norwegian patriots fought a long and effective underground war against their occupiers, with considerable support across the North Sea from Shetland, the run of small ships plying back and forth with supplies and commandos being dubbed the 'Shetland bus'. For mainland Britain, a much more aggressive and robust challenge to the nation itself was about to blow away any concept of a Phoney War.

CHAPTER 6
War in the West

FOR THE British, the first four months of 1940 were a process of expanding the levels of manpower and the delivery of aircraft to units as well as the consolidation of operational capabilities. Fighter forces would play a seminal role in the defence of Britain throughout the remainder of the year and see some of the most decisive encounters in the history of aerial warfare.

For the RAF, it was a time of real expansion – in terms of numerical assets and in the technical capacity of the air force to carry out its responsibilities. Much has been written about the derring-do of pilots and air crew, about the stoic determination of ground crew, fitters and technicians to keep the aircraft flying, and the senior commanders who managed the air war, first over France and then over Britain. However, the background to these events is frequently overlooked.

The decision to attack in the west was a product of failure on the part of the German political leadership to convince the British and the French that conciliation would resolve differences. It was also a failure to effectively neutralize the British resolve to stand alone, if necessary, when all external contact was cut off through a naval blockade and the sinking of merchant ships. For the Royal Navy, there was no Phoney War period. Its ships were engaged from the outset, keeping the sea lanes open and addressing the ever-present threat of the German battle groups marauding and hunting down adversaries on the high seas.

So it was that the German High Command, urged on by Hitler, approved plans to bring the British government to its knees through a process of attrition, wearing down the British resolve not only to keep fighting but also to retain an armaments infrastructure capable of carrying the fight to their enemy. It didn't work. In addition to the general expansion of the RAF, the build-up of frontline forces continued unabated during the opening months of war. During the period from January to April 1940, monthly production of medium bombers increased from 96 to 130, of light bombers from 86 to 91 and of fighters from 157 to 256. Overall, including reconnaissance, naval, trainers and miscellaneous types, monthly production totals across all classes of aircraft increased from 802 in January to 1,081 in April, a cumulative total of 3,462 in the first four months of 1940. The Germans estimated UK production at 3,500 and were essentially correct. However, as we shall see, their estimate for the year as a whole fell far short of the true figure.

The haste with which Hitler sought to deploy his forces westwards was driven largely by his desire to engage the enemy on the battlefield, where it could be destroyed before it could grow and expand its capability. He was convinced that Britain would advance into Belgium and the Netherlands, which reinforced his determination to employ blitzkrieg tactics before ground forces could organize themselves into defensive positions. It was there that he wanted to destroy Britain militarily and break its back, if not its spirit, so that the Kriegsmarine could mine the coastal waters and starve Britain into submission over the long term.

The fact that this plan was delayed until the spring of 1940 benefitted the Wehrmacht, enabling them to deploy later models of medium tank, the Panzerkampfwagen III and IV. The numbers of these in frontline service increased from 314 on 1 September 1939 to 715 by 10 May 1940, succeeding and replacing the much smaller Panzerkampfwagen I and II light reconnaissance types for major assault operations. Each type had been ordered into development during 1935. The Panzer IV and its derivatives would become the main German tank throughout the war. This land force, integrated with the air force, would prove overwhelming during the attack in the west.

On paper, the Allied countries of western Europe (France, Britain, Belgium and the Netherlands) had the numerically superior force, with a total of 144 divisions, 13,974 guns, 3,383 tanks and 3,099 aircraft. Against this combined force, the Wehrmacht had 141 divisions in the west, 7,378 guns and 2,445 available aircraft. However, against the Allies' 719 bombers the Germans had 1,559, while the Allies had 1,590 fighters compared with the Luftwaffe's 1,220. When examined more closely, if the blitzkrieg eliminated the Continental forces, Britain alone had only 540 fighters based back in the UK and any outcome would swing in favour of the defending force.

The dictates of Clausewitz, that Prussian military theorist of the early 19th century, maintained that an attacking force must outnumber the defender threefold in order to achieve victory over the entrenched resistance. However, Clausewitz was referring to land-based forces, long before the advent of air power and the employment of blitzkrieg created a new equation that could tilt victory in favour of the force with the most resilient air component. The Spanish Civil War and the 1939 attack on Poland had shown German forces the value of using closely interconnected instruments on land and in the air to overwhelm a numerically superior force. And this was the least developed element in the operational use of the RAF alongside the British Army.

At the end of March, Hitler had given orders to switch to an offensive in the west by mid-April, within days of achieving victory over Denmark and Norway. However, the Luftwaffe got tied down in the protracted refusal of the British to leave Norway to the Germans, so the start of the offensive was pushed back to early May to allow for reconsolidation of Luftwaffe units. Ironically, diplomatic papers in the British embassy in Norway revealed to the Germans plans for the British government to invade Norway imminently (Plan R4). The Nazi propaganda machine used this to justify its action in that it was preventing aggressive attacks on Germany by creating a defensive buffer.

CASE YELLOW

The overall plan for the invasion of France, *Fall Gelb* ('Case Yellow'), depended upon overwhelming force by the Luftwaffe, with Luftflotte 2 under Gen Kesselring and Luftflotte 3 under Gen Sperrle. These units had been deployed to the French border in September and October and had been conducting repeated reconnaissance and surveillance flights since the outbreak of war. The British had little chance to absorb lessons from the attack on Norway before their intelligence revealed ominous moves by Germany to begin an attack in the west. During the afternoon of 9 May, Germany issued an ultimatum to Holland and all Allied forces were put on alert.

Other matters, too, were sending shock waves through the British establishment, where Prime Minister Neville Chamberlain had presided over a government that was unable to mobilize a satisfactory response to Hitler's aggressive movements. On 7 May, the first day of a three-day debate about national policy with respect to the war, Leo Amery – a politician and journalist noted for his opposition to military appeasement – stood to deliver a rousing condemnation of events to date. With a faltering voice, falling to barely a whisper at the end, he spoke the words that would transform the way Britain would fight Hitler. Beginning by looking at the Speaker, then turning his gaze to fall on

Chamberlain, who had just returned to the chamber, pointing a finger at him as if in condemnation, he uttered the words that marked a turning point in the MPs' attitude to the war:

'This is what Cromwell said to the Long Parliament when he thought it was no longer fit to conduct the affairs of the nation: "You have sat too long here for any good you have been doing. Depart I say, and let us have done with you. In the name of God, go."'

At the end of the third day of debate, Chamberlain attempted to form a coalition with Labour and the Liberal Party. However, they were unwilling and indicated that they would only join such a government of national unity if it were led by a Conservative other than Chamberlain. The King wanted Lord Halifax to fulfil this role, but he turned it down. When it was put to him, only a man who had voiced long-standing condemnation of Hitler would do. That man was Winston Churchill. He became Prime Minister on 10 May, the decisive day when Allied forces would experience the full force of the Wehrmacht.

The first German attack on the morning of 10 May used paratroops under an assault detachment led by Hauptmann Koch to seize the fortress at Eben-Emael, Belgium, with cargo gliders employed for the first time in combat. As in Denmark and Norway, paratroops were dropped on key airfields to prevent them from being used by the Allies and to keep them open so that German transport planes could fly in more troops and logistical supplies. Co-ordinated assaults took place across Holland, Belgium and Luxembourg, with heavy air attacks on airfields and communication centres in France. German forces quickly occupied Luxemburg and began the push on Belgium through the Ardennes. Still the French resisted the order for the RAF to bomb, before Air Marshal (Air Mshl) Barratt seized the initiative and ordered an attack. Thirty-two Fairey Battles were sent in to strike enemy columns. Coming under heavy fire, 13 were shot out of the sky, the remainder returning with considerable damage.

Surprise was a key element of German strategy, the shock provided by howling Stuka dive-bombers being backed up with raids by conventional bombers throughout the day, pounding supply lines and enemy positions. Overall, some 1,180 German aircraft were employed – including 341 dive-bombers, 970 fighters and 270 heavy bombers – and sprang unexpected raids on the command centres. Having learned nothing from Poland, which they saw as a unique case, the Allies were totally unprepared for the attack. The Germans had expected the British to mount diversionary attacks on the Ruhr but when these failed to materialize the Luftwaffe was able to transfer defending fighter units from that area to consolidate attacking forces in France and the Low Countries. No persistent

Allied opposition transpired and the response from Britain and France was reactive rather than tactical.

Belgium had about 200 operational aircraft and the Netherlands had 125 fairly obsolete craft that could play little role in defence. It was left to the French and the British to defend the whole of western Europe. On the first day, the Luftwaffe targeted more than 45 airfields, each of which sustained considerable damage, and 30 French aircraft were lost. RAF Fighter Command put up a fierce attack, with Hurricanes from Nos 1 and 73 Squadrons in action primarily against small numbers of unescorted German bombers. During the day, they were moved to different airfields to provide better cover for Allied bombing operations.

A NUMBERS GAME

On the day that war broke out in the west, the RAF had five squadrons (Nos 1, 17, 73, 242 and 501) in 67 (Fighter) Wing; ten squadrons (12, 88, 103, 105, 114, 139, 142, 150, 218 and 226) in 71, 75 and 76 (Bomber) Wings; one photographic reconnaissance and one reserve squadron under the authority of the British Air Forces in France (BAAF) under Air Mshl Barratt. Established on 15 January 1940, the BAAF provided a unified command of RAF units in France.

The Air Component of the British Expeditionary Force (BEF) came under Air Chf Mshl Blount and incorporated ten squadrons (3, 79, 85, 87, 213, 242, 253, 607, 615, 504) under 14 (Fighter) group, of which the majority were based at stations in England and would have a chequered operations diary that saw them transfer first to French airfields and then back to the UK under the general withdrawal from the Continent. But these were defensive operations. The option for attack was within the preserve of the AASF under Air V-Mshl Patrick Playfair, formed on 24 August 1939 out of No. 1 Group Bomber Command.

With ten squadrons, the AASF was assigned to an offensive strategy and from 15 January, along with the Air Component of the BEF, it came under the authority of the BAAF. With a pitifully inadequate complement of Battle and Blenheim types it would fall prey to Luftwaffe fighters and pay the price for inferior aircraft.

During the afternoon of 10 May, No. 3 Squadron flew in to France from Kenley in south-east England, followed by No. 79 Squadron from Biggin Hill. Both were equipped with Hurricanes. The fighting was intense but uncertain due to the rapidly evolving situation, with the RAF flying more than 200 sorties during the day, some individual pilots logging three or four sorties each. There were claims that 42 German aircraft had been brought down for the loss of five Hurricanes and ten badly damaged, a further five eventually being written off. However, the performance of Bomber Command was compromised by the inadequacy of their light and medium bombers, which seemed to have no real success stemming the tidal assault of the ground forces. Indeed, Bomber Command suffered a loss rate of 40 per cent of aircraft sent out against German forces in Luxembourg, compared to a loss rate of 9 per cent on raids over Holland. Both of these figures paled in comparison to the 83 per cent loss rate of fighters attacking Waalhaven in the Netherlands due to a focused attack on the bombers by Luftwaffe fighters and from ground forces.

Day One of *Fall Gelb* saw carnage on all sides. The Germans lost 353 aircraft and 904 air crew while the Allies lost 410 aircraft and 115 personnel. This lower aircraft to personnel ratio was due to the fact that most Allied aircraft were knocked out on the ground. With 54 aircraft destroyed and 67 air crew lost, the RAF had taken to the skies and engaged the enemy in the air, and this was displayed in the expected spread of casualties per aircraft.

By the third day, the Germans had control of an air corridor into Waalhaven. This enabled Ju-52 transport aircraft to bring in troop reinforcements, emphasizing the unique nature of this air war. Compared to World War I, this war was proving very different, thanks to the addition of the new element: air support. No longer did success depend upon the taking of land. Troops could be flown direct to their assigned locations in the theatre of war while the air was contested by aerial combat, whittling down the defenders and driving them back. Frequently, the arrival of ground forces raised the intensity of the fighting but the final objective was closer than it would have been without aerial warfare playing a pivotal part in the fortunes of both attackers and defenders.

The inadequacy of the British bombers became evident as the percentage loss of Battle squadrons committed to raids as part of *Fall Gelb* increased from 40 per cent on the first day to 100 per cent on the second and 63 per cent on 12 May. While the efficacy of the bombers may have been in doubt, the bravery of the pilots was not. For example on 12 May, Flight Officer D.E. Garland, the pilot of Battle P2204, and navigator Sergeant T. Gray were both posthumously awarded the Victoria Cross for persistence in attacking the Veldwezelt bridge over the Albert Canal in Belgium from low level and under incessant anti-aircraft fire. Their aircraft crashed and burned out near Lanaken. The citation acknowledged the 'heroism displayed by the crews in undertaking a virtually suicidal task'.

Yet this is just one among countless acts of bravery against overwhelming odds which, while recognized at the highest level, brought a sense of hopelessness. This was expressed in an urgent message to Air Mshl Barratt from the Chief of the Air Staff: 'We cannot continue indefinitely at this rate of intensity... If we expend all our effort in the early stages of the battle we shall not be able to operate effectively when the really critical phase comes.'

FOR OUTSTANDING BRAVERY

Although prevented from flying aircraft in combat during World War II, women carried out jobs and responsibilities vital for oiling the machinery of warfare. All too often, however, acts of bravery went unrecognized or, in the heat of conflict, were overshadowed by the sheer intensity of events.

One such act of bravery that was properly recognized took place on 31 May 1940 when an Avro Anson (R3389) of No. 500 Squadron returned to RAF Detling, Kent, after attacking shipping in Boulogne.

Cpl Daphne Pearson was at the station at 1.15 am when the Anson undershot the runway trying to land on one engine, causing the undercarriage leg to collapse and a fire to break out. Pearson dashed to the burning aircraft and as she was pulling the pilot, Plt Off D.E. Bond, from his seat he muttered that there were still bombs on board and that they could explode at any minute. She pulled him further away just in time to save his life as the bombs detonated, spraying the area with shrapnel.

For this outstanding display of bravery, Daphne was initially awarded the Empire Gallantry Medal in July 1940. However, when the George Cross was instituted by King George VI in September 1940 she was asked to hand back the Empire Gallantry Medal so that she could receive the nation's ultimate acknowledgement of bravery, making her the first woman to receive the George Cross.

On 13 May the weather was poor, which made it difficult for the British to conduct reconnaissance flights in order to provide intelligence on the worsening situation. The Luftwaffe continued to attack communications and supply conduits far to the rear of Allied lines and Hurricanes sprang an attack on German forces pursuing the retreating elements of the French 7ème Armée. During the morning, six two-seater Defiants from No. 264 Squadron, Martlesham Heath, Suffolk, attacked Ju-87 Stuka dive-bombers but were themselves set upon by Bf-109 fighters, with five being shot down and the sixth badly damaged but repairable.

On this day also, the Dutch government reported to London that their air force had ceased to exist and that the country was on the verge of capitulation. Plans were formulated to evacuate the Dutch royal family from Ijmuiden on the British destroyer HMS *Codrington*. All this, just as the Belgian Army was retreating to new positions to defend Antwerp and Louvain. However, frantic appeals for more fighters resulted in 32 Hurricanes, together with their pilots, being sent across from England to reinforce depleted squadrons. The following day, German forces consolidated their positions to link up with paratroops who had been dropped on the first day and to prepare for an all-out assault on Rotterdam.

WAR ON CIVILIANS

As the intensity of the assault grew in scale there were decreasing opportunities for the RAF to stem the tide of German incursions. As had been the case with Poland, the Luftwaffe was deployed on offensive operations with little regard for the civilian population. When there was fierce resistance in Rotterdam, a major harbour and point of maritime trade, on 14 May, a concentrated bombing raid forced an early capitulation. This important town surrendered two hours later after being reduced to what Gen von Waldau reported as 'a pile of rubble' where once stood a major centre of trade and commerce.

The destruction of Rotterdam unfolded when Gen Lt Rudolf Schmidt, commanding the XXXIX Armeekorps, issued an ultimatum demanding a surrender by 2.10 pm, some 50 minutes prior to a planned artillery barrage and air raid. Dutch soldiers fought back fiercely and a stalling action on the part of the town's negotiating body attempted to delay the response to see how the fighting was progressing. Because of the request for extended clarification on demands for the city's surrender, Schmidt ordered a postponement of the barrage. Luftflotte 2 was unaware of the extension and sent off 90 Heinkel He-111s of KG54 in two formations, approaching Rotterdam from separate directions. About 36 of those bombers spotted red flares on the ground, which indicated that there were friendly forces in the vicinity, and aborted, but three leading aircraft failed to see the flares. The other 54 bombers failed to hear frantic attempts by their controller on the radio and continued with the attack, placing their bombs precisely on target but inflicting extensive damage and causing 750 Dutch civilian casualties.

Across France, heavy bombing raids were conducted by the Luftwaffe. The Belgian city of Namur came close to falling as the French defensive line along the Meuse river began to crumble. On 14 May, of 71 RAF bombers sent out from bases in England more than half were shot down or crashed due to errors. Estimates of losses varied between 50 and 70 per cent. However, so confused were operations in those first two weeks of the German assault that the records are incomplete and it is impossible to know the detailed story of these hectic days. What is certain is that in the first three weeks of conflict, cumulative losses would amount to 75 per cent of aircraft sent out on sorties, with 100 Battle bombers lost, along with 119 air crew.

The result of these unsustainable losses changed the direction of the strategic planning and removed the Fairey Battle from all but night operations. The aircraft themselves were completely unsuitable for combat, with no self-sealing tanks, no armour protection, minimal and largely ineffective bomb aiming equipment and crews who had been given little training for operational techniques, which were anyway already outdated and unacceptable. Had the British public known at the time that RAF flight crews were being sent out on missions that introduced words such as 'suicide' into official top secret reports back to London, public morale that had held firm so far might have evaporated. The detailed figures for loss rates on sorties and on the total inability of Bomber Command to hit all but the largest and most visually obvious of planned targets remained a secret for at least a decade after the war.

However, it was not only the Allied air forces that were losing aircraft. On 15 May, the Luftwaffe lost 104 aircraft with 52 destroyed and 52 damaged, some of which could be repaired. Daytime Luftwaffe activities concentrated on attacking rail targets and disrupting the movement of French reserves to prevent the consolidation of ground forces and on raids across the communications network. In this, the Luftwaffe was particularly successful.

Already, under the onslaught from the air, refugees were fleeing the guns. They blocked routes, inhibiting the movement of military forces on metalled roads suitable for mechanized traffic. Movement around the remaining open countryside was an exercise in land navigation as civilians carried belongings on carts, wagons, tractors and dilapidated vehicles. Mothers with prams were followed by young girls with their own little prams with dolls inside. Wrecked army trucks and burned-out buildings razed to the ground by dive-bombers clogged intersections and men in uniform speeding along the verges on half-track vehicles added to the sense of panic, even among those paid to stand and fight.

It was a similar story for the air crew, who were also falling back and walking away from the advancing spearhead of the German Army. One such was Flg Off Edward Hall of No. 73 Squadron, RAF. He wrote in his diary:

'Every mile was littered with its complement of fuel-less cars, abandoned completely by their owners who had preceded on foot. Somehow we gradually worked our way in the tightly wedged phalanx, happily to discover that it occupied but two-thirds of the road, the remaining third being kept open by military police although with considerable difficulty, for the exclusive use of military traffic also bound south. As for any traffic proposing to travel north, well, that was palpably absurd. We lost our way and had to swing back in a wide curve towards our destination. And as we drew near to it ... [we were amazed] to see a column of RAF personnel marching briskly along the road leading from it in the opposite direction to us. We stopped and enquired if we were ... [heading in the] right [direction] for the [aero]drome only to be informed that they were just coming away from it – evacuating it in so much of a hurry that those for whom there was no transport had to take up their packs and walk.'

Pressure for France to give permission for attacks on the Ruhr, denied during the initial phase of the assault, was granted on the third day but poor weather prevented these until the night of 16/17 May. A raid on the Ruhr the previous night involved 99 aircraft of Bomber Command, which were assigned 16 separate targets. In the mix were 39 Wellingtons, 36 Hampdens and 24 Whitleys. Eighty-one of these aircraft reported bombing their assigned targets, but there was scant evidence that any of these aircraft had actually dropped bombs on intended targets. One report announced that a dairyman, Franz Romeike, had been killed – Cologne's first casualty to air bombardment – and a further report in a local newspaper said that he had gone to the toilet, turned on an outside light and promptly invited a rain of bombs! What is known is that one aircraft was lost, when it was blown off course and flew into a hill.

DARK DAYS

On 15 May, the French Premier Reynaud implored Churchill to send more aircraft, believing that without them France was doomed. The bombing raids had had no measurable effect on German activity in the Ruhr, the bombers had no real idea of where they were and there appeared little reason to mount these operations if they weren't going to produce useful results. Just the day before, Reynaud had pleaded for more fighters but on 16 May Fighter Command C-in-C Hugh Dowding refused to send any more, asserting that to do so would expose Britain itself to great danger and that without the force he already had he would be unable to repel a German assault on Britain, which was universally believed to be coming in due course.

Churchill flew to France and met with Reynaud, who restated his passionate plea for more aircraft. Despite Dowding's opposition, Churchill telegraphed London and ordered six more squadrons to be sent across the Channel. More measured minds resisted and the Cabinet agreed with the Chief of the Air Staff Cyril Newall that there were simply insufficient intact resources in France to accommodate that number of additional aircraft. So, the squadrons that would have gone were kept on the English side of the Channel and sent on sorties from their home bases to conduct attacks before landing and refuelling in France, returning in daylight.

By denying France additional aircraft, the resources were retained in Britain and a Home Defence force was kept intact against the time when the Luftwaffe would turn its full fury on the British Isles. Many French citizens felt they had been abandoned by the British, despite the logic of Dowding's refusal. Through no fault of its own, France was becoming a drain for man and machine alike. Such a view can still be heard today, despite the unlikeliness that the ultimate defeat of France could have been prevented had the entire complement of Fighter Command been sent across the Channel. The fact that it was not would prove crucial in the coming months when Britain did indeed face the full might of the Luftwaffe, alone.

Unbeknown to the British, a directive from Hitler dated 24 May authorized the Luftwaffe to commence a 'full scale' air offensive against England, starting with a 'devastating retaliatory attack' for the British bombing of the Ruhr. Two days later, the Luftwaffe delivered the result of an analysis that cast doubt on whether a conclusive result could be achieved by attacks on British imports alone and that 'disruption of the utility system (gas, water, electricity) could be of decisive importance'. To do that, the skies above would need to be cleared of fighters, mainly clustered on airfields in the south-east corner of England. The industrial heartland of England could only be laid open to attack if the RAF itself was defeated.

It's clear, then, that long before Europe was occupied, plans were being laid for a major offensive against Britain. C-in-C Dowding had made the correct judgement. The RAF would need every fighter it had to repel the massed formations of bombers Göring planned to send once France had been secured.

The race to evict British troops and airmen from France gathered pace during the second half of May. With intense aerial support, the German Army made great progress, with Panzer divisions sweeping across north-western France not, as the French military had feared, in a sickle-shaped sweep to take Paris, but in a dash to the Channel to squeeze the Allied armies against the coast. It was a brilliant piece of strategy; by cutting off the British in the north, remaining French forces to the south would be denied reprieve and support, the overwhelming force of the German Army cutting the Allied defence in two.

By 19 May, the situation was chaotic. Conditions were getting much worse, with the Air Component of the British Expeditionary Force (BEF) commanding operations in the north while the Advanced Air Striking Force (AASF) controlled operations in the south and flew support for the Army. However, the headquarters of the British Air Forces in France (BAFF) had to relocate south to Coulommiers, which split it away from overall contact with supreme headquarters. While Bomber Command continued with its bombing campaign, with No. 2 Group under the dual command of Bomber Command and the BAFF, the French operations were also split by the German wedge, now in control of the central region of France across to the Channel.

OPERATION DYNAMO

To the British commander, Gen John Gort, the situation was becoming hopeless and, without telling his French counterparts, on 20 May he began planning for a mass evacuation of British troops across the Channel from the area around Dunkirk. There was little confidence that the French could hold out. The Germans were encircling a wide swathe of north-west France from the border with Belgium and up to Zeeland, down as far as south of Boulogne. Allied forces in that area were trapped and vulnerable to the Panzers and to sustained attack by the Luftwaffe. Known as Operation *Dynamo*, the evacuation was put in the hands of Vice-Admiral (V-Adml) Bertrand Ramsay from his command bunker below Dover Castle on the coast of Kent. That same day, Brigadier General (Brig Gen) Gerald Whitfield was sent to Dunkirk on the French coast to organize the evacuation from the ground.

By 21 May, the whole structure of operations on the Continent had changed, with bomber squadrons withdrawing back over the Channel to conduct raids from English soil. No. 2 Group operated primarily from East Anglia while Fighter Command began to organize around a command structure that could best counter German air attacks launched from occupied France. The following day, Churchill instructed the BEF to attack to the southern edge of the German lines to co-ordinate with Gen Georges Blanchard's First Army to join up with other French forces. Gen Gamelin had been dismissed three days earlier due to a feeling that he was out of his depth and Blanchard was now supreme commander of French forces. However, realizing the magnitude of the situation, Gort abandoned this plan and, along with Blanchard, made his way behind the Lys canal all the way to Gravelines. The sluice gates of the canal had been opened to flood the countryside as a defence against the advancing German Panzer divisions.

Two days later, on 24 May, the Germans occupied Boulogne and surrounded Calais. Here, German engineers rapidly built five bridges over the much-inflated canal, the route to Dunkirk blocked by a single British battalion. RAF Fighter Command flew patrols along the coast of northern France and inland as far as Saint-Omer but another two aircraft and six pilots were lost.

The day before, at the orders of Col-Gen von Rundstedt, Fourth Army commander Generalfeldmarschall Günter von Kluge brought the Panzers to a halt and, in a remarkable message sent in open transmission and without code, stated: 'By order of the Fuhrer ... the Canal line is not to be crossed.' Later, during the afternoon, after consultation with Göring, Hitler ordered the Luftwaffe to defeat the encircled British and French troops and prevent their escape.

The British and French troops were trapped in a pocket behind a line running generally Ghent–Tournai–Arras–St Pol and inside this 127-mile line there was no escape by land. It had been wrongly believed by the Germans that any evacuation would take place through Antwerp and the temporary halt to the German advance was also used to bring up stores and additional supplies. The decision to halt German forces has been debated ever since and various historians and writers have reached a range of conclusions. In the overall story of the air war, the evacuation of more than 300,000 men off the beaches of Dunkirk is not of great moment, except to relate the cover that was accorded by the RAF from airfields in England.

There was some logic to the decision to halt the advance. Von Rundstedt had already expressed concern about how vulnerable his flanks were and about the supplies for his armour as well as tracked and wheeled vehicles. He had good reason for this. The pace of the German advance had been as expected by many of the doctrinal advocates of blitzkrieg warfare but was not wholly accepted by the logistics, transport and supplies branches of the Wehrmacht. Some units were perilously close to running out of fuel, and post-war examination of the quantities being brought forward showed that about 10 per cent of the vehicles would have run dry within 12 hours. Moreover, the Luftwaffe units were losing aircraft and men and there was still a contested region to the south where fighting was intense and continued to absorb resources.

There was also the question of the type of ground versus the kind of vehicles and tanks available on the periphery of the contested pocket. Von Rundstedt was concerned about this and wanted to hold the Allies static. He accepted that this was a role for air power – to go in and destroy the remaining equipment so as to deny it to the enemy. No one on the German side seriously anticipated an evacuation by sea off the beaches of Dunkirk.

First-hand sources suggest that Hitler was undecided about what to do with the British. Hitler had a fascination with Britain and watched films depicting great triumphs in the establishment of the Empire. On many occasions, he expressed his admiration for the way the British ruled India with relatively few military personnel. Likewise, in later months, German pilots came to have high regard for the way the RAF fought in the skies over England, seeing 'an adversary worthy of us' as Galland would say. By contrast, the Poles were (inaccurately) dismissed for having been easily overcome and the French were deemed equally ineffective in their defence of France from the air. Somewhat counter-intuitively, then, between Hitler and his Wehrmacht, there was a curious respect for the British.

Whether or not this affected Hitler's judgement when it came to Dunkirk is debatable. What we do know, since it was said by several German generals, not least Gen Heinz Guderian, was that allowing the British to escape off the beaches was one of the greatest mistakes in the history of warfare. This view was further endorsed by Rundstedt when he proclaimed it as 'one of the great turning points of the war'. There is another voice to add. In his memoirs written more than 15 years after the war, Gen Walter Warlimont, deputy chief of operations in the Oberkommando der Wehrmacht (OKW, Supreme Command of the German armed forces) related that:

'Late in the afternoon of 23 May, Göring was sitting at a heavy oak desk beside his train with his chief-of-staff [Gen Hans Jeschonnek] and his chief signals officer when the news arrived that the enemy in Flanders was almost surrounded. Göring reacted in a flash. Banging his great fist on the table, he shouted "This is a wonderful opportunity for the Luftwaffe. I must speak to the Fuhrer at once. Get me on."

'In the telephone conversation which followed, he used every sort of language to persuade Hitler that this was a unique opportunity for his air force. If the Fuhrer would give the order that this was an operation to be left to the Luftwaffe alone, he would give an unconditional assurance that he would annihilate the remnants of the enemy; all he wanted he said was a free run; in other words, the tanks must be withdrawn sufficiently far from the western side of the pocket to ensure that they were not in danger from our own bombing.

'Hitler was as quick as Göring to approve this plan with further consideration. Jeschonnek and Generalmajor Jodl [chief of operations of the OKW] rapidly fixed the details, including the withdrawal of certain armoured units and the exact timing of the start of the air attack.'

With most of the RAF units deployed back to the UK, Bomber Command would continue to mount raids against German forces on the Continent as the government prepared an audacious plan, calling upon the Merchant Navy, all available naval warships and even the weekend sailors with little boats tied up along the coast of eastern and south-east England. It would take everything afloat to get the men off the beaches – a task that called for protective air cover, this time coming from England itself. RAF Hawkinge and RAF Lympne were earmarked as key stations to accommodate the remnants of the Air Component and the rear headquarters was established at Hawkinge with Group Captain (Gp Capt) John Vachell in command from 21 May. Air Chf Mshl Blount arrived back from France on the evening of 26 May to take over from Air Chf Mshl Sir Joubert de la Ferté.

While the 'little ships' – manned by civilian volunteers, some of whom had set off from around the coast in East Anglia to report for duty – were to ferry personnel off the beaches throughout daylight hours, home base fighters would fly top cover to harry the Luftwaffe and keep the beaches as clear as possible of bombs and the strafing tactics of German fighters. Larger ships would berth by the River Mole and relay across the Channel for as long as it remained open.

Fighters from No. 11 Group in south-east England were insufficient in number to conduct large-scale operations. There was also concern that they may be required to counteract a possible invasion force that could be heading across the North Sea while attention focused on the narrowest part of the Channel. Prudently, the RAF maintained an equitable distribution of resources, men and aircraft to counter that eventuality. As it was, the Luftwaffe was deploying further west in occupied Europe, with bombers already probing further along the south coast of England towards the west and fighters being moved into occupied French airfields to get them closer to England.

C-in-C Dowding ordered Air V-Mshl Keith Park, commanding No. 11 Group, to run two squadrons on patrol simultaneously from an 18-squadron force, stepping up to four-squadron patrols at peak evacuation times from 29 May. By day, Blenheims attacked the encircling Germans, now within 5 miles of the coast and throwing heavy fire on the beaches.

For the men trapped on the beaches, exposed and awaiting rescue, the Luftwaffe seemed to have a free hand and the cry went up 'where's the RAF?'. The answer was: high above and just a little over the horizon, keeping at bay the bombs and the bullets that would otherwise have joined the rain of destruction already falling on the exposed ranks of waiting evacuees, adding to already intensive ground fire on their undefended positions.

On 25 May, RAF Fighter Command flew 151 sorties over the Continent providing close escort for bombers and reconnaissance aircraft. While the German Army was pressing in upon the beleaguered Allied forces in the Dunkirk pocket, the Wehrmacht was sustaining a determined attack in the south, where the French suffered heavy losses. Poor weather prevented more than half the RAF bombers from reaching their targets.

The following day – just seven days after Gen H.R. Pownall, Gen Gort's chief-of-staff, had discussed the withdrawal of the BEF from France through the still-unoccupied ports on the Channel coast – Operation *Dynamo* began. It had been hoped to use three French ports to evacuate the remnants of British troops now pressing in upon the beaches, but by 26 May only Dunkirk remained open. It was now down to V-Adml Sir Bertram Ramsay to organize the biggest evacuation of British forces since Gallipoli in 1916. From his operations bunker deep inside the chalk cliffs of Dover, Ramsay received the official command from a signal at 6.57 pm to begin operations.

Mobilization of the vast inventory of little boats around the coast of Britain had, in fact, been under way since the German offensive in the west began on 10 May. Recognizing that many more ships would be needed to resupply military forces on the Continent, on 14 May the BBC broadcast a request for owners of self-propelled pleasure boats to report to the Admiralty and offer their vessels for registration. Within 12 days, these little boats, each 30–100 ft in length, had been registered, cleared for use and requisitioned for duty. In all, more than 700 answered the call, whether willingly or not; the pace of requisitioning was such that many boats were taken without their owners' consent, simply because they could not be contacted, and at least one irate owner on seeing his boat being slipped from its moorings in the upper Thames pursued it down the river, alerting police on the way!

To give scale to the effort, during the first full day of the evacuation only 7,669 men could be recovered. This rose to 17,804 on 28 May, 47,310 the following day and 58,823 on 30 May. Peak evacuation was achieved on 31 May when 68,014 men were taken off the beaches, with 64,429 on 1 June and a further 26,256 overnight. By this time, almost all the BEF troops were back in England, yet the evacuation went on. Some 26,746 French troops were brought to England, followed by a further 26,175 by dawn on 4 June. During the morning hours of that day a force of 30,000 French troops fighting house to house to keep the Germans at bay surrendered and went into captivity. At 2.23 pm, Ramsay received the signal to end Operation *Dynamo*.

Overall, in nine days the 'little ships', together with merchant ships and naval vessels, had lifted 338,226 men off the beaches – a figure incredibly higher than the initial estimate of 45,000. Of the total, 224,585 were British, the rest (33.6 per cent) being French and Belgian troops. Most of those evacuated had been taken off from Dunkirk harbour, 239,555 of the total, while 98,671 were taken off the beaches.

A MESSAGE OF DEFIANCE

When the rescued soldiers, sailors and airmen arrived back in Britain, morale was low. There was a sense of relief that so many men had been rescued but there was also already a weariness born of defeat. Others, though, did not see it that way, preferring to view it as an expression of defiance that Hitler had not been able to take the best of British and French youth to add to the expanding population of the prison camps that had been set up across conquered states.

Defining that national resilience and determination not to give in, on 4 June 1940 Prime Minister Winston Churchill addressed the free world in a speech before the House of Commons and later broadcast universally by the BBC:

'Even though large tracts of Europe and many old famous States have fallen or may fall into the grip of the Gestapo and all the odious apparatus of Nazi rule, we shall never flag or fail. We shall go on to the end.

'We shall fight in France, we shall fight on the seas and oceans, we shall fight with growing confidence and growing strength in the air, we shall defend our island, whatever the cost may be. We shall fight on the beaches, we shall fight on the landing grounds, we shall fight in the fields, and in the streets, we shall fight in the hills; we shall never surrender and even if, which I do not for a moment believe, this island or a large part of it were subjugated and starving, then our Empire beyond the seas, armed and guarded by the British fleet, would carry on the struggle until, in God's good time, the New World, with all its power and might, step forth to the rescue and liberation of the old.'

CHAPTER 7
Background to the Battle of Britain

DURING THE historic evacuation, Dunkirk came under intense and sustained bombardment from the Luftwaffe, which destroyed most of the town, set light to oil depots and sent a pall of black smoke as a dramatic visual backdrop to the extraordinary events unfolding on the beaches. Belgium capitulated on 28 May 1940, two weeks to the day after neutral Holland had also signed a surrender document. France was still holding out and while the evacuation of soldiers, sailors and some airmen from the beaches at Dunkirk was still under way, fierce fighting persisted in the south.

There had been some restraint in the air attacks by the Germans on the evacuation due to bad weather but that improved on 29 June and the assault from the Luftwaffe intensified. Having learned the recorded times of cyclical patrols mounted by the RAF from bases in south-eastern England, the Luftwaffe timed their own attacks on the waiting evacuees with precision, avoiding the risk of encountering the RAF and being shot down. The attacks were effective: two Royal Navy destroyers were sunk that day. To the men on the beaches, the incessant bombardment seemed to be exacerbated by the apparent disappearance of the RAF. Churchill was at pains to explain what was going on:

'Unhappily, the troops on the beaches saw very little of this epic conflict in the air, often miles away or above the clouds. They knew nothing of the loss inflicted on the enemy. All they felt was the bombs scourging the beaches, cast by the foes who had got through, but did not perhaps return. There was even a bitter anger in the Army against the Air Force, and some of the troops landing at Dover or at Thames ports in their ignorance insulted men in Air Force uniform. They should have clasped their hands; but how could they know? In Parliament I took pains to spread the truth.'

Some respite from German bombing on 30 May saw the RAF fly 265 sorties during the day but with few encounters, while 11 Group flew Blenheims in dense cloud with no result. No. 2 Group mounted 68 sorties without loss. However, the attrition rate of recent days brought a halt to the attacks for several days afterwards, providing respite while replacement aircraft and crew were brought up to frontline airfields. On 31 May, while the Luftwaffe stepped up operations again, and with improvements to the weather, three raids built up during the afternoon, focusing on shipping and the little boats.

Even as the final phase of the evacuation was under way, the Luftwaffe began a concerted bombing campaign against targets further south, with a major raid being mounted against Paris on 3 June. No. 67 Wing, operating Hurricanes, was unable to respond effectively due to a breakdown in communication. Overall, although precise details from the Luftwaffe are unknown, on 3 June some 600 bombers took part in a raid, escorted by 400 fighters.

Further north, the last RAF operations in support of Operation *Dynamo* ended ingloriously the next day, in thick fog that blanketed the Dunkirk area, the Channel and even airfields along the Kent coast, where four aircraft were lost, unable to find their airfields or get down safely. On that day, too, Winston Churchill gave a full report to the House of Commons, informing the nation of 'the miracle of deliverance'.

'We must be very careful not to assign to this deliverance the attributes of a victory. Wars are not won by evacuations. But there was a victory inside this deliverance, which should be noted. It was gained by the Air Force.'

Himself a veteran of combat in three wars, and now the national leader in a fourth, Churchill was aware that the RAF had yet to show its mettle and rise to be the final barrier against Nazi occupation. However, that was what now faced the political leadership – management of an air defence of Britain that, along with the Navy, would make it impossible for Germany to invade. Churchill had a grand vision of what could be accomplished when he told the House of Commons:

'When we consider how much greater would be our advantage in defending the air above this island against an overseas attack, I must say that I find in these facts a sure basis upon which practical and reassuring thoughts may rest. I will pay tribute to these young airmen… May it not also be that the cause of civilisation itself will be defended by the skill and devotion of a few thousand airmen.'

The second phase of the German assault began on 5 June with *Fall Rot* ('Case Red') in which the Wehrmacht was to complete the overcoming of France and the Low Countries with a military defeat in the northern territories and a negotiated arrangement with the Nazis for the southern half of France – the infamous Vichy government. Before that, a violent artillery bombardment opened a long-awaited final assault, with primary attacks along the Somme valley towards Abbeville. During this attack, the French put up 250 fighters against the Germans, flew 487 sorties and claimed 23 confirmed and 35 unconfirmed victories for the loss of 19 aircraft. The Luftwaffe claimed 58 Allied fighters but the resilience of the French Air Force came as a shock to the Germans.

All three AASF squadrons were under strength and in dire need of replacement aircraft. Only 18 serviceable Hurricanes could be sent up, flying a total of up to four sorties a day. Support came from Bomber Command in Britain, with 24 Blenheims attacking enemy concentrations north of the Somme between Albert and Péronne, accompanied by two fighter squadrons. That night, 48 Blenheims pounded communication lines and infrastructure at Cambrai, Le Cateau and Bapaume. And so the struggle for national survival went on, with the French putting up strong resistance in the air and on the ground, fighting for every inch of soil and supported by the remaining RAF squadrons in France and from RAF bases in southern England.

EVACUATING THE RAF

By 8 June 1940, German forces were making fast tracks for Rouen with British forces retreating before a quickening advance. For some time, with air support, the French attempted to make a stand along the territory north of Beauvais, but to no avail. To consolidate air support, Hurricanes of No. 17 Squadron flew in to Le Mans from Hawkinge, joining aircraft from Nos 73 and 501 Squadron. That evening, it was agreed that due to the danger of being overwhelmed by ground troops, squadrons operating from England should no longer land in France before returning home. This limited the radius of operation since each aircraft now had to conserve sufficient onboard fuel to make it back across the Channel.

The same day, Hitler ordered a further directive aimed at suppressing French resistance as his forces pushed south and faced increasing opposition, the very survival of their country now clearly the focus for the French Army. It was also the day that Churchill received another impassioned request for more squadrons of fighters to bolster French air units. The Defence Committee met to consider the request and Churchill provided a summary of two alternatives:

'We could regard the present battle as decisive for France and ourselves, and throw in the whole of our fighter resources in an attempt to save the situation, and bring about victory. If we failed, we should then have to surrender. Alternatively, we should recognise that whereas the present land battle was of great importance, it would not be decisive one way or the other for Great Britain. If it were lost, and France was forced to submit, we could continue the struggle with good hopes of ultimate victory, provided we ensured that our fighter defences in this country were not impaired; but if we cast away our defence the war would be lost, even if the front in France were stabilised, since Germany would be free to turn her air force against this country, and would have us at her mercy.'

For the next several days the southward progression of German forces appeared unstoppable and air support from bases in England kept up the pressure on German supply lines and armoured columns. The RAF was fighting a very tactical operation by a Bomber Command configured and equipped for strategic warfare. On 10 June, German forces crossed the Seine. Wherever they encountered pockets of French resistance they simply went around them, isolating the French troops where they could be contained by rear echelons. With imminent threat of a German initiative along the Saar–Rhine front, the situation in France was becoming critical, and the RAF put up a sustained attack on crossings. Although the Luftwaffe failed to contest the raids, two British bombers were shot down by French fighters, who mistook them for German aircraft.

By this date the fall of France seemed inevitable. A further complication was added when Italy entered the war, ostensibly to support its ally Germany but in reality to get a seat at the table when the various countries of Europe were carved up for distribution. Led by Benito Mussolini, Italy's Fascists had common ground with Hitler and the Nazis and wanted to stand alongside Germany in the war that was rapidly engulfing the Continent. In World War I, Italy had been an ally of Britain, France and Russia but the transformation of its political core shifted its allegiance away from democracy. However, Italy was still a monarchy and King

Victor Emmanuel III (1869–1947) refused to sanction this change until pressed by Mussolini as a last resort, but only to prevent Italy losing out in the sectioning of power across the Continent and elsewhere.

Intervention by Italy would come to be of note during the Battle of Britain and drive Italy south to begin a long, drawn-out conflict across the Mediterranean coast of North Africa. This conflict zone would go on to heavily involve the RAF and the Luftwaffe when Italy failed to live up to expectations and drive the British from that front. More immediately, it resurrected plans for such an eventuality that had been drafted before the German assault on France. In this, RAF units would deploy to airfields in the south of France to attack industrial targets in Genoa, Milan, Turin and Venice. When Italy did join the war, the RAF, both in France and England, was preoccupied and there was little stomach for dispersing existing resources to attack another enemy.

Neither were the French particularly keen to attack Italy. However, the War Council in Paris had agreed at a 3 June meeting that the Allies would raid industrial and oil targets in north-west Italy as soon as possible. This enterprise was codenamed 'Haddock' and given to Air Commodore (Air Cdre) Field and No. 71 Wing at Nantes. They promptly set about configuring available airfields for a raid to be supported by French fighters. When the operation called for 20 squadrons to be sent from Britain, though, the fanciful notion was demolished by logic and the endeavour was strongly resisted by French Premier Reynaud, who feared Italian reprisals against French conurbations.

Nevertheless, on 11 June, two squadrons of Wellingtons arrived in Salon to refuel. As they prepared to take off, French locals, receiving word of their purpose, parked trucks on the runway, threatening the start of an international incident. Convinced that it was to the advantage of France, and that just a few aircraft could cause devastation in Italy's industrial triangle, while he was at the French headquarters in the small town of Briare, Air Marshall Barratt telephoned Churchill to complain. Furious that his aircraft were being held virtually at gunpoint, Barratt sped through the night and arrived at Briare only hours after Churchill had refused another request for more RAF squadrons to repel the Germans. Now the British were requesting French permission to bomb Italy! Reynaud acquiesced to this initiative and eight Wellington bombers set off for Genoa on the night of 15/16 June. Only one found the target and dropped its bombs. Next night, 14 bombers managed to find Genoa and Milan.

But things were changing fast, and having faced an impossible situation with the French Cabinet split over whether to surrender, plead for an armistice or fight on, Reynaud resigned and Marshal Pétain took his place. On 16 June, the evacuation of British troops from Brest, Cherbourg, Nantes and Saint-Nazaire got under way. Some 50,000 men embarked for Britain, leaving France to the mercy of the new government, still in charge of a diminishing resistance to German forces. Another 'Haddock' attack took place with nine Wellingtons but four were unable to find their targets in the blackness of night and on their return to Salon all were immediately ordered back into the air for a return to England. Thus ended the RAF bombing campaign from French soil.

On the morning of 17 June, the British were first made aware that the French were suing for peace. Pétain was now in charge of a demoralized, somewhat dishevelled and frustrated people, many of whom were already under German occupation, while others were fighting for their own lives and that of France. The only roads to ports out of France were heavily congested with traffic, especially those approaching Saint-Nazaire and Nantes, although exits out of Brest on the Cherbourg peninsula were relatively free.

At Saint-Nazaire, some 10,000 people were crowded into transit camps. Despite this, most of the RAF personnel were able to make it to the liner *Lancastria*, which was moored in the Loire estuary. By midday, nearly 7,000 soldiers, airmen and women with children were crammed aboard a vessel designed to accommodate 1,300 passengers. Even considering the exigencies of the hour, that was a far greater load than the ship would ever normally carry. As German bombers appeared, other evacuation ships decided to head out to sea but, rather than risk enemy submarines, *Lancastria* remained anchored. With the RAF Hurricanes at the end of their range, the Luftwaffe had a free hand and one bomber dropped up to four bombs for a direct hit on the ship. Unable to deploy lifeboats due to the volume of people on board, the liner heeled over to port and sank with the loss of more than 3,500 men, women and children. Many died in the sea as the bombers dropped flares to ignite lakes of oil spilling out across the surface.

These evacuations from the west coast of central and southern France were part of Operation *Ariel*. It was a somewhat more formal plan, and with less threat of attack than was the case with Operation *Dynamo*, and covered a vast area from Cherbourg right down to Bayonne near the border with Spain. Another evacuation plan, Operation *Cycle*, was also being staged through Le Havre. Although officially terminated on 25 June, under the terms of the armistice signed by the French, the last of these operations was not completed until 14 August. In that time, a total of 558,032 military and civilian workers were lifted out of France and brought to Britain, of which 368,491 were British military personnel.

As the attacks on France intensified, there was increasing concern in Whitehall, where strategy for the British effort was being mobilized, that the Germans might step up their efforts and push hard for an immediate invasion of southern England. The British Army was depleted in terms of men and materiel capable of mounting a significant resistance and there was a dawning understanding about how Britain would have to defend its shores. Most believed that the Navy was essential to survival, and indeed it was, for if the sea lanes could not be kept open then the country would eventually run out of food and raw materials to maintain domestic production. Germany was increasing its U-boat grip on merchant shipping and the surface fleet was a serious and very present threat to the Royal Navy.

Many saw the RAF as crucial, keeping the Luftwaffe at bay to preserve the safety of the Navy. But a new role for Fighter Command was creeping inexorably closer to the shores of Britain: Continental bases close to the English Channel had been set up from where the Germans could mount intensive raids on targets deep in the interior of Britain. The strategic plan for the RAF in war was to pummel enemy targets in Germany using Bomber Command in the offensive and Fighter Command to shoot down German bombers that were attacking Britain. Due to the distance involved and the limited range of their fighters, raids mounted by the Luftwaffe from airfields in Germany would have no fighter protection as they approached England. It was for that reason that the Spitfire had found favour as a fast, high-climbing interceptor for shooting down bombers. Like the Hurricane, it was not procured for the role of close-in combat with enemy fighters and in that job it was not as manoeuvrable as the Messerschmitt Bf-109, which in some ways was a superior fighter.

But now the balance was shifting. From airfields in Germany, the Luftwaffe bombers could not strike targets much beyond a line from Dover, across the Thames Estuary and up to places around the Wash that divides Lincolnshire from Norfolk. Operating from airfields in the Ruhr and the Low Countries, Luftwaffe bombers could extend their attacks approximately from Southampton, the west of London and up to the Humber that separated Yorkshire from Lincolnshire. From airfields in Belgium and Holland, bombers such as the Heinkel He-111 could reach targets as far west as a line embracing Plymouth, Cardiff, Manchester and Newcastle, while medium bombers such as the Dornier Do-17 and the Junkers Ju-86 could strike anywhere in the UK.

It had never really been contemplated that Britain would have to fight Germany by air against bombers operating from airfields so very close to the shores of England. Worse, the most chilling development was that the fall of France meant that the Luftwaffe could mount bombing raids on Britain with full and effective support from its fighters. Fighter Command would have to knock out the bombers while simultaneously fending off Bf-109s and Bf-110s, something that had not been anticipated when the British drew up plans for a potential air war. The situation had, however, been foreseen by the Luftwaffe. In 1938, Gen Hellmuth Felmy had reported to the Wehrmacht on an effective means of attacking Britain by air, concluding that it would only be possible from bases in Holland and Belgium.

THE FRENCH SURRENDER

On 20 June, the French Prime Minister Marshal Pétain formally requested that Germany end hostilities and placed the fate of France in the hands of Hitler and the Wehrmacht. In announcing this decision to the French public, he paid tribute to the armed services, claiming that 'French aviation has fought at odds of one to six' and that defeat had been inflicted because France had 'too few friends, too few children, too few arms, too few allies'. The following day, the remnants of the French government tried to negotiate amenable terms with the Germans, such as a negotiated settlement in which France retained an independent administration of its own territories but devoid of military equipement. Key figures were called to a clearing in the Forét de Compiègne – the railway carriage where Germany had signed the Armistice in 1918 – and delivered an ultimatum: surrender or be annihilated. The French went away to discuss the matter, announcing late in the afternoon of Saturday 22 June that for France the war was over. Hostilities officially ended on 25 June after surrender terms had been agreed with Italy.

THE BALANCE SHEET TO DATE

The figures in the lead-up to France's surrender were indicative of the ferocity of the air war since operations had begun. Between early September 1939 and 9 May 1940, the day prior to the attack in the west, the British had lost 133 aircraft and 123 personnel, the French 175 aircraft and 163 men, the Dutch 18 aircraft and 8 personnel and the Belgians 23 aircraft and 13 men. The Luftwaffe had lost 354 aircraft and 445 air crew. In total, the Allies had lost 349 aircraft and 307 men.

By the end of hostilities, on 24 June 1940, the Allies recorded a cumulative loss of 3,020 aircraft and 2,137 men while the Luftwaffe lost a total of 1,814 aircraft and 3,278 men. Joining the war late and playing a minimal role, the Italians lost nine aircraft and 21 air crew. The Luftwaffe had lost 1,460 aircraft and 2,833 men in the subjugation of France.

Despite's France's capitulation, it was not total occupation. Under the surrender terms, the German forces would occupy a line roughly down to the 47th parallel in the south and the south-east of the country but not within some distance of the Atlantic coast. This unoccupied zone was run from a government in Vichy and had responsibility for policing the population, providing workers, using French industry to supply the Germans and, when called upon, for rooting out Jews, homosexuals and gypsies and sending them to concentration camps.

As for the French Air Force, that split into separate directions: some elements escaped to England and contributed to the Free French Forces while another group stayed behind, renamed the French Armistice Air Force and under the control of the Vichy politicians. When the British attacked the French Navy on 3 July 1940, to prevent it falling into German hands, the Vichy government severed all links with the British and the Germans approved the Armée de l'Air de Vichy so that it could defend itself against further attacks.

RESISTANCE AND RESILIENCE

The last RAF operations from French soil were carried out on 18 June, the day on which Churchill uttered the fateful words that brought a sense of impending destiny to the British people, uncertain as to whether they would face the same fate as France. From that, most people drew a perverse sense of strength in that if they went under, at least everyone was in it together:

> 'What General Weygand called the Battle of France is over. I expect that the Battle of Britain is about to begin. Upon this battle depends the survival of Christian civilization... The whole fury and might of the enemy must soon be turned upon us in this island or lose the war. If we can stand up to him, all Europe may be free and the life of the world may move forward into broad, sunlit uplands... Let us therefore brace ourselves to our duties, and so bear ourselves that, if the British Empire and its Commonwealth last for a thousand years, men will say, "This was their finest hour".'

Churchill's implied cohesion of British society was an attempt to unite a nation that was still separated by rigid social boundaries. Aware that the country had to have a sense of shared work and a single set of values to get through the coming months and years, Churchill spoke for the entire country when he called for a united effort against a common enemy. Notwithstanding the exigencies of rank, the RAF played a big part in demolishing a lot of those class divisions, the sergeant pilot equal to the flight lieutenant or the squadron leader when it came to the equality of danger in the air and to the sense of value in a squadron or as a member of a flight crew.

In Britain, there was considerable uncertainty about what would happen next. There was some degree of uncertainty in the Wehrmacht, too. Hitler's long-term objective was to turn to the east; he had no argument with Britain and his expressed preference was for keeping the British Empire intact as a stabilizing force in the rest of the world. That this was in any way a logical view is dashed by understanding that Japan had been in a bloody war with China since 1937 and that its long-term goals were to expand south, liberate the 'oriental' countries from their 'Occidental' overlords and gain access to the boundless resources of neighbouring countries. Like industrial Germany, industrial Japan was outliving its capacity for autonomy within existing borders. Sooner or later, Japan would strike against British interests, not least against Singapore, which was, at the time, the world's biggest telephone switching base and the centre of radio and telephonic communications throughout South-east Asia.

Nevertheless, a very public 'peace appeal' was read out in the Reichstag on 19 July, offering Britain conciliation in agreement for a free hand on Continental Europe – an epistle that went unanswered. On 2 July, Hitler informed the Wehrmacht that, if the circumstances were right, it might be possible to make a landing in England. Neutralization of Britain's military capability was desirable so that Hitler would not be threatened by a war on two fronts when he attacked Russia. Two weeks later, Hitler urged intensification of preparations in anticipation of a landing by mid-August.

Both the German Army and Navy wanted to settle the issue over Britain without having to invade. It would be a perilous expedition at best. Unless the Luftwaffe had total air superiority over the English Channel, any invasion would be highly unlikely to succeed. Moreover, the Royal Navy would have easy targets in the form of slow-running invasion barges, which would be dispatched across the narrow neck of water, barely 20 miles at its narrowest, separating England from France. And if the Luftwaffe had not totally destroyed the RAF, British fighters would be engaging in combat over their own countryside while German fighters would have limited combat time over south-eastern England.

By the end of July the naval operations staff had decided that Operation *Seelöwe* ('Sealion') was not possible during 1940. With the British in control of the seas, the Royal Navy would be the single most difficult obstacle and without the total eradication of air and naval forces such an operation would be doomed to fail. When the arguments were laid down, Hitler conceded that an invasion should only be considered as a last resort and doubted that it would be achieved. In this, his view coincided with that of Churchill, who dismissed the idea as absurd and suicidal for Germany. However, Churchill noted that the scare of an invasion was good for the British people in that it heightened their sense of awareness and bolstered morale – because the fear of a universal threat bound people together in common cause.

Nevertheless, the OKW drew up detailed plans for how an invasion might be possible. The initial assault would take place along a wide swathe of more than 200 miles of coastline stretching from Worthing to Margate. The 6th Army would depart from the Cherbourg peninsula and land across the Weymouth area; the 9th Army would depart from Caen and Dieppe and land from just east of Portsmouth to Brighton; and the 16th Army would jump off from Calais and Ostend and land on beaches from Hastings to Margate. The shallow beaches and excellent tank country along Camber Sands and Romney Marsh were the only bright aspects of the plan. The first line of occupation would have stretched from Portsmouth across an area south of London and curved up north-east to the Thames estuary. To be secured by the 9th Army and the 16th Army, the second line would have occupied the whole of southern England from Bristol to Maldon in central Essex, north-east of London.

Despite uncertainties, Göring was granted the task of eliminating the RAF. He sought to achieve this by bombing British airfields and taking down its fighter forces. But by this time, Britain was on an effective total war footing and the infrastructure was both ready and capable of resistance. Fighter Command deployed 11 Group from a line immediately west of the Isle of Wight, north-east to a line north of London, across to Cambridge and out to the coast just south of Norwich. Everything south of this line was under its command and C-in-C Dowding had half the complement of Fighter Command in this area. Everything west of that line was under the control of 10 Group with 12 Group picking up the north to a line roughly across the centre of England north of York and south of Catterick. No. 13 Group controlled the north and Scotland.

Opposing these squadrons was Luftflotte 3, covering the south and the west of England; Luftflotte 2, in the the south-east and east of England; and Luftflotte 5 from Norway and Denmark, covering regions north of Lincolnshire. Overall, the Luftwaffe had a specific establishment of 3,609 aircraft but an actual strength of 3,358, of which only 2,550 were serviceable. Interestingly, out of an establishment of 1,313 fighters, only 1,029 were available for action. While numbers can be deceptive (establishment versus serviceability, etc) overall loss rates show why the stresses on the Wehrmacht were considerable. From the start of hostilities on 1 September 1939 to the end of August 1940 the Luftwaffe had lost 11,345 personnel to action. In just May to July the Werhmacht had lost 51,500 men – dead, missing or prisoners of war – in addition to the 16,600 lost in the campaign against Poland a few months earlier.

Britain, which had lost a third of its pilots already, needed to compound the advantage it had of being able to fly and fight over friendly territory, whereas the Luftwaffe would be over England and any aircraft shot down would have to surrender survivors to prison camps for the duration. What's more, the British knew when and where the enemy was coming – another advantage that was not fully appreciated by the Germans at the time. Enemy air fleets were first detected by 52 Chain Home RDF stations that ran along the coast from Pembrokeshire to the Shetland Islands. They would acquire and track aircraft to a maximum range of 75 miles for high-flying numbers, far less for those approaching from low altitude.

Each Group was split into Sectors, one of which was the Sector Control Station, all of which reported to Group HQ and in turn to Fighter Command HQ at Stanmore, Middlesex. The RDF Chain Home stations reported to the Filter Room at HQ, which then passed the information to Group and then Sector levels. Observer Corps posts reported raids after they crossed the coast, passing on the details about the altitude of the raiders and numbers of aircraft, before sending the information to Observer Corps centres and then on to Group HQ. They in turn sent it to Fighter Command HQ for integration with the RDF reports. This kept raid plots up to date.

In addition, information was passed up or down to Sector Control level, which could usefully alert the balloon sites to lay a barrage, forcing the enemy to fly high, thereby making bombing more difficult. At the beginning of August, Britain had 1,500 barrage balloons for passive defence with 1,300 heavy and 700 light anti-aircraft guns. Sector control would alert the anti-aircraft sites and scramble fighters, sending them to the incoming raiders. Without this, time and fuel would have been wasted in continuous patrols along the coast, which would have been patchy, leaving some raiders to get through undetected until far inland.

Fundamentally, the ability to send fighter aircraft towards the enemy depended on the controller getting information from Direction Finding (DF) stations, which reported to their local Sector Control Room. This information went up the chain of command in the same way information from the Observer Corps was handled, and was transmitted to every Sector. In this way, the loss of a single Sector Control Room would not disable Fighter Command's ability to function effectively.

Key to the RDF reports was the cathode ray screen where the radar signals would first indicate to a steely-eyed monitor the presence of a raid. Looking rather like early television screens, the cathode ray screens had a series of indicators with numbers from zero to 100 across the top from left to right, revealing the distance in miles of the incoming aircraft. At the bottom left on the screen was an indication of the bearing of the return signal from the reflected targets, and at the bottom right of the screen was the time in GMT. The blips in the CRT trace showed the intensity of the reflection, which was an indication of the size of the air fleet returning the reflected signal from individual aircraft. There were two types of blip: local structures close to the radar receiver would give large responses close to zero in miles distant, while a blip at, say 40 miles, appearing suddenly, would be a sure sign of approaching aircraft.

CHAPTER 8
The Storm Unleashed

A GREAT problem with analyzing the Battle of Britain is knowing when it started and when it finished. Books, websites, official histories and academic opinion vary, with justification; it is not easily broken down into the separate phases. What is presented here is one, albeit the 'official' RAF, view – one that we will go with that since it stands up best to detailed scrutiny. Accordingly, the struggle for survival, for the country and for the RAF alike, can be separated into five distinct phases.

The first phase covers 26 June to 16 July 1940 and consisted of a series of *Störangriffe*, or nuisance raids. These were initially ad hoc reconnaissance and probing flights by Luftwaffe units compiling a detailed photographic, visually and verbally reported status of the coastal and immediate inland areas of Britain. In addition, mine laying and general mapping activities were carried out, as well as observation of, and reports on, merchant shipping and naval operations and associated activity in ports and harbours. All of these contributed to the initial survey that was put together in the lull while the Luftwaffe awaited a final decision by the Wehrmacht and Hitler on the course of action to take. There was also a series of harassing coastal raids during the first week of this period, until an order issued by the German High Command on 2 July signalled an increase in bombing. These were mostly lone raids and lacked the anticipated co-ordination many had feared would be unleashed immediately following the collapse of France.

From 10 July – a date some historians regard as the start of the first phase proper – there were increased air operations against shipping. Dubbed *Kanalkampf*, these were battles over the English Channel that were largely concerned with shipping and naval activity. In effect proxy training exercises, they gave Luftwaffe pilots experience with a different form of warfare – hunting down slow-moving targets on water – and kept pressure on the RAF by forcing them to mount defensive operations. The Germans also started to pay some attention to the RDF Chain Home stations on the south coast during this period. Although the Germans had only vague ideas about their potential, they were aware that they were something to do with radar.

By the third week in July there was an opposing force of 606 single-seat and 101 twin-seat serviceable RAF fighters and just over 500 bombers facing 824 Luftwaffe fighters and more than 1,100 serviceable bombers. One of the areas that proved difficult to address was the decreasing number of experienced pilots. Officially, on 9 July, the RAF had 1,450 pilots. However, the actual figure at squadron level was 1,253, the majority now men who were relatively inexperienced and lacked the battle-hardened tactics of older and more tested pilots. It would become a 'boys' war' in the air – one in which the young men would have to learn how to fight up in the sky while directly confronted by the enemy.

In an effort to counter these negative ratios, each squadron was increased by four aircraft, taking the complement up to a notional 16 fighters. This put more aircraft at the disposal of pilots. To help compensate for the low numbers of pilots, 68 men from the Fleet Air Arm were seconded to Fighter Command, but only until later in 1940, when pressures in the Mediterranean theatre of war demanded their presence there.

Numbers are inadequate for assessing the odds against success on either side, the prime objective for each being the same: to erode the opposing air force beyond the point where it was sustainable, forcing an end either to defence or offence. The Luftwaffe had the advantages that it was much closer to Britain than it had been at any other time, its aircraft could carry maximum bomb loads, and its fighters could extend their reach into British skies within minutes of taking off. The RAF, meanwhile, had the advantage of fighting over their own territory and being able to recycle 'downed' pilots back into operations. What's more, they possessed other advantages that were unknown to the Germans.

Throughout this period, significant changes were taking place that placed Britain in a far better position than it had held at the start of the war. For instance, the Germans were quite unaware that, with considerable help from the Poles, the British had deciphered the Enigma coding machines that were used for transmitting encrypted messages by radio between German units and command posts and between field centres and the High Command. In practical terms, during the Battle of Britain, the information was frequently decoded too late to have any meaningful effect, although this situation would change. Throughout the war as a whole, the cracking of Enigma provided considerable help to the Allies.

Another advantage lay in the communication gathered each day by Y-stations, a listening service that together with direction finding could provide valuable information about the chatter between individuals and units speaking via radio-telephone. Added to the encrypted messages coming through the Enigma machine, Y-stations provided a better view to Britain of what was going on with the Wehrmacht than the Germans had of activity within the British command system. In fact, so parlous was the Germans' knowledge about preparations in Britain that about 20 spies were landed in England in order to report on critical aspects of the country's infrastructure. Many of them could speak little English and were apparently intended to infiltrate groups of refugees and other foreigners arriving in the UK from occupied Europe. It didn't work and they were all rounded up.

Another, more precise advantage was the forensic work conducted by Dr Reginald V. Jones who, at the age of 28, was in September 1939 the first scientist to be employed by the intelligence section of the Air Ministry. He soon displayed an aptitude for linking Enigma intelligence from Bletchley Park, the centre for decoding encrypted signals sent through the Enigma machines, to help uncover the systems being introduced by the Luftwaffe. This allowed the British to more precisely target their objectives over longer distances. Of specific interest was the *Knickebein* system, which was a developed version of the Germans' *Lorentz* blind landing system. In a special test on the night of 21 June 1940, a flight sanctioned by Churchill 'listened' for the frequencies German bombers were using, verifying Jones' predictions and making it possible to develop a wide range of jamming methods – techniques that 'bent' the beams, causing the Luftwaffe to drop bombs on vacant countryside rather than the intended populated areas.

Perhaps the most effective advantage of all was the system of Fighter Command control channels formulated by C-in-C Dowding and described earlier – the link between detection by RDF and by Observer Corps posts, and the precise positioning of individual squadrons on to specific streams of incoming raiders. Before the implementation of this system the probability of any one individual aircraft engaging the enemy was around 30 per cent. After it was put in operation for the Battle of Britain, it achieved at worst 75 per cent and sometimes 100 per cent of specific intercepts per aircraft. The Germans had nothing like this and would only introduce an effective air interception structure using radar quite late in the war.

A NEW LEVEL OF ATTACK

The second phase of the battle began on 17 July, when the Luftwaffe stepped up its attacks on coastal shipping, naval targets and airfields, with night raids on RAF airfields and aircraft production plants. It was a concerted effort to starve the British people into submission by preventing food and essential supplies being delivered by sea and to deny the RAF its airfields so that it could not attack German bases on the continent.

The third phase of the battle ran from 13 August to 6 September and was planned by Germany as an all-out effort to destroy the RAF. It was defined by a strategy agreed by the Luftwaffe on 6 August that was largely based on incorrect intelligence. Believing the RAF to be already seriously deflated and close to defeat, Göring had been given the impression that an all-out assault would quickly clear the skies over Britain. The ensuing operation was known as *Adlerangriff* ('Eagle Attack'). *Adlertag* ('Eagle Day') was set for 13 August.

On that first day, poor weather kept most of the bombers from Luftflotte 2 grounded during the morning, but a few Dornier Do-17s from KG-2 set off just before dawn. Controllers working though the RDF stations detected formations beginning to build up in the Amiens area and soon two formations of 30 aircraft were sighted. Finding no escorting air cover waiting to accompany them – the fighters had been told to stand down because of cloud and mist – and unable to be contacted by radio, they set off across the Channel for Eastchurch on the Isle of Sheppey, Hornchurch and Manston. Then, in addition to the 60 German bombers already coming in, a further 100 were observed forming up over Dieppe, 40 more were detected off Cherbourg and a smaller group was forming up not far from the Channel Islands.

Nos 43 and 601 squadron set out from Tangmere to guard the west flank of 11 Group while Spitfires and Hurricanes from Kenley guarded the Thames Estuary. By late morning, more than 100 RAF fighters were in the air facing up to 300 enemy aircraft, the defenders organized into sectors rather than operating as independent squadrons. This was the secret to positioning fighters on to bombers and prevented time-wasting formations operating individually. Dornier 17s from KG-2 had no fighter escort but headed for Coastal Command bases at Eastchurch and Sheerness dockyard, but 74 Squadron engaged above mid-level cloud and the first Spitfire and Hurricane units with cannon armament joined the fray.

During the day, aircraft from 10 Bombengeschwader participated in raids on what would become one of the most intense periods of the battle. The first

German loss was a Do-17P off the coast of Kent, brought down by Sqn Ldr 'Sailor' Malan at 6.20 am. While conventional bombers went for airfields and RAF facilities in a wide swathe of the south-east of England, a test unit known as Erp-210 (Erprobungsgruppe 210) flying the brand-new Messerschmitt Me-210 headed for fast attacks on Rye, Pevensey and Dover in addition to nearby airfields.

In service little more than a year after its first flight, the Me-210 was very similar in appearance to the Bf-110 but with a top speed in excess of 360 mph and, as such, faster than any other aircraft extant. Other units involved included Stg-2 (Sturzkampfgeschwader 2) and Stg-77, each with Stuka dive-bombers. These were adept at hitting small targets and ideal for striking at the Chain Home radar masts, but were highly vulnerable to attack by Hurricanes and Spitfires. Stg-77 went for ships and installations in Portland Harbour, where flying boat operations were based.

Three RAF squadrons – Nos 151, 111 and 74 – covered convoys in the Thames, and the area around RAF Hornhurch and RAF Manston (both in Kent) respectively. Next, No. 238 Squadron was sent up to cover RAF Warmwell while No. 257 was ordered to patrol the area around Canterbury. Four more squadrons – Nos 601, 213, 64 and 87 – were ordered to support those already airborne and consolidate the air defences. The weather having cleared around midday, there was an increase in activity during the afternoon. Operations began around 4.00 pm with a major attack along a 40-mile-wide front. Around 40 Junkers Ju-88 twin-engine bombers from KG-54 and elements of LG-1 from Luftflotte 2 headed straight for the Supermarine works at Southampton, to Middle Wallop and further to the west. Here, 30 Stuka dive-bombers preceded 50 more of the same type, these escorted by Bf-109s from JG-27. Another contingent of Messerschmitt fighters from JG-53 swept in between the Isle of Wight and Lyme Bay. In response, No. 152 Squadron sent in its Spitfires, which, because the German bombers' fighter escort had had to return to base due to fuel exhaustion, were able to set upon the Stukas with great vengeance.

The German attacks that day were disorganized opportunities that were frittered away, the air crew believing that they had the RAF on the run and that their job was all but done. That this was emphatically not the case was brought home by the fierce resistance put up by No. 56 Squadron against a swarm of Ju-87 and Bf-110 aircraft, which forced the intruders to drop their bombs in the Canterbury area, their intended target of Rochford being covered in cloud. The Stukas were finding it hard to survive the remorseless attacks by Spitfires and Hurricanes. As an example of tactics developed by the Luftwaffe to avoid interception, when 40 Ju-87s trundled in to attack the airfield at Detling they were protected by German fighters, which tactically drew away the defending fighters of No. 65 Squadron. Detling suffered significant damage, losing 22 aircraft and 67 men, including the station commander, Gp Capt E. David.

Elsewhere, attacks on shipping continued throughout the day with Heinkel He-111 bombers attempting a precision night attack on the Castle Bromwich Spitfire works. Bombs were dropped across a scattered area close to Wolverhampton and Herefordshire. Both the RAF and the Luftwaffe suffered significant losses, with Fighter Command losing 47 aircraft, 19 of which were Spitfires and Hurricanes, while the Germans were down by 52, including 25 single- and twin-engine fighters. With longer-term implications, the Luftwaffe lost 28 bombers that day – aircraft that could never return to threaten England. Ferocious as the fighting had been so far, however, the worst was yet to come.

On 14 August, the Luftwaffe organized some 500 sorties, opening with a high-speed dash to Manston where No. 56 Squadron was taken by surprise by the suddenness of the assault, which saw two dozen twin-engine Bf-110 fighter-bombers racing in to strafe the airfield. As they dropped their bombs, a main force of Stukas split into two streams, attacking Hawkinge and Dover. Fighter Command drove off attacks on the former while other aircraft attacked the Folkstone Gate Lightvessel sinking it. It was noted that survivors were strafed in the water by German attackers. This was a not-uncommon occurrence but one that was not universally practised.

During the afternoon and evening of that day, random attacks by bombers and ground-strafing fighters swept in along a 100-mile front, Do-17s attacking Pevensey RDF station but others effectively countered by an increasingly skilled use of the radar defences.

It should be noted that it was not only England that came under attack. He-111s from Vannes in Brittany attacked targets in Belfast, Northern Ireland, hitting the Short factory where the RAF's new long-range bomber – the Short Stirling – was in development.

By the end of the day, the RAF had the upper hand: for the loss of eight fighters, the Luftwaffe lost ten Bf109s. Overall, the British lost a total of 15 aircraft, the Germans 19. Losses the following day would be the worst the Germans had suffered to date.

Reports flowing back to the OKW were aggressively over-optimistic, supposed 'intelligence' reports from Göring's Luftwaffe claiming that 300 RAF fighters had been destroyed, that 30 airfields and major factories had been reduced to rubble and that 40,000 tons of merchant shipping had been destroyed. From his lofty position, Göring criticized the Luftwaffe's planning methods, blaming strategists for selecting inappropriate targets, leaving the vulnerable Stukas and twin-engine Bf-110s undefended, and faulty integration between the senior echelons and the air crew. In future, he dictated, three Bf-109s would be assigned to each Ju-87 as escort. This was a foolish move. The logical path would have been to withdraw the Stukas completely – something they were forced to do from 18 August when 18 Stukas were lost, either destroyed or seriously damaged.

Events would later show 15 August to be the most intense – arguably the most important – day of the battle, with the Germans throwing up more sorties and a greater number of aircraft than at any other time. The RAF was forewarned of these through the various intelligence nodes, such as intelligence information and the Y-station communications. These picked up the early sweeps by German fighters along the south coast and inland, and reconnaissance sweeps by a Do-17 that preceded the main strike. As a result, two patrols from 11 Group were set up in the Thames Estuary. However, when the attack came, a large force of Stukas flew in from the Pas-de-Calais, escorted by Bf-109s; 40 of the Stukas were intent on attacking Hawkinge and Lympne. Twenty-four subsequently turned off to attack Folkestone, but sufficient damage was done to put Lympne out of action for the next three days.

By early afternoon, a formation of 30 aircraft was spotted east of the Firth of Forth heading for either Scotland or the north of England. Coming in slowly, they were identified as Heinkel He-115 seaplanes. These feinted in the direction of Montrose before 41 Squadron of 13 Group from Catterick headed out to engage them.

The Luftwaffe had mistakenly thought that Fighter Command had mustered all its resources down into south-east England. Luftflotte 5 was therefore instructed to attack airfields in the north, believing them to be undefended targets. However, a navigation error put a force of 65 He-111 bombers too far north, where they were intercepted 40 miles off the coast by 41 Squadron. The German formation was stacked in threes at 18,000 ft with the Bf-110 escort fighters positioned 1,000 ft higher. As 41 Squadron pounced, the formation began to break up, some heading for cloud cover, others breaking away completely with the twin-engine escorts forming up in a defensive circle, more to save themselves than the bombers they were protecting. As the German formation split in two – one heading south, the other for Tyneside – it came under attack from 79 Squadron heading for Newcastle, where they were hit by 605 Squadron, most of the bombs falling in the sea.

Throughout the afternoon, further German formations came in from bases in Denmark to attack the east coast down as far as the Humber, where 50 Ju-88s were addressed by 12 Group. Several British targets were hit and a few Blenheim fighters were successful in attacking the German aircraft. Previously, the Blenheim has been described as a light bomber but several squadrons were equipped with the Mk 1 to operate as a 'home fighter' with not a little success, including No. 219. The intensity of the attacks brought a determined response from the RAF, individual pilots resorting to frantic pursuit to knock down the enemy, as fighter pilot Hugh 'Cocky' Dundas later recalled in his book *Flying Start*:

'I set course and rammed the throttle "through the gate", to get the maximum power output, permissible for only a limited period of time. Some of the others were ahead of me, some behind. We did not bother to wait for each other or try to form up into flights and sections. We raced individually across the coast and out to sea. About 15 miles east of Bridlington I saw them, to the left and slightly below – the thin pencil shapes of German twin-engine bombers, flying in a loose, straggling, scattered formation toward the coast.

'I switched on my reflector sight, setting the range for 250 yards, turned the gun button to the "fire" position. Wheeling down in a diving turn, I curved towards the nearest bomber, judging my rate of turn and dive to bring me stern. A light winked from the rear-gunner's position and tracer bullets hosed lazily past. When I opened up with my eight Brownings [machine guns] the return fire stopped. The bomber turned and lost height. First a gush of black smoke, then a steady stream poured from its engine cowlings and it fell steeply toward the calm summer sea.'

During the afternoon of 15 August, a sophisticated complex of raids began to unfold. Sixty Bf-109s dashed ahead of Dorniers from KG-3 while some Bf-110s headed for the RAF experimental station at Martlesham. Some reports indicated that Stukas were used for pinpoint attacks on Bawdsey Manor, one of the sites where Watson-Watt developed RDF. Meanwhile, Spitfires and Hurricanes tangled with intruders over Kent, presaged by another gaggle of German fighters hoping to clear a swathe for oncoming bombers. Later, about 80 German bombers were addressed by 10 Group as they made their way along the south coast and the Swanage and Portland area, but again the Stukas found it hard going and struck out for home, jettisoning their bombs and pursued by defending fighters. Off the Isle of Wight, a further 60 Ju-88s, with 40 Bf-110s as escort, fought their way doggedly towards Southampton facing five squadrons of Spitfires and Hurricanes, which were unable to prevent some damage to facilities on the ground.

In the early evening, Air V-Mshl Keith Park faced a major challenge as another big raid assembled, comprising Dorniers from KG-1 and KG-2 escorted by Bf-109s. Park's pilots were already heavily stressed from having flown two or three sorties that day. Nevertheless, they were now sent up again, five squadrons put to the air to intercept the Germans. Fighting back, some intruders got through and hit West Malling rather than the intended target of Biggin Hill.

The final major event of the day was a small raid led by Walter Rubensdörffer, commanding Erp-210. This headed for RAF Kenley at high speed but the low setting sun caused the group to overshoot to the north-west and hit Croydon. The marker was set by this first attack on what was considered a large urban suburb of London, civilian targets having until now been off limits under a general agreement adhered to by both sides. Some historians attribute this attack on Croydon to a decision by Churchill to bomb Berlin.

On 15 August, the Luftwaffe boasted that it had sent up more than 2,000 sorties while Fighter Command had flown 974 in what was generally regarded as the 'Greatest Day' of the battle. There were wild claims and much speculative propaganda as each side claimed superiority in the air. In fact, the Germans lost 83 aircraft either destroyed or seriously damaged while the RAF lost five – the most imbalanced ratio that would be recorded for the entire battle.

Despite this, the Germans remained convinced that the RAF was all but on its knees. The record shows the opposite. While the number of serviceable aircraft was oscillating up and down over the days, the number of RAF pilots was steadily building. In July, there were about 1,200 pilots available, increasing to 1,400 by 1 August, about 1,450 in September and 1,600 by October. The following month, it stood at 1,800. The numbers of serviceable fighters had fallen slightly during July but held steady and began to increase during August and September. Most of that was due to the Civilian Repair Organisation (CRO).

THE CIVILIAN REPAIR ORGANISATION

The CRO had been formed on 11 September 1939 as an organization that could use civilian light and heavy engineering facilities that had been converted from peacetime production into repair and replacement factories for returning military hardware to operational use. On 14 May 1940, management of the CRO was placed under the Ministry of Aircraft Production (MAP) and a high number of small, medium and large firms set to work restoring damaged and wrecked airframes and returning them to service use. The first such unit was set up at the Cowley works of Morris Motors, where production of military vehicles shared workshop space with aircraft repairs.

Supporting units were also established to deliver aircraft that had been put back into serviceable condition to bases. Initially, aircraft were returned to operational duty after passing through the Air Servicing Unit airfields, but then channelled through the CRO. By the end of 1940, almost 5,000 aircraft had been put back into action by the CRO.

The fact that the RAF was defending the country by countering incoming air attacks rather than risking offensive strikes against airfields under German control in occupied Europe meant that some aircraft that came down on British soil could eventually be returned to action and that pilots who parachuted to the ground could be returned to their units. By contrast, German pilots parachuting to the ground became prisoners of war (POWs) and every Luftwaffe aircraft that came down in Britain, damaged or not, was lost to the enemy. German pilots who parachuted into the English Channel were collected by the same rescue boats that collected downed RAF pilots, and became POWs.

The psychological stress of flying across the Channel to attack an enemy country was immense. Pilots dreaded being shot down into the water, potentially to drown before they were rescued. Limping back to north-eastern France in a crippled bomber, they were easy prey to Spitfires and Hurricanes. More than a few German fighters, damaged but still flyable, were jumped by swooping RAF Spitfires just when they believed their escape to be secure. This was in part because by late evening the sun was in the west – and shining in the rear-view mirrors of aircraft returning to France – which meant the pilots could see little to the rear and were even more vulnerable to sudden attack.

THE FATE OF POLISH PILOTS

Following the fall of Poland in September 1939, the Polish Air Force was formed in France by arrangement between the French government and the Polish government-in-exile. Despite their defeat, the Poles remained convinced of the right of their cause, anticipating the day when they could return to their home country and free it from oppression. Accordingly, during the battle for France and the Low Countries between May and June 1940, 174 Polish airmen were assigned to combat units. The French, however, completely disregarded the experience and the fighting qualities of the Polish airmen, providing them with inferior training aircraft and inadequate equipment. Nevertheless, the Polish pilots shot down 52 enemy aircraft and damaged several more before France capitulated.

The first of the 8,384 Polish airmen who would make their way to Britain by the end of July 1940 landed at Eastchurch, Kent, on 8 December 1939, two days after leaving France. They called it 'The Island of Last Hope'. The British at first believed the contemptuous attitude of the Nazi propaganda machine and its claims that the Polish pilots were inept and incompetent, and that their national air force had been defeated in three days. It was, therefore, with some reluctance that the Polish airmen were integrated into the RAF. However, their capabilities soon became self-evident. This, and an acceptance that these were, after all, the people for whom Britain had gone to war, meant that dedicated 'Polish' RAF squadrons were soon formed – notably Nos 302 and 303 with a total of 66 pilots – and a further 79 Polish pilots were dispersed in other squadrons.

Here, they acquitted themselves with valour. In all, during the Battle of Britain, Polish pilots accounted for 203 of the 1,733 enemy aircraft downed during the conflict – almost 12 per cent of the total. Over the course of the war, Polish air crew with the RAF were credited with 769 victories in air combat, with a further 252 damaged and an additional 'probable' of 177.

The Poles acquitted themselves well in other areas of life in Britain, too. Several Polish men went on to marry British women and settled in the UK after the war. Others returned to their Communist-controlled homeland and faced accusations of espionage and subversive intentions. Some prominent flyers from the Battle of Britain were subsequently imprisoned and others were sentenced to death. Shamefully, during the Cold War, Britain failed to secure safe haven for men who had fought for freedom in a foreign land. The debt Britain owed to the Poles who battled the enemy at risk to their own lives could never be repaid.

A PROFOUND SENSE OF DUTY

The Battle of Britain was frantic, sometimes chaotic, never executed in the air as it was planned on the ground, intensely frightening, violent and without compromise. Sometimes it was tinged with elation, sometimes tainted with horror, always grinding away at sanity, never less than remorseless and as unforgiving as it was bloody.

Yet just seven years earlier, on 9 February 1933, a motion had been passed 275 to 153 at an Oxford Union Society debate – dubbed the 'Oxford Oath' – that

'This House will under no circumstances fight for its King and Country'. Despite the outcome, however, it should be noted that the young men of the Oxford Union who reached this judgement hadn't yet faced the test of fear brought on by an immediate and enveloping challenge to the very institutions that they held dear. What's more, when their way of life came under direct threat from an evil totalitarian force, they were shaken from their clinical debate in more comfortable times. So it was that in 1940, many of those students willingly threw themselves into the defence of Britain to stem the tide of Nazi aggression. Not just for 'King and Country' but for deeper reasons. For a very personal determination, as Battle of Britain veteran Bob Doe said, not to have 'some Nazi jackboots striding up my Mum's garden path!' That was the essence of why brave men went to risk, and to lose, their lives in the skies over England in 1940. There is no myth in that. But there is true heroism of the kind that legend remembers.

The real story is certainly of heroic deeds, but it is more than that. It is about a generation who emerged from their rural idyll, from towns and villages across the nation, to answer the call to arms, to rise further into the skies over Britain and defend their country, their principles about faith and freedom, and to do it through devotion, dignity of purpose and with a profound sense of duty.

There was an unavoidable inevitability about where they were, doing what they did and experiencing emotions that only those who have flown in combat can ever truly understand. As Sqn Ldr Peter Townsend wrote:

> 'Some of us would die within the next few days. That was inevitable. But you did not believe that it would be you. Death was always present, and we knew it for what it was. If we had to die, we would be alone, smashed to pieces, burnt alive, or drowned. Some strange, protecting veil kept the nightmare thought from our minds, as did the loss of our friends. Their disappearance struck us as less a solid blow than a dark shadow which chilled our hearts and passed on.'

There is much here to compare with the tale of Henry V's Englishmen at Agincourt, the universally feared English archers who, in raising their two bow fingers to the French, gave a timeless signal of defiant contempt for boastful claims by an enemy perverted by its own ambition. In another battle, for Britain in 1940, the RAF pilots once more donned the mantle of knightly deeds to rise against defiant contempt through valour and the defence of country against an aggressive enemy.

CHAPTER 9
The 'Hardest Day'

WHILE 15 August was regarded as the most intense day of attacks by the Luftwaffe, the events of three days hence would nominate 18 August as the 'Hardest Day' of the air battle. After a day of fierce fighting on 16 August, a lull saw drastically reduced activity on 17 August – both sides were weary and regrouping for a revitalized effort – when the RAF would lose 53 aircraft (all except eight being Spitfires and Hurricanes) and the Luftwaffe lost 73 either destroyed or damaged. Of the German total, 18 were Ju-87 Stukas. The type would never recover from these losses and was removed from operations over England, their use not worth the loss of so many. They had their value, but not in the air war over Britain and in no place where they were vulnerable to the new generation of fighters.

The events of 18 August began around midnight with a raid on Aberavon, Coventry and Liverpool, while other raiders dropped almost 600 incendiaries and 22 high-explosive bombs on the Spitfire works at Castle Bromwich. In one remarkably successful stalking exercise, a single Blenheim Mk 1 fighter picked up a lone Heinkel He-111 bomber some 15 miles south-west of Chester, observing lights from its rear to track it out past Newark, over Lincoln and out to the North Sea. There, they shot it down 10 miles west of the Cromer Light Vessel. However, such lone encounters were rare.

As the sun rose on the Hardest Day, some reconnaissance aircraft were picked up, one a high-flying Bf-110 that was shot down from an altitude of 31,000 ft over Manston. Throughout the day, wave after wave of attacking bombers forced routes past defending Spitfires and Hurricanes with aircraft streaming across in parallel and converging groups. Each side reached the peak of capacity in both attack and defence, with no respite from dawn to dusk. As the results came in, Göring vented his fury on the Jagdwaffe – the German fighter units and their pilots – which had been unable to prevent the Stuka losses. The Luftwaffe also found its Bf-110 too unwieldy to outfly the nimble Spitfires and Hurricanes, losing 14 to enemy action while 19 Bf-109s were also taken down.

Also on that day, Winston Churchill visited the underground operations room for 11 Group at RAF Uxbridge. As he sat silently, teeth clenched around his unlit cigar, he watched the build-up of enemy aircraft approaching from across the Channel. On asking how many reserves there were, C-in-C Dowding replied that there were none. Later, on getting into his car he uttered the now historic words: 'Never in the field of human conflict was so much owed, by so many, to so few.' Two days later he stood in the House of Commons and repeated that phrase and later still would record it for broadcast by the BBC.

Eager to be as close as possible to the action, and with uncanny prescience, Churchill visited Uxbridge again on 15 September, after which, referring to the individual lights illuminated as each squadron went into action, he wrote in his diary that 'all of the bulbs glowed red', indicating that every squadron was in the air fighting the Luftwaffe.

Faced with an unsustainable rate of attrition, both in aircraft and air crew, and with many of the British aircraft manufacturing plants beyond the reach of German aircraft, on 19 August Göring ordered missions to proceed 'as long as enemy defences are still strong'. These were to be flown only by individual aircraft and when weather conditions were favourable. He was intent on destroying Britain's ability to reconstitute its forces and replenish depleted units, by wearing down the enemy 'day and night'. He explained that:

'We have entered the decisive period of the war against Britain. Everything depends on using all possible means to defeat the enemy's air force. To achieve this our first aim is to destroy his fighters. If they avoid combat in the air, we shall attack them on the ground or force them to accept a fight by using bombers to attack targets within the range of our fighters. Moreover, we must constantly intensify the battle against enemy bomber units by attacking their ground support. When the enemy air force has been defeated, the Luftwaffe will continue its attacks on vital targets to be specified then.'

The supply of pilots to the RAF had been steadily increasing while the numbers available to the Luftwaffe were at times down by one-third on the required complement. In Germany, there were divisions over the best way to use the fighters, which caused argument between the Luftwaffe High Command and the pilots themselves, a lot of which stemmed from Göring's arrogant nature. There had been too little attention paid to the degradation of the pool of fighter pilots: on 1 May, the Jagdwaffe had 1,010 operational pilots but during that month 6.8 per cent were lost; on 1 June, the total available had fallen to 839, a further 7.8 per cent loss; on 1 July, there were 906 but losses during the month amounted to 124 or 11 per cent of the total; by the end of August, there were 735 Bf-109 pilots operational – a 27 per cent loss from the number registered just before the campaign in the west began on 10 May.

The root cause of the problem for the Luftwaffe lay in the inability of the Jagdwaffe to provide sufficient air cover for the bombers to survive. At one point in early September, Göring visited his fighter units in the Pas-de-Calais and berated them for not doing more to protect the bombers. When asked what he needed to get the job done, the rising star in the fighter force, Adolf Galland, replied that he would like a squadron of Spitfires! That answer focused clearly on a persistent criticism of Göring's demand that the single-seat fighters should stay close to the bombers so that they could protect them from the RAF. While the Bf-109 had a comparable performance to the Spitfire, and in some respect to the Hurricane at the higher end of its performance capabilities, at slower speeds it lacked the acceleration and agility of the two RAF fighters.

In answering this question, to the annoyance of Göring, Galland touched a nerve that would put him in opposition to the diehard followers of the senior leadership. But in fact he was correct. The experiences of the young German fighter pilots made it clear that rather than staying clustered close around the bombers, lumbering along at little more than 200 mph, they would be more effectively employed leaping ahead of the bombers to engage and destroy the enemy. Galland offered two options: give us the freedom to engage the enemy on our own terms, where the Bf-109 was equal to the best the RAF could put up, or give us an aircraft with the performance of the Spitfire at slow speeds if you need us to protect the bombers.

TOO FEW

Meanwhile, the RAF did not have it all its own way; the second half of the third phase of the Battle of Britain saw a significant threat emerge from its own steady loss of pilots. Historians are split in their conclusions about that critical phase between 24 August and 6 September. Records show that the RAF lost 295 fighters in action while receiving a total of 269 from the production line and from the repair depots. However, this should take account of 171 badly damaged aircraft as well, making 466 removed from immediate availability. Moreover, with 231 pilots either killed, missing or wounded, the weekly attrition rate was about 12 per cent of the total of approximately 1,000 throughout Fighter Command. In August, the Operational Training Units (OTUs) turned out about 260 fresh fighter pilots to replenish squadrons that had lost 300 that month and this accounts for the reduction from 26 to 16 in the average complement of pilots per squadron. In peak periods, the situation was far worse; between 8 and 18 August the RAF lost 154 fighter pilots while only 63 new trainees reported as replacements. From 24 August to 6 September, more aircraft were destroyed in attacks on airfields in the south-east of England than were being replaced.

For all these reasons, had the Germans kept to their strategy of pounding away at airfields and engaging Fighter Command in the air to destroy aircraft, extrapolation of all the trends shows that by the end of September the RAF would have been defeated.

The fourth phase of the Battle of Britain began when the Luftwaffe turned away from trying to grind down the RAF and concentrated on attacking the cities, inaugurating what would become known as the Blitz (short for blitzkrieg). The realization that defeating the British was more difficult than they had predicted prompted the usually optimistic Nazi spin-doctor Dr Joseph Goebbels to inform his propaganda ministry that it had to 'prepare the nation gradually for the possibility that the war may continue through the winter'. This managing of expectations was important. While Britain was working at peak effort to survive both a submarine blockade of its ports and the repeated bombing of its towns and cities, civilian Germans had up until now had little experience of war – so far, it had always been on, or over, foreign countries. This meant, for instance, that unlike London, there were no blackouts to conceal the brilliant lights of Berlin's night life. Goebbels' propaganda machine therefore needed to work hard to reassure the public and maintain morale when they were informed that the war would drag on.

It is too easy to divide the various phases in the Battle into well-defined objectives and target packages. In reality, there was more of an overlapping transitional switch than a sudden change. For instance, on 24 August the OKW began the shift towards city targets. During a raid on London the following day, 100 bombers attacked the British capital and on 31 August the Luftwaffe ordered Luftflotten 2 and 3 to prepare a 'retaliatory attack on London' in response to a British raid on Berlin six nights earlier. The following day, in addition to attacking industrial targets and 30 factories, the Luftwaffe High Command ordered the secondary use of city bombing in order to terrorize the population with a 'big attack on London', which was distinct from the disruptive attacks on armament and port facilities.

The fourth phase of the Battle therefore began on 7 September with a massive raid on London that involved 400 bombers and 600 escort fighters, mainly targeting areas around the East End. A sustained assault, it went on during the latter half of the day and into the night.

This series of raids was greater than anything the city had experienced to date. It was a visible sign that the Luftwaffe had switched its tactical goal in favour of a more generalized desire on the part of the German government to wear down the British people and in some way cause a revolt. Leading Nazi figures persisted in their desire to bring Britain to its knees and then do a deal that would give them a free hand in the rest of the world.

There was some precedent to this. During World War I, German raids on the East End of London caused dock workers and their families to march on Buckingham Palace, where they attempted to tear down some of its railings to protest at the inequalities that condemned them to live in barely habitable dwellings. From that day onward, guards were posted at the palace, where they remain today.

The main action on 7 September began in the late afternoon and started fires that were seen as far away as Cambridge. As night fell, the six o'clock BBC news brought alarming information that did little to assuage the fears of people all over Britain. Until now, aerial activities had consisted of gladiatorial combat high in the skies over England, peppered with attacks on strategic targets across the country. Now, this shift in targets from military bases to civilian conurbations led to a belief among the general public that an invasion was imminent. There was no other means of getting information out than through BBC radio stations. People across the country therefore rushed home to turn on their sets and to make preparations.

Shocked by the apparent suddenness of this switch in strategy by the Germans, people passed on information as they travelled out of London on their way home. For instance, a man on a train from Liverpool Street station described how he had witnessed the docks beginning to burn and how he had heard that reports were coming in of a massive invasion force crossing the Channel. As people watched from a wide radius out across the south of England, the fires built in intensity as the sustained assault went on through the night – a night that came early to the East End that day as thick black smoke roiled over the area, blotting out the sun and only adding to the sense of hopelessness.

Children in the East End of London, 1940, sit outside the ruins of their bombed house and wait for word about where they will sleep that night. David Baker Archive

Firefighters struggle to extinguish the fires, some conflagrations left to burn themselves out. David Baker Archive

Not since 1666 had the capital city seen such devastation in a single night. Bombs were dropped on Nunhead, Beckenham, Rochford, Brentwood, Dartford, Stone Purfleet, Cory's Wharf, oil installations and Shorehaven before the bomb patterns crept closer to central London, to Woolwich, Plumstead, Falconwood and Crayford. Merchants' warehouses, storehouses, manufacturing plants, the Shell-Mex installations and barges and river vessels caught light as much of London erupted under the intense bombardment, with high explosives and incendiaries raining down, adding to further raids already delivered on Camberwell, Croydon, Putney and Kensington.

All the major London docks were on fire by mid-evening, the eruptions and explosions of highly combustible materials and products exploding with great ferocity. The raids had come with such sudden and unexpected fury that the Army was officially ordered to stand by and told that invasion was imminent. In the very darkest night of a black and fateful year, there was a universal belief that Hitler's Panzer tanks would be rolling up the beaches of southern England at the crack of dawn. Despite all this, however, German expectations of a collapse in morale were confounded as the attacks were instead met by a universal resolve to stoically resist the aggressor.

The sudden intensity of the raids activated the first combined operation involving massed formations of RAF fighters, putting together resources from 11 Group under the command of Air Chf Mshl Trafford Leigh-Mallory and 12 Group under Air V-Mshl Keith Park. Encouraged to merge operational commitments towards a single objective, this was known as the 'Big Wing', and had emerged as a result of experience over Dunkirk in June. It was a concept urged on by Leigh-Mallory and by Douglas Bader – a fighter pilot who had lost both legs in a flying accident in December 1931 and who became the only legless fighter pilot in the RAF. Bader carried considerable influence, not least because of his total disregard for formality and established chains of authority to get things done.

The Big Wing had been put together from three squadrons at RAF Duxford, near Cambridge, which was geographically placed to serve a wide area of central and southern England. The Big Wing was therefore ideally situated to respond to the raids on London building up on the afternoon of 7 September. Scrambled to cover North Weald, north-east of London, it arrived too late to intercept the main force but managed to shoot down 11 German aircraft for the loss of one fighter. Park was bitterly opposed to this ad hoc gathering, loosely assembled for a mass attack upon enemy formations, but Bader was convinced that what had worked over Dunkirk could work over England. However, there were flaws in the plan: the Spitfires had to climb at the slower speed of the Hurricanes, wasting time in reaching altitude; and the formation, once assembled, was unwieldy and frequently late in arriving where it was required.

It was an argument that would rage long after the war was over and brought Park and Leigh-Mallory into bitter conflict. In the end, it was C-in-C Dowding who was blamed for maintaining a separation between 11 Group in the south and 12 Group in the Midlands, his view being that it was better to nibble away at the enemy rather than engage in set-piece battles that could erode defensive forces unproductively. Dowding would pay for that view after a series of clashes with the Air Ministry over his tactics during the battle, which resulted in his dismissal in November 1940, after which Churchill sent him on a procurement mission to the USA.

A THIN LINE

After Luftflotte 2 had completed its assigned raids, late in the evening Luftflotte 3 moved in from the Caen area to stoke up the fires already alight across London. Casualties were mounting and the Fire Brigade was challenged to address all incidents – some impossible to suppress. In one tragic incident, for instance, the Tate & Lyle factory burned furiously, turning sugar and molasses into sticky rivers of molten sugar that crept out like flows of lava on to the surrounding streets and into homes, setting them alight. The entire Silvertown area had to be evacuated.

After the high explosives came the incendiary bombs that torched gas lines and burned out power supplies and junction boxes. Mercifully, though, the casualties from these were far fewer than feared.

By dawn on 8 September, 600 fire appliances had been hard at it all night, and 292 people had been killed with a further 1,285 seriously injured. The last bomber had departed at 4.30 am. The Luftwaffe had operated throughout the night without serious challenge due to the absence of an effective night-fighter force. Remember, these were just the early days of round-the-clock bombing! In all, the Luftwaffe lost 48 aircraft, of which about half were escorting fighters during daylight hours, while the RAF lost 57, half of which were Hurricanes. For the British, the positive aspect of the Germans' switch in tactics was that Fighter Command was relieved of the relentless pressure that had previously been placed on their airfields and men. The negative was that 12 Group had repeatedly failed to protect 11 Group airfields; the efficient and co-ordinated control of Fighter Command operations trumped by internecine conflicts between Park and Leigh-Mallory, and only loosely held together by the sensitive and considered management of Hugh Dowding.

Climbing into his Hurricane at Northolt airfield, Park flew east across London and saw for himself the damage that had been caused. He later commented: 'It was burning all down the river. It was a horrid sight. But I looked down and said "Thank God for that", because I knew that the Nazis had switched their attack from the fighter stations thinking that they were knocked out. They weren't, but they were pretty groggy.'

Another advantage in the shift in targets from airfields in the south-east to cities further inland was that the German escort fighters, particularly the Bf-109s, were now so stretched in terms of range that they had a mere ten minutes of combat time over the target. A more powerful and arguably more effective fighter with longer range was at this time coming off the drawing board and into German factories – the Focke-Wulf Fw-190 was a beefy, bull-nosed machine powered by a 1,660 hp BMW radial engine that gave it a top speed in excess of 400 mph – but it was still some months away. For now, the Luftwaffe had to rely on the Bf-109E and F models, powered by a 1,200 hp Daimler-Benz in-line engine to produce a top speed of around 355 mph.

For seven days, the pilots and ground crew of Fighter Command had a respite; on some days, pilots would not get scrambled at all. This allowed for some rest, recuperation and opportunities to repair aircraft and get damaged buildings and support facilities properly back in order. Reflecting afterwards, pilots and senior officers judged that had this not occurred, the narrow margin between success and defeat reduced to a very thin line.

Over the next few days, the raids were repeated and by 14 September they had a particular intensity; Luftwaffe air crew returned with vivid descriptions of seeing almost the entirety of London under thick palls of smoke, fires burning to light the dark shroud that hung above, of smoke drifting lazily out across the Thames Estuary, of cratered airfields south of London with bombed and blasted buildings. Such sights made many secure in their certainty that the RAF was all but defeated. However, doubt that this was actually the case began to creep in and on 14 September, Hitler questioned whether the entire effort should be called off. In response, the Luftwaffe Commander Hans Jeschonnek pleaded to be allowed to carry on just a little while longer in order to unleash total devastation on the urban areas of Britain and bring the people to their knees. The following day, the assault began that would decide the outcome of the Battle of Britain.

A PERFECT ENGLISH SUMMER'S DAY

On Sunday 15 September, the Luftwaffe mounted an intense effort to defeat the RAF and break the back of the British people. This time, in order to maximize their potential success, the bombers would come over the Channel at relatively high altitude; they never knew why but the Germans had noted that whenever they flew above 20,000 ft the RAF was late intercepting their formations. This was due to the inability of the RDF stations to detect aircraft flying above this altitude.

In the fighter units on the Pas-de-Calais, the pilots were frustrated and angry in equal measure, as later expressed by Adolf Galland: 'Failure to achieve any notable success, constantly changing orders betraying lack of purpose and obvious misjudgement of the situation by the [High] Command, and unjustified accusations had a most demoralising effect on us fighter pilots, who were already overtaxed by physical and mental strain.'

In one of those fortuitous but unintended encounters, on this very decisive day Churchill and his wife had decided to visit Air V-Mshl Keith Park at 11 Group's HQ at Uxbridge. At 9.30 am, RDF and observers noted formations gathering over the Channel near Dover and towards the Thames Estuary. Squadrons were therefore sent up from Hornchurch, Gravesend and Croydon. When the bombers turned back for the Continent the fighters were ordered to stand down in what was a not-uncommon occurrence. An hour later, more formations were observed, with estimates of several hundred enemy aircraft slowly assembling in the skies just over the Channel. While Park kept up a running commentary to Churchill, more aircraft continued to assemble – at least 200 bombers with an undetermined number of fighters. By 11.00 am, the formations were heading in a direct line for Dungeness, so 11 Group ordered up Spitfires and Hurricanes from 12 squadrons across airfields at Biggin Hill, Northolt, Kenley, Debden, Martlesham, Hornchurch and Warmwell. About 30 minutes later, a further 11 squadrons were scrambled as the German bombers approached over the west Kent coast. To consolidate the air defence, Park decided to call on Leigh-Mallory's Big Wing and apply that to the defence of London, leaving 11 Group squadrons to do as much damage as possible to the oncoming raiders in the south-east.

By noon, the lumbering bombers had made landfall between Maidstone and Ashford and Spitfires were directed to intercept them, experiencing exceptionally heavy combat as they engaged the intruders. Several hundred Bf-109 fighters were milling around across a wide area as the enemy force staggered on towards London. The forward gunner in a Dornier Do-17, Hans Zonderlind, recalled:

'All around us were dogfights as the fighters went after each other, then as we were getting ready for our approach to the target, we saw what must have been a hundred RAF fighters coming at us. We thought that this must have been all the RAF planes up at once, but where were they coming from, as we had been told that the RAF fighters were very close to extinction.'

With the fighting getting more intense, additional Spitfires and Hurricanes arrived on the scene to engage an ever-increasing number of targets, as described by Sqn Ldr J. Sample from 501 Squadron:

'Each of us selected his own target. Our first attack broke them up pretty nicely. The Dornier I attacked with a burst lasting several seconds began to turn to the left away from his friends. I gave him five seconds, and he went away with white smoke streaming behind him. As I broke away and started to make a steep climbing turn, I looked over the side. I recognised the river immediately below me through a hole in the clouds. I saw the bends and the bridges and idly wondered where I was. Then I saw Kennington Oval, and I thought to myself, "That is where they play cricket".'

It was now 12.15 pm and the Bf-109s were being forcibly detained all over the sky above Kent as Bader's Big Wing arrived, on time for once, putting 52 fighters to the defence of London. Nine squadrons struck simultaneously with devastating force and brutal effect, hammering hard into the bombers, freed for the most part of their escorts, still reeling under intense harassment to the south-east of London and out of range. In all, more than 160 Hurricanes and Spitfires pounded the Dorniers as they struggled to find targets, turn away, drop their bombs to lighten the load and run. Rapidly, the organized assault of the Big Wing turned to a chaotic shambles – to the benefit of the RAF – as individual pilots, ecstatic with the sheer intensity of their impact, hurtled around the sky hunting down the German bombers. Whether by virtue of the brief seven-day respite or by sheer dogged determination, there was an upwelling of intensity and adrenalin-fed excitement as pilots threw themselves into the fray.

With the bomber formations heavily disrupted, the damage to London was less than predicted, although bombs fell in Battersea, Lambeth, Clapham, Victoria and all the way across to Westminster. One Hurricane pilot had a near miss when the bomber he attacked blew up with such intensity that it sent his aircraft spinning out of control. As the crew of the bomber baled out and came down over the Oval cricket ground, the Hurricane pilot drifted down on his parachute and landed precisely in the middle of a dustbin!

Back on the Continent, Kesselring's bombers were being counted back in as the fighters were being refuelled and re-armed ready for the next wave. In Britain, the same procedures were being carried out at Fighter Command stations across the south-east, and further north where the Big Wing landed for more fuel and more ammunition.

BY THE BOOK

Credit for a significant shift in the way fighter pilots conducted aerial warfare has been given to South African Adolf 'Sailor' Malan, who on 8 August 1940 was given command of No. 74 Squadron. He wrote 'Ten of My Rules for Air to Air Fighting', which became something of a mantra for the young pilots. The rules were:

'Wait until you see the whites of their eyes
While shooting think of nothing else, brace the body, keep both hands on the stick
Keep a sharp lookout
Height gives you the initiative
Always turn and face the attack
Make decisions promptly
Never fly straight and level for more than 30 seconds
When diving to attack, always leave a portion of your formation above as top guard
INITIATIVE, AGGRESSION, AIR DISCIPLINE and TEAMWORK
Go in quickly – punch hard – get out'

AS A member of the US diplomatic corps observing events, the military attaché in London, Raymond Lee, reported that:

'I can't for the life of me puzzle out what the Germans are up to. They have great air power and yet are dissipating it in fruitless and aimless attacks all over England. They must have an exaggerated idea of the damage they are doing and the effects of their raids on public morale... Just as I finish writing this, the heavy guns commence giving tongue and the little Irish maid comes in to turn down the bed. She went over to Victoria to see the plane which crashed there and is very pleased because she saw the dead German crew extracted from the wreckage.'

The weather on this Sunday epitomized a perfect English summer day – skies blue and clear, strong sunlight. This provided a bewildering contrast to the mayhem in the skies, which paused for a while as the forces regrouped before another gladiatorial clash. At 1.30 pm, reports began to come in that a truly massive formation of more than 150 Dorniers and Heinkels was forming up across the Channel in the Calais-Boulogne region. As time would show, the Germans were about to phase the assault so that after the first wave had been countered by 11 Group, the second wave would come in as the RAF pilots were on the ground refuelling and re-arming. With diminishing resources to play with, the Germans were trying tactics that could multiply the effect and compensate for fewer numbers. Even the timing of the initial wave was measured carefully so as to catch the Spitfires and Hurricanes on the ground in the two hours required to turn them around from the morning foray and get them back in the air.

At 2.15 pm, the enemy made landfall between Dungeness and Dover and again most of the bombers were thrown off course by the attacking squadrons that did manage to get airborne. The formations came across at 15-minute intervals, the total force numbering between 150 and 200 aircraft with approximately 400 escort fighters – a mass of 600 aircraft heading for London spread out across 30 miles of sky. Large numbers of bombers reached London, but 49 fighters from the Big Wing slammed into them once again, with other squadrons excitedly converging on the attacking pack, increasing the total number to more than 170 Spitfires and Hurricanes mauling and hacking at the Dorniers and Heinkels.

The western flank of the formations banked off to their left and came back on London from a westerly direction. Escorts were able to stay with the bombers longer due to the disposable fuel tanks that they carried beneath the central fuselage, which could be jettisoned, and the fact that the Bf-109s were engaged heavily by the Spitfires and Hurricanes, drawing them away from the bombers so that other squadrons could attack them unprotected by fighters. When the fuel tanks were dropped, the fighters became more agile, but with little fuel remaining their combat time was further limited. This was due to the fact that they were further from bases in the Pas-de-Calais region than they would have been had they been dogfighting over Essex, Kent or Sussex.

The bombers had their own defensive armament, which meant that the tactics adopted by the intercepting fighters had to be very different from those used when attacking fighters. Engagements between fighters resulted in high aerobatics and extreme manoeuvrability with fleeting seconds to get a 'bead' on the opponent; knocking out the bombers was best achieved through 'slash-attacks', getting in fast with a closing speed from the stern, sometimes in excess of 100 mph, where a one-second pause could mean a miss distance of 150 ft.

At the peak of the battle, the RAF had 300 fighters in the air attacking the intruders. The ferocity of the turmoil was evident all across the sky above London and South East England, where threads of wispy contrails were woven across the azure blue like chaotic spider webs, without form or structure but painting the sky with evidence of mortal carnage. Indeed, so prolific were these contrails tracing the flight paths of warring factions that clouds began to form and the sky lost its light.

The sheer energy of the pilots of Fighter Command demonstrated a new and deeply determined resilience – one that caused the German bombers to flee to other less contested regions of the sky, disassembling the precise formations the bombers had held earlier that day when they first reached England's shores. Others fled for home, a few being intercepted and brought down over the Channel. As they withdrew, the attraction of pursuing these wounded and damaged remnants was great and some RAF pilots found themselves very nearly over the French coast before they turned back for home, pursued themselves by Luftwaffe fighters hunting stragglers preying on the afflicted. And yet the battle wasn't over. Even as the exhausted airmen were regrouping for another scramble, yet another formation of German raiders was picked up dashing for Southampton in the final raid of the day. On this decisive day of the Battle of Britain, the Luftwaffe lost 80 aircraft to the RAF's 37 destroyed, damaged or written off. These were losses the Germans could not sustain. The decision to switch tactical direction in order to bring Britain to its knees turned out to have been flawed and failing.

A TACTICAL RETREAT

Göring held a conference on 16 September to review the overall situation, which was attended by the senior leadership of the various Luftflotten. His assessment was that the RAF would be destroyed in a maximum of five days. He therefore ordered a sustained blitz against London and other major cities; small raids in inclement weather, larger formations when the weather permitted. In addition to the urban areas, priority targets were ports and aircraft factories, to be hit day and night, with emphasis on fighter patrols to engage the RAF wherever possible. There were very few who now felt that Göring retained a grip on reality; the Luftwaffe senior leadership knew that they were battling against the odds – that no matter how they pounded the cities, the British public would never give in. And all the while, as that seemingly pointless exercise was being sustained, the Luftwaffe was slowly bleeding to death.

As attention switched from day to night attacks, the RAF made preparations for interception by moving six Blenheim aircraft of 600 Squadron to Redhill, from where they could carry out rapid response. What's more, Redhill was home to a Beaufighter that had been specially equipped with radar. This quickly came into its own, resulting in a Ju-88 being engaged and shot down over the sea.

AN ADAPTABLE WORKHORSE

The Bristol Beaufighter emerged in 1938 as the first purpose-built high-performance fighter equipped with 'airborne interception' (AI) radar, at the time a highly secret application of ground-based RDF to airborne night interceptions. The type had flown for the first time on 17 July 1939 and the primary production version, the 1F, was placed in production at the Bristol factory at Weston-super-Mare and at Filton, Bristol. The RAF received the Beaufighter 1F at Tangmere on 12 August 1940. By the date of its deployment to Redhill, it was still undergoing intensive trials and evaluation.

Powered by two 1,670 hp Bristol Hercules radial engines, the Beaufighter had a top speed of more than 330 mph and a range of up to 1,470 miles, although this figure is for any aircraft greatly dependent on weather conditions, load carried and the condition of the aircraft. The Beaufighter turned into a veritable workhorse for specialized combat operations, seeing service in North Africa, the Middle East, the Far East and other theatres of war. Armed with four nose-mounted machine guns, it had a maximum load of 2,127 lb (in the form of a torpedo) and was very successful against ships or, with eight wing-mounted rockets, against precision land targets attacked from low level.

The introduction of the AI-equipped Beaufighter in September 1940 marked another turning point for the RAF – one in which technology in the form of advanced radar was starting to play a significant role – and heralded a new generation of high-performance aircraft. The success of this type saw it remain in service for 20 years, until it was retired in 1960.

The application of the Beaufighter on the night of 16 September was a key turning point – one that the Luftwaffe air crews came to fear. Operations this day were largely restricted due to weather, causing Park to make subtle changes to the way 11 Group operated. He observed that, in general, the squadrons took too long to form up and that others failed to make any effort to do so at all, heading directly for the enemy formations without any cohesive integration with other squadrons. To improve the overall allocation of roles, he organized the Spitfires from Biggin Hill and Hornchurch to engage the Bf-109s flying top cover on the bombers, allocating the three Hurricane squadrons from Tangmere and Northolt to attack the bombers flying at medium altitude.

TAKING TO THE TUBE

Plans to put Londoners down in the Tube during raids were implemented early in the Blitz. With the power to the rail lines switched off, many people spent the night on the greasy tracks, lying on newspapers. There was little opportunity for sleep. There was a lack of adequate air conditioning, and uninterrupted noise and disturbance from tired children excited by the drama, babies crying, restless parents, old people unable to look after themselves, the sick and the injured requiring attention. All of this added to the nightly grind, made worse by the fear that the day would bring scenes of more death and destruction, crumbling buildings, the sick on stretchers, the dying in the back of ambulances. Then there were the constant warnings of burst gas mains and the sudden discovery of unexploded bombs. This was the reality of modern aerial warfare for civilians who endured the first sustained campaign of terror-bombing.

To find safety during the 'Blitz', when German bombers raided London and key cities across Britain, civilians found haven in the capital's Underground, electrical power to the train lines having been switched off to allow extra resting space. David Baker Archive

17 September started badly in poor weather. There was little expectation of major raids, though 17 German and 13 RAF aircraft were lost. The following day, a

sustained bombing campaign was carried out over London but the loss ratio still favoured the British. Spasmodic attacks were mounted against other towns and cities in Britain, including Birmingham, Swansea and Southampton, the latter coming in for some intense bombing. By the end of the month, the attrition rate was alarming senior members of the Luftwaffe High Command. Göring, however, held to his consistently expressed belief that the RAF was on its knees and the country was being burned into submission. Between 7 and 30 September, the Germans lost 433 aircraft against 242 for the RAF.

The fifth and final phase of the Battle of Britain began on 2 October. It would last until the end of that month. Now, the Luftwaffe would restrict its daytime operations to light bombing while maintaining a sustained assault on London night after night. During these intense periods of heavy bombardment, great and heroic episodes of sacrifice became commonplace as the citizens of Britain's capital, the hub of what was still then a global empire, struggled hour by hour to survive and to carry through until, once again, day dawned and the clearance of rubble, the extrication of the dead, the care for the injured and the rehousing of the homeless could be undertaken. With each new dawn, people who had spent the night taking refuge in the London Underground – the 'Tube' – came out to go about their work.

The light daylight raids were conducted by fighters adapted to carry bombs – particularly the Bf-109-7 'Jabo', which was equipped with a single 500 lb bomb under its fuselage. Crossing the Channel at high altitude and consuming more fuel due to the weight, after releasing its single load there was little opportunity for realizing the full potential of the aircraft as a dogfighter, the limited range still remaining in the depleted fuel tanks eaten up with getting back to France. These raids began to dwindle away as the weeks wore on and by the end of the month the only daylight attacks focused on the airfields in the south-east. Yet, the Blitz continued, night after night, beyond 31 October – the date that is officially considered to mark the end of the fifth and final phase of the Battle of Britain. Appropriately, this was the quietest day for four months; not a single German or British aircraft was lost in operations over England.

THE TALLY

An assessment of the gains and losses by both the Luftwaffe and the RAF reveals concerted British success in wearing down the numerical forces available to the Germans. The British had lost 1,542 air crew killed, 422 wounded and 1,744 aircraft destroyed. The Germans had lost 3,510 air crew killed or captured for the duration, 735 wounded and 1,977 aircraft destroyed. Overall, the Germans had been badly mauled in the offensive in the west and their drive on Britain. In the five months of May to September 1940 inclusive, the Luftwaffe lost 3,064 aircraft, some 57 per cent of the 5,349 aircraft it had on strength on 4 May. Of that total, the Germans lost 65 per cent of their original bomber complement, 57 per cent of their single-engine fighters (the Bf-109), and 94 per cent of their twin-engine fighters (Bf-110).

Moreover, in the three months from October to December 1940, the Luftwaffe lost 384 bombers out of an average complement of 1,412 at the beginning of each month – a 27 per cent attrition rate. Most losses were a result of having been driven to conduct bombing operations by night in poor visibility with only minimal losses in actual combat. During October, bomber losses amounted to 171, of which only 64 (37 per cent) were during operations, followed by 17 per cent in November and 48 per cent in December.

Moreover, the ratio of fully operational crew numbers to authorized aircraft dropped to an unacceptable level. Having already been heavily affected by losses during the campaign for France and the Low Countries, it is perhaps not surprising that between 7 July and 21 September the Luftwaffe bomber crews declined as a percentage of paper complement from 75 per cent of operational levels to 59 per cent, with a steep decline after the city-bombing began on 7 September. More telling perhaps than any other figure is that the number of authorized aircraft available for service in the respective Luftwaffe units declined from 99 per cent in September 1939 to 91 per cent when the May offensive began, and to 80 per cent at the end of the year.

During September and October, Hitler did little to discourage plans for the invasion of England, despite increasing doubt, matching Göring's view that such an objective was possible. Both the Army and the Navy were against an invasion for highly practical reasons. As dictated by tides, weather patterns and the general preparation of barges, tugs, naval equipment and men and materiel, the earliest possible date for such a cross-Channel invasion had been 24–27 September. This was changed to 8 October once it was realized that the Luftwaffe would not have destroyed the RAF by the earlier dates. But Hitler was also personally worried that any major attack on British cities would bring a response from RAF Bomber Command. Even the very Luftwaffe bomber crews who had conducted bombing raids on Britain expressed horror that such destruction might ever be meted out to German cities and recorded those views for posterity.

On 14 September, Hitler informed his commanders that in spite of 'the enormous' success of the Luftwaffe the conditions for an invasion did not yet exist, but that any dates beyond mid-October would risk poor weather conditions in the Channel. For this reason, on 19 September orders were issued for assembled barges and tugs to be brought together in case an invasion was authorized, to be dispersed due to the destruction wrought upon them by Bomber Command.

On 2 October, however, Hitler ordered that all preparations for an invasion were 'to be largely dismantled'. The opportunity for Germany to invade Britain had evaporated because the RAF had successfully fought off the Luftwaffe. In a war of attrition, the British were winning.

On 18 December 1940, Hitler issued another directive, ordering the Wehrmacht to make preparations to 'crush Soviet Russia in a rapid campaign' and to do that even before the end of the war with Britain. Called Operation *Barbarossa*, it would be the biggest land invasion in recorded history and set in motion the process that would eventually result in the catastrophic collapse of the German war machine and Nazi Germany. This is what the British government had been waiting for: a switch in the relationship between Germany and Russia and the entry of the USA into the war, diverting attention from the UK and greatly expanding the production and manpower base of the Allied nations. Both would occur in 1941.

CHAPTER 10
On the Offensive

THE TACTICS employed by Luftwaffe fighter pilots during the Battle of Britain were very different to those used by the RAF. A Staffel of approximately 12 aircraft was made up of four Schwärme and led by a Staffelführer. Each Schwarm was led by a Schwarmführer and each pair, or Rotten, by a Rottenführer. Each Rotte would operate as a single fighting unit, slightly staggered in broadside and elevation so that one covered the other. In this manner, the pilots were able to extract the maximum potential from their aircraft while enhancing the co-operation between fighters. When turning a Schwarm, the formation was able to execute a 90-degree change in direction by making relatively tight arcs, reversing the positions of the aircraft by having one overlap the one next to him, maintaining a constant high speed and completing the change quickly.

The RAF, meanwhile, entered the war believing that gunnery in the air was something that could be learned at squadron level. Many pilots therefore arrived for operational duty never having fired their guns. Fighters flew in 'Vic' formation, a triangle with one aircraft at each corner. A variation, known as the 'finger-four' retained the triangle shape but added a fourth plane, positioned directly in a line from the lead aircraft through the left rear fighter to an equidistant location in a line behind. Usually, each squadron would have four Flights, each of which was given a specific colour, but each Vic would operate as a single attacking unit. Even in the turn they were schooled to retain the same formation, the inner aircraft having to throttle right back and make a tight change of direction, while the lead and outer aircraft in the formation had to accelerate to make it around a quarter-turn. This was cumbersome and unwieldy – especially in battle – since only the lead pilot could focus on the target ahead rather than giving their full attention to maintaining the tight formation and the avoidance of collisions with their wingmen.

As the Battle of Britain unfolded, the RAF changed its tactics and dispensed with the Vic formation. Where previously Dowding had taught his fighter pilots to converge their fire at 1,200 ft and thus hit the bomber while still out of range of his opponent's guns, now they harmonized guns to converge at 750 ft and placed greater emphasis on speed, agility and the ability of the individual pilot to get in fast, take deadly aim, fire a burst and get out.

The initiative seized during the Battle of Britain would write the handbook on fighter tactics that was used for this war and during the entire post-war period. It gave Fighter Command the confidence to replace a defensive with an offensive role, and to take the fight to the Luftwaffe over France, to Germany and to other occupied countries. The air combat operations of 1940 were therefore a pivotal turning point for the RAF, and not only for its fighter operations. With new and more capable heavy bombers coming on line, by the end of 1941 the war itself was shifting from a Continental conflict to a truly global affair, with a sequence of technical, operational and production developments that would transform possible defeat into assured victory for the Allies.

Away from the action in the skies, other activities were building an investment for expanded production and the delivery of greater numbers of aircraft to the RAF. Created on 15 May 1940, the Ministry of Aircraft Production (MAP) took over responsibility from the Air Ministry for supplying aircraft from the factories to the squadrons. Under Lord Beaverbrook, it was also responsible for the supply, inspection and repair of aircraft and all their armament and equipment, for design and development, and for storage up to delivery. It was apparent early on that transforming a peacetime administrative organization into one fit for wartime was fraught with difficulty and that many challenges lay ahead.

One of the drawbacks of this organization was the lack of new types specified or developed, the emphasis being on pushing out increasing numbers of the same designs, namely the Wellington, Blenheim and Whitley bombers and the Hurricane and Spitfire fighters. However, once it was felt that change was essential for an effective production programme and a new and ambitious development plan for new and more capable aircraft, Colonel (Col) Moore-Brabazon (later Lord Brabazon of Tara) replaced Lord Beaverbrook on 1 May 1941.

As the MAP evolved, in September 1942 Col John J. Llewellyn took over from Moore-Brabazon and a month later Air Chf Mshl Sir Wilfred Freeman took on the job of chief executive. Under his authority, great strides were made in transforming production and introducing new types. It was within this nexus of overriding authority over industry, manpower and production that the post-war future of the British aircraft industry was defined, one in which government would take greater control of private industry – something the Labour government from late 1945 defined – forging a precedent that successive Conservative governments struggled to disengage from.

BOMBS AWAY

If 1940 was characterized by the clash of fighter forces, the remainder of the war would witness the remorseless rise of the strategic bomber. This would inflict upon Axis countries – Germany and eventually Japan – a rain of ruin unlike anything experienced to date. When the Americans entered the war at the end of 1941, they began earnest development of high-flying bombers with pressurized crew compartments, and the capacity to unleash enormous destruction on industrial and urban areas and to eventually drop single atomic bombs on two cities in Japan. The way to that end was pioneered and lit by the RAF over Germany between 1941 and 1944.

The British bombers that would emerge during this period had far greater bomb-carrying capacity than equivalent types operated by the Luftwaffe. They were also more heavily armed and had much greater range. They were each designed for a strategic role, not for supporting blitzkrieg warfare, as the German bombers were. The distinct separation from land operations made RAF Bomber Command ideally suited to a strategic role and a potent successor to Trenchard's Independent Air Force of 1918, which had itself justified the formation of an independent air arm, separate from the Army and the Navy. Where Fighter Command had done much to shield Britain from invasion, in Bomber Command the RAF had the powerful means to carry the fight right to the heart of the enemy and to inflict damage on an unprecedented scale.

The Luftwaffe had little or no experience with strategic bombing prior to 1940, having developed a class of military aircraft designed to support ground operations and at best to prepare the battlefield ahead of engagements by the German Army on the ground. This changed during the Blitz, from 7 September 1940 until February 1941. Under the codename 'Loge', attacks on London were conducted for eight weeks, after which, from mid-November, the target areas were enlarged to include other cities and in particular the industrial heartland of the West Midlands, such as Birmingham and especially Coventry. This campaign continued until February 1941.

The figures were staggering. During the period of the Blitz, the Luftwaffe dropped a total of 16,500 tonnes of bombs on London, killing 28,500 people and wounding a further 25,500, with total injuries estimated at 139,000. Incendiaries and high-explosive bombs wrought destruction on a colossal scale, as did the new 'fire bombs' pioneered by KG-100, which dropped a total of 10,000 such devices. These were small in size but devastating in their effect.

Elsewhere in the UK, this intense period of bombardment resulted in an additional 12,500 deaths. In order of tonnage dropped, the Liverpool and Merseyside area received 1,700 tonnes, Birmingham 1,600 tonnes. Glasgow and Clydeside 1,200 tonnes and Plymouth 1,100 tonnes. Twelve other cities were also bombed, though less than 1,000 tonnes each.

Consistent bombing of cities and industrial plants was having some effect but not the conclusive result that Hitler and senior leaders in the Luftwaffe hoped for. With prompting from the Kriegsmarine, its C-in-C Erich Raeder proposed a seminal shift in strategy by switching from the destruction of industrial plants to attacks on merchant ships, which were vital for maintaining a lifeline to beleaguered Britain. In Directive 23 issued by Hitler on 6 February 1941, the attack on the British war economy was now to be carried out primarily by the German Navy. This change of tack went largely unopposed by the Luftwaffe, which was now resigned to the fact that the air raids on the UK had failed to bring the RAF to its knees, had failed to bring the country to the bargaining table and now had failed to significantly reduce or hinder Britain's production of war materiel.

The fact was that although the Luftwaffe had dropped a total of 41,000 tonnes of bombs on Britain during the Blitz, there had been only a moderate reduction in the munitions output by British industry, which continued to rise slowly throughout this period. Probably the most noticeable effect was the redistribution of manufacturing; in an attempt to escape the specific targeting of factories and production facilities, the locations of which were known to the Germans, British firms had had to relocate.

On the British side, by observing and absorbing all the details of the German offensive in the air, the government had been able to collate information that would help the RAF develop a strategy for its own bombing campaign. Assessments of raid damage indicated that a focused targeting of specific sites was of greater benefit than haphazard raiding, and that incendiaries were more effective than high explosives because they were more disruptive. Based on these analyses, the RAF's bombing strategy was modified, and there was a shift in policy towards demoralizing the German public through economic warfare and the destruction of Germany's manufacturing base.

In general, Bomber Command never did adopt a policy of specifically killing civilians through carpet-bombing, having noted that the Blitz on Britain failed to achieve for the Germans the desired objective through 'terror bombing'. Unfortunately, though, Bomber Command was ultimately forced to adopt a strategy of area bombing because the equipment provided to its air crew was inadequate for precision bombing from altitude. Plans are only as effective in application as the means to deliver them. That said, the significant improvement in the capabilities of a new generation of bombers did make possible a wide range of options.

NEW TOOLS

During the first three years of the war, RAF Bomber Command had three principal types – the Blenheim, Whitley and Wellington – which it used to varying effect for the strategic bombing of German targets. However, these were inadequate for the anticipated operations to come. The RAF had always been influenced by high strategic goals, believing that the only way to win a war was to conduct an intensive bombing campaign, both to destroy the ability of an enemy country to produce equipment that was essential to the war effort and to bomb the factories and other places of work that kept the country in general going. To do that they needed a very large bomber force.

Three major types of British four-engine bombers emerged between 1940 and 1942, intended to carry out strategic bombing on a scale unimagined before the war: the Short Stirling, the Halifax and the Lancaster, the latter a development of the short-lived, two-engine Manchester. There would be other types, too, including the de Havilland Mosquito, a very fast twin-engine aircraft with a top speed of 380 mph, which was introduced initially into operational service as a bomber in May 1942 but was subsequently adapted for reconnaissance and as a night fighter. With a primary structure built of wood, it was unique in its adaptability for operations and its multiplicity of roles. Yet more aircraft would be procured from the USA and operated by Bomber Command. These included the Boeing B-17 Fortress, the Douglas Boston, the Lockheed Ventura and the North American B-25 Mitchell, all in relatively small numbers.

The first four-engine monoplane bomber operated by the RAF, the Short Stirling was designed in 1936 to specification B.12/36. This would be the template requirement for the Halifax and the Lancaster, each bomber being named after a British city. The Stirling was powered by four 1,650 hp Bristol Hercules engines, had a top speed of 270 mph and a range of just over 2,000

The Boeing B-17E was the first US bomber to reach England in mid-1942 at the start of a long campaign to carry the war to the very heart of Germany itself. USAF

Production was key to winning the air war, as here Boeing B-17s are built for service from England in the fight against Nazi Germany on an unprecedented scale. Boeing

miles when it was laden with 3,500 lb of bombs, or 590 miles with a maximum bomb load of 14,000 lb. This was a major increase in capability when compared to that of its nearest predecessor, the Wellington. Built under subcontract to Short Brothers of Rochester, Kent, from Short & Harland at Belfast, the Stirling had a bad reputation, as a result of both the design of the bomb bays, which prevented some RAF bombs being carried, and its marginal performance.

The first Stirling entered operational service with No. 7 Squadron at RAF Leeming, Yorkshire, in August 1940, replacing that squadron's Hampdens. The latter had only limited load-carrying capacity of 4,000 lb, a cruising speed of just over 160 mph and a maximum range of 1,200 miles fully loaded. The arrival of the Stirling was anticipated with marked enthusiasm. As the type began to be used, however, it was noted that its attrition rate was higher than others of its general type, such as the Halifax and the Lancaster. This was likely attributed to its lower operating altitude (15,000 ft), where it was more vulnerable to anti-aircraft flak and to interception by night fighters.

The Handley Page Halifax was initially designed to a specification that called for two Rolls-Royce Vulture in-line engines. Due to shortages of the Vulture, the requirement was changed and the Halifax emerged powered by four 1,280 hp Rolls-Royce Merlin Mk X engines – variants of the type used by the Spitfire and the Hurricane. The Mk 1 made its first flight in October 1939 and entered service with No. 35 Squadron in November 1940. Various adaptations and variants evolved, with armament changing between marks as operational experience dictated. For instance, the Mk 1 incorporated two 0.303 in guns on the nose and four in a tail turret, with some aircraft having beam guns in the centre fuselage. Later marks would dispense with the beam guns, retaining one 0.303 in gun in the nose and with four in tail and dorsal turrets. With a maximum bomb load of 13,000 lb the Halifax had a range of 1,260 miles, increasing to 1,869 miles with a 5,800 lb load.

The Lancaster had evolved rapidly out of the Avro Manchester into arguably the most famous bomber of World War II. A single example of one has been preserved in flying condition in the RAF Battle of Britain Memorial Flight. The Manchester from which the Lancaster emerged was designed to the same specification as the Halifax and the prototype made its first flight in July 1939, powered by two 1,769 hp Vultures. In its brief life, the Manchester experienced several changes. For example, it initially had three vertical fins but this was quickly reduced to two and their surface area was increased. The Manchester entered service with No. 207 Squadron at RAF Waddington, just outside Lincoln, in November 1940 and the first operational flight occurred on the night of 24/25

February 1941. Operations lasted little more than a year before the type was withdrawn in favour of its four-engine protégé, the Lancaster.

The Lancaster took the essentials of the Manchester, but the two Vultures were replaced with four 1,460 hp Merlin engines and the overall layout was refined into a much more efficient aircraft, initially without the characteristic dorsal and ventral turrets. In early models, those plus nose and tail turrets (the ventral eventually removed) housed four 0.303 in machine guns. With a cruising speed of 210 mph, a range of 1,660 miles with a 14,000 lb bomb load and a service ceiling of 24,500 ft, the Lancaster was adapted over time and ultimately became the only aircraft to carry the 22,000 lb Tallboy bombs. The Lancaster made its first flight in January 1941 and joined No. 44 Squadron at Waddington for service trials in the September.

These three heavy bomber types would be the main force behind Bomber Command's increasing pressure on German industry, its transport systems, marshalling yards, ports, harbours and – increasingly – on the towns and cities that housed the German workforce. Thanks to these activities, a great deal of experience and many operating practices, techniques and tactics had been built up and acquired by Bomber Command by the time the Americans became operationally involved during mid-1942.

NEW TARGETS

Despite contemporary newspapers and later history books' tendency to focus on Fighter Command during the testing months between May and October 1940, the challenges faced by Bomber Command and Coastal Command were equally as intense, if not quite so spectacular to watch.

In the Battle for France, Bomber Command had lost 145 aircraft on sustained but largely unproductive operations, supported by a force only half the strength it was when the German offensive opened in May 1940. However, there was little means of verifying just how accurate or productive these raids actually were since evidence was drawn directly from the verbal reports of the air crew themselves, which, while made in good faith, were frequently incorrect and misleading.

The next challenge came in the uncertain days between the Battle for France and the Battle of Britain, when some 3,000 German barges were seen assembled in coastal harbours facing the North Sea and the English Channel. Bomber Command was tasked with destroying as many of these as possible. With daylight raids attracting unsustainable levels of attrition, Bomber Command resorted to night raids in an effort to keep pressure up on the Germans while remaining within the limits of acceptable losses. As the Battle of Britain was being waged over England, Bomber Command was therefore opening a 'second front' in its raids on German targets.

In reality, though, absence of verification veiled an appalling performance on the part of the bombers – one that was only revealed when cameras, whose shutters were automatically triggered when the bomb load was released, were fitted to the underside of the planes. In the meantime, back on the ground Bomber Command was going through a change of leadership and faced inherent uncertainties as to the precise nature of its task.

These were days when the Whitley, the Blenheim and the Wellington were the sole means of delivering a meaningful attack on Germany itself. By the end of 1940, the Air Ministry had delivered a protracted list of priorities, top of which was the German oil industry, followed by specific industries that sustained the enemy's war effort: railways, marshalling yards and freight facilities in important German cities and airfields from where attacks on Britain could be mounted. However, attacks on German cities were deemed particularly important for boosting morale in Britain. Despite moral objections from some religious leaders and a few atheists alike, opinion among the majority of the British public favoured vengeful destruction of German towns and cities with little thought for the suffering this would cause. Despite this appetite for destruction, though, attacks directly on German cities was slow in coming.

In reaction, in part, to the bombing of civilian areas by the Luftwaffe during the Battle of Britain, the War Cabinet approved a raid on Berlin, which was at the very extreme end of the range available to aircraft of Bomber Command. This was duly conducted on the night of 25/26 August 1940. In all, 103 aircraft were assigned to the German capital city, as well as to Bremen, Cologne and Hamm. Hampdens and Wellingtons went to Berlin, where they did little damage within the city boundary, the only noted destruction being a wooden summerhouse, injuring two people. It was an inauspicious start to what would develop into a major campaign by the largest strategic bombing force ever assembled. But that would take some time to accomplish.

Air Mshl Sir Richard Peirse took over Bomber Command in October 1940, replacing Air V-Mshl Portal, who was promoted to Chief of the Air Staff and was essentially in charge of the RAF. Now, Bomber Command had a strength of 532 aircraft, of which 217 were Blenheims and 100 were Wellingtons. Over the next five months, the Blenheim inventory fell to 150 and the 85 Battles were all retired. So, when Peirse assumed command, he had a workable inventory of just 230 aircraft capable of winter night operations. This was reduced to ten when servicing problems and the employment of inexperienced crew was taken into account. As a result, in the winter months the numbers of aircraft dispatched on raids fell dramatically in proportion to the potential capabilities of the force.

Acting upon Hitler's Directive 23, issued on 6 February 1941, the Kriegsmarine stepped up U-boat operations that year. In response, Churchill specified targets that supported the German U-boat submarine war as top priority for Bomber Command; it was more important that Britain's maritime lifelines were kept open than that the overall German war effort was eroded. This therefore became the prime objective between March and July 1941. With three submarine building yards, Kiel was a prime target and well within reach of bases in England. Hamburg had two U-boat yards, and there were others at Bremen and Vegesack. The marine diesel engine works at Mannheim were also targeted. Another engine factory at Augsburg, Bavaria, was too far for the shortening nights and long flights, which would have exposed the bombers to attack. When the capital ships *Scharnhorst* and *Gneisenau* slipped into Brest harbour on 22 March 1941, Bomber Command singled out those as targets for a major raid too.

At this point, Peirse objected that his force had been removed from the strategic assault on Germany's oil and manufacturing industries to support what he considered a tactical Navy issue. Portal, however, was disinclined to object. He knew that Bomber Command was probably far from effective in its attacks on strategic targets. What's more, he was concerned that the new aircraft coming into service had to be operated effectively and efficiently. In order for this to happen, an assessment of just how accurate the bombing campaign was would be crucial, especially in light of the number of resources it took to manufacture the aircraft and train the crews.

On 9 July 1941, Bomber Command was directed to switch priorities back to the strategic offensive to dislocate the German transport system and to destroy the morale of both the civil population and, in particular, the industrial workers. Peirse's plans were back on track and the bombers were returning to the strategic role he wanted to pursue. To do that, accuracy and capability were essential but there were problems.

Examination of current bombing practices and their effectiveness had exposed weaknesses in capability that made it impossible for the RAF to effectively knock out Germany's oil industry or its supplies. This was tantamount to an admission of failure. News got worse a month later when a report dated 18 August 1941 revealed just how limited the effectiveness of this campaign had been to date. Known as the Butt Report, it had been commissioned by Professor Frederick A. Lindemann (Lord Cherwell), a physicist and confidant of Churchill and chief science adviser to the Cabinet. Using photographs taken by the bombers on night operations, it was an alarming confirmation of claims by air crew about the lack of success achieved in bombing prescribed targets. Based purely on photographic evidence and excluding statements made by the crew, the report concluded that of all aircraft dispatched, on average only one in three got to within 5 miles of the target, two in three when attacking French ports, one in four over targets in Germany, and one in ten over the industrial Ruhr. When there was a full moon, the rate was two in five, or one in 15 on moonless nights. In highly detailed analysis conducted after the war, it was judged that almost half of all bombs dropped during the 12 months up to May 1941 fell in open country.

However, figures in the Butt Report excluded aircraft that had set off but had to return due to technical failure, those shot down on the way, weather avoidance carrying aircraft away from their designated locations, or those that could simply not visually find the target. Including all of these, of aircraft assigned to a target only 5 per cent dropped their bombs within 5 miles of where they were intended.

These statistics sent shock waves through Bomber Command and raised consternation at the Air Ministry and in the Cabinet. Bombers were deemed to be the tip of the spear in terms of striking back at Germany and bringing the Nazi regime to its knees. Only fighters could have won the Battle of Britain but only the bombers could do the kind of damage necessary for Britain to have any chance of winning the war. There was no obvious solution, no magic technology to provide a quick answer. The way the aerial war was carried out would have to be adjusted so as to be deliverable within the limitations of navigation, bombing aiming and execution.

Lindemann concluded – and recommended to the Cabinet, through a paper circulated on 30 March 1942 – that any attempt at precision bombing of pre-selected targets was futile. The only real capability lay in area bombing, thereby creating a new definition of a strategic offensive. In what was known as the 'dehousing' plan, Lindemann proposed that Bomber Command should be used to drop very large quantities of bombs on cities, with a view to destroying the homes and shelters of the workforce involved in industrial production.

The exposure of the flaws in the capabilities of the bomber force prompted a tirade from the Army and the Navy. Both proposed that finite resources – financial and material – would be better spent on land and sea warfare rather than, in their view, being wasted in the air. Seeing in this critique a means of filling their own funding shortfalls, senior soldiers and sailors pushed the argument that the war could only be won by men fighting on land or at sea, engaging the enemy directly.

Churchill, however, was committed to the use of air power as the second front of the war against Germany and strove to balance the needs of Bomber Command with competing pressures for money, men and materiel from the other two services. So the dehousing plan became the fixed imperative for the RAF, maintaining a prewar focus on pre-emptive attack rather than reactive defence as the way to win the war. As events would show, this was not altogether possible, even with limitless resources, and was just one weapon in the arsenal of victory.

Interestingly, there were subtle variations among those who agreed with the dehousing strategy. Some believed that the way it would be of greatest value was not in the wholesale destruction of cities and the escalating impact on production workers, but rather through the enemy resources such a campaign would tie up. This included the civil defence, anti-aircraft troops and fighters that the enemy would have to build in order to counter the destructive potential of the RAF.

Yet all of these were theoretical ideas based on analysis and paper calculations. In reality, Bomber Command would be asked to conduct an experiment in an entirely new form of warfare; the magnitude of the effort and the levels of destruction anticipated through area bombing at night were unlike anything experienced so far. Despite this, it was the only policy the RAF could adopt, because it lacked the means to do anything else. And that alone was an important factor in Churchill's determination to stick with strategic bombing. He wished to maintain a belief among the general public that the government was doing something to keep up the pressure on Germany. He also believed that eventually Germany would attack Russia and that America would have to enter the war. It was important that he maintained a sense of action – at home and abroad.

DEFENDING THE REICH

Unfortunately for the British, the enhanced effort and the greater tonnage of bombs delivered by the new aircraft entering service met increased resistance from an emerging series of German night fighters, which posed a greater threat to the nocturnal raiders. Although the provision in Germany of an effective air defence system had been slow to develop, under Gen Josef Kammhuber various measures were put in place, with varying effect.

By July 1941, there were 134 twin-engine night fighters deployed, most of which were based in Holland. On German soil, the operation of the flak barrage compromised the interception of incoming bombers by preventing the defending fighters from getting near their targets, for fear of being hit by the anti-aircraft guns. Next, a range of powerful searchlights were deployed as a continuous barrier along the coast in an attempt to light up the intruders without risking defending

An anti-aircraft searchlight on the roof of the Royal Chelsea Hospital, London, in April 1940, a month before the German invasion of France and the Low Countries. David Baker Archive

fighters being shot down. This, too, proved ineffective as the RAF got its aircraft through the searchlights before the fighters could find their prospective targets.

The solution was radar stations. Known to the British as the Kammhuber Line, this was in principle the equivalent of the Chain Home RDF stations that skirted the coast of the British Isles. Eventually, this defensive line grew into a complex system of three barriers, each about 20 miles in length and up to 12 miles in depth, the forward boundary housing a Freya radar that was capable of detecting aircraft at a range of 62 miles.

The three defensive lines laid down by the Kammhuber Line proved a formidable challenge to Bomber Command as they attempted to reach the Ruhr and head deeper into the German heartland. Nevertheless, that was Bomber Command's objective. In this, they were successful. By November 1941, the RAF had extended their penetration of enemy territory and broadened the base of operations as increasing numbers of aircraft rolled off the production lines and into service. However, all of this came at a price.

Throughout the period July to November 1941 losses had grown. These were commensurate with the intensity of the effort but were disproportionately high when compared to the results obtained.

GERMAN RADAR SYSTEMS

Named after a Nordic mythological character, Freya was a development of naval radar, tests for which had begun in Germany in 1937. Radar as a means of detecting objects too far away to be visible to the naked eye had first been developed in Germany long before the British gave it serious attention in the 1930s, but the British were way ahead of the Germans in deploying an operational system – one that proved very valuable during the Battle of Britain. Urged on by the demands of the military requirement, development of German radar accelerated in the early years of the war into fully operational systems, which, as represented by Freya, were more advanced and sophisticated than the British system. Using a radio frequency of 1.2 m, versus the British 12 m frequency, it had a greater ability to pick out smaller targets in the air. What's more, since it had a smaller and more flexible mounting, it was much easier to operate.

Intelligence information about the existence of Freya originated from a Danish officer, Thomas Sneum, who secretly took photographs of installations and, in a remarkably audacious effort, managed to fly to Britain with the pictures. From these, Dr R.V. Jones of the intelligence section of the Air Ministry was able to work out its true purpose. Further information about the German air defence system came from photographs taken by a reconnaissance aircraft. These led to a commando raid to obtain critical intelligence about what the Germans referred to as the *Würzburg* system – a smaller radar system designed to position Luftwaffe fighters on incoming enemy aircraft. The raid in February 1942, known as Operation *Biting*, targeted a *Würzburg* radar at Bruneval, some 12 miles north of Le Havre, and successfully retrieved pieces of radar equipment that were vital for helping the British to gain a full understanding of how it worked.

Operating in the 54–53 cm band (553–556 MHz) and with a power output of 7–11 kW, *Würzburg* was complementary in that it took the initial low-resolution detection of a target by Freya and displayed a high-resolution location that could pinpoint the intruder. With an effective range of 18 miles, it was accurate to about 80 ft. Some 4,000 were produced. After the war, the equipment was used by the Dutch in the early development of radio astronomy.

BOMBER COMMAND VITAL STATISTICS

By way of illustration, the British produced 41 heavy bombers (Halifax, Manchester and Stirling) in 1940, increasing to 498 in 1941 (including the first Lancasters) and 1,976 in 1942. However, the balance of medium bombers (Hampden, Hereford, Wellington and Whitley) produced went up from 1,926 in 1940 to 2,777 in 1941 (of which 1,816 were Wellingtons) and 3,463 in 1942. In this category, the Wellington dominated production, output growing from 997 in 1940 to 1,816 in 1941 and 2,702 in 1941. Added to these were the light bombers (Battle, Blenheim and Mosquito), production declining from 1,753 in 1940 to 1,393 in 1941 and 814 in 1942. The Battle was out of production in 1941 and production of the Blenheim was in decline as limited numbers of Mosquito rolled off the production lines to replace it.

From these figures it could be assumed that the strength of Bomber Command was growing: output delivered 3,720 bombers of all types in 1940, 3,707 in 1941 and 5,492 in 1942. Yet it must be remembered that many of these aircraft were replacements for those that had been lost. The attrition rate was high – Bomber Command shared with the German U-boat fleet the highest loss of life of any branch of the armed services among all the combatant nations. By the end of the conflict, of the 125,000 air crew from across the Commonwealth who served with RAF Bomber Command, almost 60 per cent had become casualties. Some 55,000 of that total were killed in action or through accidents – half of all flying crew.

Because of the high loss rate, the number of serviceable aircraft in squadrons on average hovered between 374 and 419 for any given month during 1942. The gradual shift towards heavy bombers, however, had a significant impact on the bomb lift in terms of tonnage available to the RAF, increasing on average for any one day from 510 tonnes in February 1942 to 824 tonnes by the end of that year. Of those totals, the most significant was the contribution made by the 'heavies', which grew from 137 tonnes in February to 667 tonnes in December.

The Butt Report had made clear the inability of Bomber Command to fulfil its obligation. When the 4,065 individual photographic frames exposed by camera-carrying aircraft as they delivered their bombs over a period of 100 nights were analyzed, it became was clear that something had to change. The immediate response was to withdraw from the heavily defended transportation nodes, the marshalling yards and the industrial heart of the Ruhr, and instead reassign aircraft to easier targets in an effort to balance the equation – by reducing the number of casualties and raising the effectiveness of the operation. Yet, while this strategy would balance the books, it would not win the war.

The figures that most alarmed the Air Ministry were the nightly losses. These had to be explained by Peirse when he was summoned to meet Churchill at Chequers on 8 November 1941. In particular, he was asked to account for the unusually heavy losses of the preceding night, when of the 169 aircraft that set out for Berlin only 73 reached the general area of the city, with only minimal damage reported, 11 people killed and 44 injured. This was the last raid on Berlin until January 1943. Instead, on the night of 8 November, 75 aircraft went to bomb Cologne, 55 Wellingtons and Stirlings went to Mannheim, and 30 more aircraft went on roving patrols. Still more bombed Ostend and Boulogne and carried out mine-laying duties near Oslo. Of the 392 aircraft that set out that night, 37 were lost – an unacceptably high 9.4 per cent.

Overall, the picture was poor. For the period from 7 July to 10 November 1941, Bomber Command had conducted operations on 93 nights, a total of 11,991 sorties on which 414 aircraft (3.5 per cent) had been lost. But if the night figures were bad, the daylight figures were totally unsustainable: of 83 daylight operations supporting 1,567 sorties, 112 aircraft failed to return – a loss of 7.1 per cent.

The deliberations at Chequers produced a gloomy conclusion without a ready solution and on 13 November Peirse was informed that Bomber Command was henceforth to conduct only limited operations. This would remain the case for the next three months, and in fact no operations at all were conducted between 10 and 15 November.

For several months, then, the fate of Bomber Command hung in the balance. Many options were weighed up and consideration was given to reducing its strength and changing its role – from a strategic to a tactical function, supporting the increasing demands of the British Army as it strengthened and expanded operations in North Africa.

This was not received well. As the most senior officer in the RAF, Portal – despite the implications of the statistics – had for months argued the case for an even more robust and capable Bomber Command. He pointed to the new generation of aircraft, such as the Lancaster; a new tranche of technical equipment, which would allow more accurate bombing by night; and a larger force to simultaneously position several hundred aircraft over the same target. In a letter to Churchill dated 25 September 1941, Portal had also argued for a force of 4,000 bombers, with which he boasted he could blast the German war machine and bring an end to Nazi Germany within six months. Refraining from engaging in such an ambitious commitment, Churchill supported Portal's underpinning rationale and told him to get on with the job using the equipment he had. That was wise. Other factors were about to enter into play.

The final decision issued on 14 February 1942 supported the continued, pre-planned expansion of Bomber Command but changed the mission to general area bombing of built-up areas. In reality, this had already been the general policy adopted by the RAF for some months, in an attempt to minimize losses.

A NEW PHASE

Just eight days later, on 22 February 1942, Bomber Command got a new leader – Air Chf Mshl Sir Arthur Harris. With prewar experience of the RAF in India, Harris was determined to produce positive results, not by taking an easy oath and reassigning operations to less heavily defended targets, but by maximizing the potential, raising the morale of the air crew and effectively utilizing the new aircraft and the latest technology.

Bomber Command in early 1942 was no larger than it had been a year earlier. With demands from Coastal Command and support for Middle East operations, Harris therefore inherited a force of 469 night and 78 day bombers (56 Blenheims and 22 Bostons purchased from the Americans). Fortunately for the British, though, new technology appeared on the scene at this time, in the form of 'Gee' – a device that greatly increased navigational accuracy by tying aircraft location to the relative position of the target and so made it easier for pilots to find a specified location in the dark. Gee worked by picking up signals from three widely dispersed locations in England to a maximum range of 400 miles from an altitude no lower than 20,000 ft, then measuring the time delay between any two transmitted radio signals to produce a position fix. This was accurate to within a few hundred feet.

Developed initially as a blind-landing system, Gee was used operationally for the first time on the night of 8/9 March 1942, when it was fitted to a single Wellington of No. 115 Squadron for a raid on Essen. With the Wellington as the lead aircraft on which all the other 211 aircraft formed up, the raid was expected to hit the Krupp works. Although the exact target was missed, an astonishing 33 per cent of the aircraft reached the area and dropped their bombs; compared with an average of about 20 per cent in like-for-like raids.

Following this successful inaugural flight, Gee would grow both in importance as a target-location aid but also one that was used for plotting a flight path home, lowering the percentage of aircraft that lost their way back from 3.5 per cent to 1.2 per cent.

The first major success for Gee occurred on the night of 13/14 March, when 135 aircraft targeted Cologne. It was a moonless night, so the lead aircraft, equipped with Gee, lit the targets with flares and incendiaries to provide a visible marker for the following aircraft, which carried mixed bomb loads. Great damage was caused and the general assessment was that this one raid, in which just one aircraft was lost, had been five times as successful as the most effective raid on this city to date.

The tide had turned. The fortunes of Bomber Command now pivoted on the availability of new and more capable aircraft, particularly the Lancaster, the generation of technical equipment and the experience of the air crew. What's more, another player had joined: the Americans were now fully engaged in a war against Hitler and would send masses of airmen and aircraft across the Atlantic for what would quickly become known as the Combined Bomber Offensive. However, before we explore this crucial phase that would ultimately signal the end of the war, we need to turn our eyes east to Russia and Japan.

CHAPTER 11
Strategic Air Warfare

THE EXTENSIVELY planned German invasion of Russia began in the early hours of 22 June 1941 under the codename Operation *Barbarossa*, after the 12th century Holy Roman Emperor Frederick I. Tearing up the agreement reached with Stalin in August 1939, Hitler sought to destroy the Soviet Union, take Moscow, decapitate the Communist leadership and annihilate the country as an independent state by occupying all territories, initially up to the Ural Mountains. It was the greatest land invasion in history along a continuous battle front of almost 1,000 miles, extending from the Baltic to the Black Sea – equal to the distance between London and Rome, or Washington DC to Houston, Texas.

Prior to the invasion, despite his pact with Hitler, Stalin considered Germany the most dangerous threat to Soviet security and as early as December 1940 had warned his generals that it was only a matter of time before Germany launched a pre-emptive attack. However, Russian armed forces had been denuded in strength, experience, capacity and resources by Stalin's great purges of the late 1930s, in which 30,000 personnel of the Red Army had been killed, including 15 of the 16 army commanders, 50 of the 57 corps commanders, 154 of the 186 divisional commanders and 401 of 456 colonels. This wholesale purging of the Red Army set back the Soviet Union at least a decade in its capacity to field a capable and effective defence against the Wehrmacht. Nevertheless, Stalin gave his army four years in which to build back its capability. In the meantime, nervous of provoking an attack, great efforts were made not to give Germany any excuse for invasion. Thus it was that when various intelligence sources indicated an attack was imminent, they were either ignored or their warnings were played down.

THE SOVIET AIR FLEET

Even prior to World War I, Russia had a history of aircraft with very long range and outstanding performance, supported by advanced mathematics and robust engineering practice. The Imperial Russian Air Service had been formed in 1912, empowered by a tradition of aeronautical science and engineering established by the Aerodynamic Institute, which had been formed by Nikolai Zhukovsky in 1904. When war broke out in 1914, the Air Service had a complement of 263 aeroplanes, second in terms of size only to France. After the Bolshevik revolution on 20 December 1917, the organizational structure for the various air units was formed, followed on 24 May 1918 by the 'Workers and Peasants' Red Air Fleet'. After several name changes, it became the Voyenno-Vozdushnye (Soviet Air Forces), or VVS.

Emphasis on aircraft design and production favoured long-range bombers, which drew on engineering for a tradition of long-range transport types, which Stalin had favoured as exemplars of a progressive and record-breaking Soviet state. Russia had made considerable advances with rocketry in the mid-to-late 1930s, too, although much of that capability had been squandered during the purges when leading scientists were sent to the gulags. Nevertheless, prominent designs and associated manufacturing teams produced credible and effective aircraft based largely around the declared requirement for long-range bombers for a strategic application and on nimble and fast interceptors for defence.

While there was emphasis on the need for aviation to support the Army and for bombers to strike at the heartland of an aggressor, technical development of new and innovative concepts saw Russia field the first low-wing, cantilever monoplane fighter. This entered service as the Polikarpov I-16 in 1935. Powered by a 1,100 hp nine-cylinder radial engine, the I-16 had a top speed of 325 mph and a range of 430 miles. With two cannon and two machine guns, it was a credible interceptor when it was first introduced and saw service in the Spanish Civil War fighting for the Republicans, and performed well against the older German types. However, it was very rapidly outclassed.

In production from 1940, the Yakovlev Yak-1 was in service at the time of the German invasion. So good was its basic design, which was made from wood, and performance that it became the basis for a series of developed variants. However, at the time of the invasion fewer than 100 were in service, with more than 300 still in need of final assembly and delivery to units. What Yak-1s there were proved an equal match for the Bf-109E, although they were outclassed by subsequent developments of the German fighter; like most Soviet fighters, the Yak-1 suffered from its armament being too light. Despite this, it was well liked by its pilots.

The emerging team of Mikoyan and Gurevich produced a series of fighters, the MiG-3 being available from 1941 with almost 1,000 in service. However, there were fewer than 500 pilots who could fly them. Here, as elsewhere, the purges had taken their toll on operational readiness; the pilots who were available were inexperienced and lacked the flying time essential for maintaining familiarity and competence. Although the aircraft was good for its time – with a top speed of more than 310 mph and a range of 510 miles – the MiG-3 carried just three machine guns with the potential for six air-to-air rockets and therefore lacked potency. It was no match for the Bf-109 or the Fw-190, which were already in operational deployment.

Technically, there could be few such reservations about the Lavochkin-Gorbunov-Gudkov LaGG-3 fighter, which was available for service in 1941, in time for *Barbarossa*. However, despite numerous modifications, upgrades and improvements after its initial deployment in 1940, the type was not liked and never really acquitted itself well in combat. It had a very high top speed, equal to that of the British and German single-seaters, but it lacked reliability and was prone to break apart when its wooden structure was struck by cannon shells. Like so many Soviet aircraft of the era, a lack of experience and know-how in the post-purge workforce that remained available gave it a flawed performance and a questionable reputation, which resulted in it being dubbed the 'mahogany coffin'.

Bombers developed by Ilyushin included the DB-3 and the 3A. The majority were the latter type, a design that made its operational debut in 1937. In terms of sheer capability, this was the best twin-engine bomber in the world. Markedly more capable than the Luftwaffe's He-111, the DB-3 could carry a maximum bomb load of 1,100 lb and had a range of 2,500 miles or 1,900 miles with a 2,200 lb load. On very short missions it could carry a 5,500 lb bomb load. As part of an improvement programme, the DB-3B would eventually have a range of 2,400 miles and carry a defensive armament of three machine guns and one cannon.

Ilyushin had pushed hard on new technologies and a complex manufacturing process that compromised production, leading to delays getting the type into service. But where it was employed, it showed good results, the type being the first Soviet aircraft to bomb Berlin, on the night of 7/8 August 1941. In an effort to correct production problems, Ilyushin produced a developed version designated Il-4. This had greatly improved performance and was used on several raids on Berlin. About 6,700 DB-3 and Il-4 bombers were built during the war.

Designed in a Soviet prison by Vladimir Petlyakov, who had been arrested on a charge of delaying another project, the Pe-2 escort fighter was introduced in March 1941 and proved to be an outstanding aircraft. It was employed in the role of tactical bomber following modifications made during its development. These were based on Russian analysis of Luftwaffe Blitzkrieg operations, which were seen to be successful. Petlyakov was given just over six weeks to turn it into a dive-bomber – which he did. As it transpired, the Pe-2 went on to do work as an escort fighter, for which the specification had first been set, and to carry out ground attack and conventional bombing duties. More than 11,000 were built during the war. Powered by two 1,200 hp 12-cylinder liquid-cooled piston engines, it had a theoretical top speed of 360 mph but there were instances when the aircraft outran attacking German fighters by dashing away at more than 400 mph.

The Pe-8, meanwhile, was the only Russian four-engine strategic bomber produced by the Soviet Union during the war. Introduced into service in 1940, more than four years after its first flight, only 93 were built for a role that evaporated as the ground war placed the priority on tactical air support rather than very long-range bombing missions of German strategic targets. This went against the long-held Russian preference for large aircraft – a prejudice that had resulted during the interwar years in the emergence of several types that claimed phenomenal distance and endurance records. The type of war the Soviets faced after June 1941 was, however, altogether different, which rendered this sort of aircraft all but redundant. Nevertheless, with a maximum bomb load of 11,000 lb and a range of 2,300 miles, the Pe-8 was unique.

At this point, mention must be made of the Tupolev TB-3, a contemporary of the Pe-8. It had a similar capability to the Pe-8, but saw high losses and had a redundant role. In the second half of 1941, the few that had not been destroyed by the Luftwaffe were retired ignominiously. In many ways, this aircraft was an anachronism in that it was created out of assumptions made during World War I that the very long-range bomber could do sufficient damage to a country's economy and its industrial base to make it a flagship weapon. Thus, it was believed, if the Tupolev TB-3 was ever used it could destroy an enemy's prospects of a sustained war. And after the experience of that first Great War, anything that could achieve this end was worth investing in, if only to avert the prospects of a protracted conflict and save countless lives at home. In reality, though, it was too big and too slow to really count, struggling to achieve a cruising speed of little more than 120 mph.

After the Pe-2, Andrei Tupolev's Tu-2 was the most important bomber of the Soviet Air Force, being one of the most useful and adaptable twin-engine aircraft of its day. Liked by pilots and ground crew, the Tu-2 had a top speed of more than 320 mph and a capacity for carrying a 3,300 lb bomb load or an additional 5,000 lb externally. The type was in the final stages of development when the Germans invaded but it quickly entered service and, with the Pe-2, shared the roles of army support and anti-armour attacks that were so important to turning the tide of land battles.

Later in the war, the Russian aircraft industry developed more powerful and reliable designs. Unquestionably capable and on equal terms with the best the Luftwaffe could put up against it, the Lavochkin La-5 fighter boasted a top speed of more than 400 mph under ideal conditions from its 14-cylinder, 1,960 hp Shvetsov radial piston engine. With two 20 mm cannon and a capacity for two bombs of up to 220 lb each, it was a credible ground attack aircraft as well. However, it was not in service until mid-1942, when it was sorely needed for some of the most demanding fights of the war. In 1944, a development – the La-7 – arrived as the definitive fighter of type before the end of the war.

So it was that on the eve of *Barbarossa* the Soviet Union had 316 divisions, up from 131 in January 1939, and 5.7 million men under arms, more than double the 1939 figure. Over that period, the number of guns and mortars increased from 55,800 to 117,600 and the number of tanks from 21,100 to 25,700. In theory, the Red Air Force had 19,500 aircraft, making it the largest air force in the world, of which about 5,540 were deployed in five military districts in the west of the country and considered available for service – a vast quantity were not operationally suitable for service. Of this total, the Germans assessed only 4,700 to be of combat status, of which 2,850 were of modern standard.

Technically, the Russian aircraft were more advanced than the Germans believed but this was offset by the fact that the VVS was still in a state of total reorganization and also suffering the consequences of damaging purges and inadequate training. The Germans also dramatically underestimated the role that civil aviation would play when pressed into war duty by Moscow, and the production capability of the Soviet aircraft factories, unaware that Stalin had already begun withdrawing those facilities far from the frontline and back towards the Urals. This move would accelerate after the invasion.

HEGEMONY

The Germans came to Russia well prepared – for battle, for occupation and for turning its vast land area into settlements where professional and agrarian Germans could begin a new life. They would be aided in this by native people, who would be made into slaves; Hitler regarded slavery in much the same way European settlers in North America had in an earlier century when they exploited the native population. Indeed, Hitler was fascinated with the occupation of North

America and the establishment of the USA and sought to achieve the same result in the East by creating his Greater Germanic Reich. This deep-seated purpose is frequently avoided by historians when they examine the complete restructuring of human demographics that energized his military adventures, yet it explains the intensity and abominable thoroughness, brutality and inhumane nature of the campaigns.

For Operation *Barbarossa*, the Wehrmacht mobilized 153 divisions in four Army Groups: Norway, to head across to Finland and support their fight against Soviet occupation; North, heading for the Baltic States and Leningrad to seal off the sea approaches and squeeze the Russians out of that area close to southern Finland; Centre, dashing straight for Minsk, Smolensk and Moscow; and South, to drive across Ukraine for the wheat and into Rumania to secure the oil. In that it was driven by a need to feed both its people and its industry and to provide room for a growing population, for Nazi Germany this was unlike any of its previous campaigns. It was defined by the long-term planning that was behind its execution and its completion, which anticipated a hegemonic Nazi state from Ostend to the Urals and from the north of Norway to the Mediterranean coast of North Africa.

It was intended that behind the frontline would come engineers to begin the transformation of the land; Einsatzgruppen (paramilitary death squads) to liquidate partisans and Communist officials, gather up gypsies, Jews and political extremists; and the SS to filter the population into three groups: those with long-term potential as slaves for transforming the land; less fit and older people with some work potential, to be exploited while they lived; and the useless, feeble-minded and debilitated, who were to be immediately exterminated.

As an overlying administrative objective, both the Army and the Luftwaffe had organizational responsibility for siting certain military bases for operations further to the east and for establishing the location of supply depots for ground and air support. Primary objectives focused on achieving victory over Russia at the border by setting up a Blitzkrieg-induced dash east, simultaneously on all fronts. Disposition of Luftwaffe forces took account of the need to maintain defences against Britain and threats from the south, specifically along the Mediterranean. If North Africa were to be secured by the British, the threat to Italy would be compounded. That concern had already siphoned off Luftwaffe units that could otherwise have consolidated *Barbarossa*.

Luftflotte 1 under Gen Keller, but quickly replaced by Gen Korten, was assigned to Army Group North; Luftflotte 2 under Gen Kesselring supported Army Group Centre; Luftflotte 4 under Gen Lohr supported Army Group South; and Luftflotte 5 under Gen Stumpff was assigned to special operations and equipped mostly with Ju-88s, Stuka dive-bombers and Bf-109F fighters. On 21 June 1941, the Luftwaffe had a total complement of 4,882 aircraft, of which 1,440 were single-engine fighters and 1,511 were bombers, of which 2,770 were deployed in support of the invasion. Ground forces comprised 6,900 armoured vehicles including tanks, 600,000 motor vehicles, nearly 700,000 horses (invaluable in the muddy terrain encountered) and 3.8 million men.

The offensive began when aircraft of KG-2, -3 and -58 crossed the border and hit airfields crucial to clearing the skies of the Soviet Air Force. In total, the four air fleets mounted an offensive force of 1,400 aircraft on the first day, consisting of 510 bombers, 200 Stukas, 440 fighters, 40 destroyer and 120 long-range reconnaissance aircraft. This was aerial warfare on a colossal scale across a vast land area and would require up-to-date reconnaissance to prepare raids, strikes and attacks proportionate to the resistance of the Soviet forces.

Using fragmentation bombs to destroy aircraft taken by surprise on the ground, strafing operations supported the Army units as they poured across the border and made lightning pace pushing east. Not until the afternoon did the Luftwaffe encounter any Russian aircraft. When they did, although most of the Russian planes were slower than the Bf-109s, they were more agile and difficult to shoot down. Nevertheless, in less than nine hours the Russians lost 1,200 aircraft. In total, on the first complete day of operations the Germans destroyed 1,811 Soviet aircraft – 822 in air-to-air combat and 1,489 on the ground via Stuka attacks and high-level bombing, which were particularly effective because the Russian aircraft had been parked in precise rows close together.

Where they encountered German aircraft in the air, the Russian pilots fought like fanatics, on several occasions physically ramming the enemy aircraft in a desperate bid to bring them down. These determined pilots wrought havoc wherever they appeared, causing surprisingly high losses for an air force the German pilots had been indoctrinated to believe comprised half-educated savages. Nevertheless, surprised by the attack and shocked by the intensity of the attacking force, the Russian resistance quickly crumbled due to the destruction of equipment on that first day.

Over the following five days, the Luftwaffe achieved almost complete control of the air – which was their purpose – and struck at troop concentrations and rear echelons withdrawing from the rapidly shifting battlefront. By this time, German troops were 200 miles inside Russia and close to the Northern Dvina River. By the end of the month, all Soviet opposition in the Baltic region had collapsed. On the central front the Luftwaffe hammered home waves of destructive attacks on airfields and troop concentrations, supporting the advancing units of the German

Army. A complete disaster for the Russians occurred when an enormous pincer movement was carried out by two Panzer divisions in mid-June which encircled Białystok and met up east of Minsk.

Several days later, on the night of 29/30 June, the Luftwaffe focused on support for the ground troops, JG-51 hitting hard at a concentration of Russian bombers and destroying 114, raising to 1,000 the total number of aircraft destroyed by this one unit since operations had begun a week earlier. Two other Jagdgeschwadern reported similar tallies. After mopping up round Minsk, by 9 July the Germans held almost 288,000 Russian prisoners captive, had killed or wounded at least that number, and had destroyed more than 2,500 Soviet tanks. Ten days later, two Panzer groups encircled the Smolensk pocket, capturing a further 100,000 Russian soldiers together with 2,000 tanks and 1,900 pieces of field artillery. On 22 July, a month into the offensive, 127 Luftwaffe aircraft bombed Moscow but met with more than 300 searchlights and a barrage of anti-aircraft artillery.

It was here that the Germans believed they had the defeat of the entire Soviet Army within their grasp, and an independent analysis at the time would have concluded that this was indeed the case. However, there were subtle shifts in the pattern that was developing. The Russians had withdrawn a lot of their production facilities – factories that would have been exposed to German bombing had been moved out of harm's way – and after the initial shock there was a determined reaction to halt the aggressor at all costs. Time was needed to replenish the lost men and materiel, to build new aircraft and to stem the German rush eastwards, because, according to Russian legend, there were two enduring Russian generals who always ensured that no invader of Russia would remain and survive. Their names were December and January. Eventually, the Russian winter would come.

The Luftwaffe, too, was suffering by this point; it had outpaced the supply lines and was beginning to feel the consequences. This was not a new situation: it had previously been faced by the German Army in France during late May 1940 when their tanks had rolled to a halt short of Dunkirk, partly through lack of supplies. The deeper the Luftwaffe sent its flying units into Russia, the more difficult it was to keep the fuel and ammunition flowing. In several respects, the advance had been swifter than expected and the full panoply of logistical support was being left behind, the supply lines frayed and unsupported. Units reported as early as 5 July that they were running dry and the broadening funnel effect of the widening front made this worse. As losses mounted, the resources diminished and the length of the frontline increased. Where it had been 1,000 miles at the start of the air campaign, by the end of the year the front stretched almost 1,900 miles, from Rostov-on-Don to Murmansk, embracing an area of aerial conflict across almost 580,000 square miles – more than the area of Spain, France and the British Isles combined.

What was becoming clear was that the flexible supply chain imposed for the French campaign in 1940 was not applicable in this theatre of war in 1941. Supporting the Army's advance, fighter and bomber units were required to move at the pace of the forward echelons. But hauling around entire groups consisting of many squadrons and units was not as easy as plunging forwards in a Blitzkrieg attack. Losses began to mount and aircraft could not be repaired due to a lack of spares and workshop facilities. In 12 days during August, a Fliegerkorps reported the loss of 10 per cent of its aircraft with 54 per cent damaged but repairable. In total, by mid-August the operating elements of the Luftwaffe in Russia had lost 3.9 per cent of its air crew killed, 5.7 per cent wounded and 2.9 per cent missing – a total casualty level of 12.5 per cent.

STALEMATE

After a short respite in operations, allowing the logistical supply elements to catch up with the advancing armies, the advance resumed at the end of August with the Luftwaffe adhering to the flexible supply chain that was still modelled on its operations in France. This may have been plausible for north-western Europe but it was inadequate for the Eastern Front. Surging forwards in the south-east, the various Wehrmacht Army groups began to converge and line up, enclosing a vast area around Kiev and capturing a further 655,000 Russian prisoners. Progress was now dependent on the weather and on local conditions. Hitler had amended the plan and instead of racing for Moscow, Army Group Centre had split in two to support its flanking armies, North and South. While Army Group North had secured the north-west territories of the Soviet Union and placed Leningrad (the modern St Petersburg) under siege, Army Group South had decimated resistance in the general direction of Ukraine and Rumania. Hitler now refocused the effort on Army Group Centre moving to take Moscow. The Luftwaffe was to play a vital role in pushing east to complete the rout of Russian air and ground elements.

The main drive east resumed on 30 September with Gen Guderian's Panzers moving up from Ukraine and pressing toward Orel. Two days later, the main German offensive began, supported by 1,387 aircraft. Movement was now so swift that the Russians had no time to prepare a defence. By 5 October, Russian reconnaissance aircraft noted a German column 15 miles long advancing along the Smolensk–Moscow highway. In rapid order, supported by a blistering attack from the air, the regions around Bryansk and Vyazma were encircled and a further 658,000 Russian prisoners taken.

Known as Operation *Typhoon*, the march on Moscow progressed slowly, with the troops encountering increasingly unfavourable waterlogged territory. Aircraft became bogged down and were unable to take off. The primitive dirt strips from which air operations had been mounted only weeks before became wheel traps, cutting operational sorties from 1,000 per day to 559 on 8 October and to a mere 269 the following day. What's more, the lack of progress in improving the flow of fuel, ammunition and provisions fell far short of satisfying the requirements of the German logistical supply chains. The OKW had simply refused to accept that this was an important part of their planning and the lack of provision showed in the reduced capacity to continue with the same intensity.

In an attempt to halt the eastward advance, Russian Army engineers blew up the Istria waterworks on 24 November, flooding more than 30 villages. These were rapidly submerged, swelling two major rivers from the six reservoirs that were drained in this process. While the loss of Russian life in those villages was significant, the action played a major role in delaying the German advance as winter set in. German expectations that the Russians were all but defeated were further confounded when Stalin transferred 1,500 aircraft, along with 18 divisions and 1,700 tanks, from the Far East, together with 1.1 million men. Despite this, the Russian forces still only marginally outnumbered the German Army in that area.

Nevertheless, there were significant advantages for the Russians: their troops were used to the sub-zero conditions; their engines for both vehicles and aircraft ran on coarser-grade fuel from local sources, which the Germans could not use; their aircraft were designed to operate in freezing conditions; and the extremes of winter restricted supplies and logistics getting through to the German frontline. As the weather worsened and the ground froze, providing better traction for wheels and tank tracks, operations were marginally better but this was only a temporary respite from the inexorable decline in fortunes for the Wehrmacht.

As the Army moved towards Moscow, the Luftwaffe became decreasingly important while the Russian air forces found resurgent energy and pressed hard upon the German Army. A counter-offensive from Gen Zhukov threatened to pull apart the entire front but the operational resilience of the Luftwaffe fell further and rates of aircraft availability fell to 40 per cent for the bomber force and remained close to 53 per cent for all types.

When operations drew to a halt in December 1941, the losses to both sides were colossal. Some 21,000 Russian civil and military aircraft had been destroyed, against 3,800 aircraft and 13,700 personnel lost to the Luftwaffe, of which 8,400 men were wounded and repatriated back from the front. More German casualties were now caused by the winter weather (-38° C) – the worst across the entire European continent that century – than by enemy action.

Between the attack on 22 June and 1 November 1941, the Luftwaffe suffered average losses of 741 aircraft each month, approximately 30 per cent of the total average monthly strength of 2,462 aircraft. Against an average monthly crew strength of 2,963 men, losses were around 318, nearly 11 per cent, with a total loss of almost 43 per cent over that four-month period. While the attrition rate was no higher than the monthly average during the Battle of Britain, the sustained drip-feed of weekly casualties was draining the replacement cycle of new aircraft coming off the production lines. What had been unsustainable over the four months of the conflict over Britain was becoming equally unsustainable over Russia.

Production of German aircraft lagged behind requirements. The need for increasing numbers of aircraft soared as the intensity of operations provided no respite in which to rebuild unit strength. Despite the ferocity of successive conflicts from the invasion of Poland to the Russia campaign, there had been no major increase in either quotas or deliverable airframes. Industry had produced 10,247 aircraft of all types in 1940, increasing to just 12,401 in 1941. In that same period, counting only operational units, the Luftwaffe had lost approximately 12,000 aircraft. Overall, the losses were below production levels.

The decline in sustainable unit inventories and the high rate of attrition resulted in an actual strength of around 4,300 aircraft compared with almost 5,300 authorized, and a total loss for 1941 of 5,000 aircraft, or 115 per cent of actual strength. When assessed on these terms, the inevitable demise of German air power was unquestionable – a reality that was borne out by the almost total depletion of the bomber force. From an authorized strength of 1,950 bombers, the Luftwaffe had only 468 in commission on 6 December 1941.

Responsibility for this appalling picture lay squarely on the shoulders of the poor management displayed by Ernst Udet, with additional blame going to Göring and Luftwaffe chief of operations Hans Jeschonnek. Little guidance had been given to manufacturers and there was a general sense of apathy regarding the impending consequences for the lack of quotas throughout the most urgent categories of combat aircraft.

A WORLD AT WAR

While the Germans were regrouping, holding the line against a resurgent Soviet defiance and a credible consolidation of Russian forces in the defence of Moscow, developments were moving fast towards the involvement of the USA – but in a far removed theatre of war forced by a pre-eminent attack from Japan. Since July 1937, China had been engaged in a war with the militaristic regime in Tokyo and a government firmly set upon the domination of East and South-east Asia as it fought for resources and materials to support a burgeoning population and a growing industrial base.

For several years, Japan followed a stridently nationalistic imperial foreign policy, demanding access to food, materials and labour, which it was unable to provide itself in sufficient quantities for national growth. For six years prior to the attack on China, Japan had orchestrated skirmishes and armed action to provoke China, which was at this stage going through its own struggle between democratic government and a growing Communist movement energized by rebel activity within the country and a civil war orchestrated by its revolutionary leader Mao Zedong. For centuries prey to the imperialist ambitions of European countries and the USA, China was made up of a set of separate, semi-autonomous provinces and lacked the industrial muscle and internal cohesion of those countries seeking to exploit its weakness, politically and militarily.

The invasion of China by Japanese land and air forces began on 7 July 1937, greatly aided by Japan's air power. Infamous incidents in the capital city of Nanjing in 1937 and the rape of Nanking's female population damned the Japanese in the eyes of the world, but meant that it gained favour with the Nazi government in Germany, which professed shared goals of eradicating inferior races to clear space for what they considered superior racial groups. This lay at the core of Japan's hegemony throughout the region until 1945 and would result in the two powers – Germany and Japan – joining together within the Axis, which already included Italy's Fascist government in hock to Hitler. This was beneficial to Germany; Japan was well equipped technically to carry the conflict to a wider theatre than China alone and had a proud history in aircraft engineering.

Recognizing the surge in experimental aviation that blossomed across Europe from 1908, in 1910 Capt Kumazo Hino and Capt Yoshitoshi of the Japanese Army were sent to France to learn to fly. A few French aeroplanes were then imported to Japan so engineers could begin adaptation of foreign designs and use them for flying tutorials. From 1910–15, Japanese designs replaced foreign types and three manufacturers came to dominate production: Mitsubishi and Kawasaki, which began as separate aviation departments of parent companies, and Nakajima, which was financed by the Mitsui family as a start-up company.

Until the early 1930s, these companies relied heavily on imported types from France, Britain and Germany and their engineers and technicians were schooled in the USA before returning home. Independently designed Japanese aircraft began to emerge in 1936, fuelled by the imperialist ambitions of the Japanese government and its warlike defence establishment. The following year, the industry was veiled in secrecy and there was considerable growth in its capitalization. A law was also passed by the government that stipulated licensed operation and control of equipment and production. A major expansion boost in March 1941 preceded on 17 October 1941 the appointment of Hideki Tojo as prime minister – the architect of war crimes and atrocities in the years to follow.

The Japanese produced 445 aircraft in 1930, expanding to 952 in 1935 but by 1941 output had soared to more than 5,000 airframes. It would peak at 28,180 in 1944. Employment in the Japanese aircraft industry ran at approximately 230,000 in 1941 but would reach 820,000 by August 1945, of which 545,000 were building airframes and the remainder producing engines and propellers. By far the largest output came from Nakajima, which built 37 per cent of all Japanese combat aircraft, followed by Mitsubishi with 23 per cent and Kawasaki with almost 15 per cent. The remainder was spread among a wide range of second-tier manufacturers. In terms of engine output, Mitsubishi led with almost 36 per cent of the 41,534 engines produced between 1941 and 1945, followed by Nakajima (31 per cent) and Hitachi (11.6 per cent). Here, too, the remainder were made by lesser manufacturers.

The remarkable rise of Japan's indigenous aviation industry was built almost entirely on the design and manufacture of military aircraft, stimulated to a great degree by British influence. When British aircraft manufacturers fell on hard times at the end of the 1914–18 war, as the government summarily terminated production orders without compensation, they turned to export markets to replace lost revenue. As an ally of Britain, France and the USA, Japan was a lucrative customer for existing aircraft and, being a maritime nation like Britain, was attracted to the aircraft of the Royal Naval Air Service. Encouraged to develop naval aviation, Japan bought aircraft from Britain and used British experience with naval aviation to create their own carrier fleet. This they would later use to attack US bases in the Pacific from December 1941.

Influenced by the British organization of land and sea power, Japan developed both army and navy air forces, the former situated on land bases and the latter on carriers and shore installations. Each went through a variety of name changes but in quality and quantity of equipment the Japanese Navy Air Force was the strongest and most influential naval force during World War II. Both services experienced a major growth in size and in re-equipment from 1937, supporting militaristic activities against China and preparing for the expansion southwards in December 1941.

Technically, both army and navy air forces were well equipped, highly trained, fanatically motivated and supported with technically advanced aircraft. Too numerous to identify in detail here, type description is best told through the evolving air warfare operations as different aircraft were employed for specific operations. The first and most popular of those was the naval attack on Pearl Harbor on 7 December 1941, a day that President Roosevelt advised the world would 'live in infamy'. It was an action that would carry strategic war to both hemispheres and see the greatest expansion of air power in the 20th century.

CHAPTER 12
A Clash of Carriers

WHEN THE USA went to war with Germany and Japan in 1941 it was infinitely better prepared to join the Allies in a fight against totalitarianism than it had been in 1917. It proved a formidable force – one that would develop naval air power to a new level and see the introduction of the aircraft carrier as the new flagship of naval force, replacing the battleships that had pioneered an arms race at the turn of the century.

War came to the USA following the attack on Pearl Harbor by Japan on 7 December 1941 – an act that had been precipitated by a US embargo on trade with Japan in retaliation for its invasion of mainland China four years earlier. Strained by the pressures on financial and material resources that resulted from its military actions, many senior Japanese political and military leaders argued against a breakout south to occupy countries in South-east Asia, including French Indo-China, Vietnam, Cambodia, Thailand, Burma, Malaya, Singapore and the Philippines. Despite this, an aggressive push to secure the vast resources that could fuel Japan's economy, seize the Orient from Occidentals and control the sea lanes that kept the British Empire thriving proved too attractive an option, even given the risk of failure. And yet the acknowledged might of the USA and its manufacturing and production potential were never very far from the thoughts of those tasked with planning the big land invasions to the south. Indeed, the threat the US posed was deemed so great that Adm Yamamoto was instructed to plan and deliver a knockout blow on the US Pacific fleet at its base in Pearl Harbor, situated in the Pacific Ocean west of the Hawaiian Islands.

Japan had been preparing for such a war for some time and had the means to carry it out. Recognizing that neither the USA nor Britain had significant airpower in the region, Japan turned to its naval forces to strike swiftly and decisively in an attempt to remove the immediate threat posed by US aircraft carriers. It was not a false expectation that success could be secured and the Americans could be evicted; Japan had the third largest navy in the world and, unlike Britain and the USA, its maritime forces were focused regionally rather than being spread around the globe defending their respective interests. With 12 battleships, 20 aircraft carriers (15 of which were large fleet carriers), 18 heavy cruisers, 28 light cruisers, 195 submarines and 349 destroyers, the Imperial Japanese Navy was an impressive assembly of naval power – on paper.

But wars are not won on statistics alone and the political and leadership divisions between the air arms of the Army and the Navy – fuelled by an intense hatred of one another – caused problems. Each claimed to have a superior capacity for carrying out military duties. However, when it came to it, the rational pre war planning for effective deployment in battle order and in the field failed to be supported by the Japanese in reality. Where in planning it had been specified that each air unit should have an additional one-third of the complement of equipment used operationally, to back up losses and the inevitable levels of attrition of men and essential materials, no such reserves were assigned to combat units. There were also no maintenance units dedicated to the operational combat groups and there was a total lack of understanding about how to deploy combat aircraft in poor and undeveloped countries lacking proper airfields, support facilities or the essential infrastructure for maintaining operational capabilities. All this would come to haunt operational commanders and doom Japan to fail in its military aspirations as it moved south into less developed countries.

TRANSFORMATIONAL CHANGE

The development of the aircraft carrier into an effective and autonomous fighting entity occurred slowly during the interwar years, although Japan recognized the inherent value of disengaging the carrier from its formative role as a platform for reconnaissance, gun-spotting, anti-submarine work and anti-air functions to stop an enemy doing the same to its own forces. Naval aviation therefore became a proactive tool rather than part of a reactive defence system. This higher value placed on carriers made it imperative that the Japanese carry out a pre-emptive naval strike to neutralize enemy forces and reduce the threat to its own fleet. Unlike US and British opponents, this pushed the specification for Japanese carrier planes into lighter aircraft with longer range so that they could reach out further in their operating radius.

An important part of this assemblage of carriers, aircraft and fighting doctrine was the use of mass air power from the sea. This resulted in all Japanese carriers being integrated into a single Air Fleet in April 1941. Known as the Kidō Butai, it comprised three carrier divisions and was completely different to the American system, in which the carrier divisions were linked administratively but not operationally. Under the Kidō Butai, the two aircraft carriers in each division could exchange aircraft and crews and operate as a single entity. All three divisions could be brought to bear on a single objective, thereby increasing the mass of air power applied. In fact, the amount of firepower that could be focused on a single target was unprecedented.

In taking on the Americans, Yamamoto was resigned to the fact that any expansion of territorial gains would incur the wrath of the USA. For this reason, he insisted, against sceptical advice in the war cabinet, that an attack on the central Pacific was vital to neutralize US carrier power. Believing that it was inevitable that Japan would have to fight America at some point, he said it was better to strike the first blow and weaken the enemy. In so doing, his actions would transform a regional bid for territory into a major war with the world's most powerful economy – an instrument of major production capable of outperforming the relatively constrained Japanese resource base.

Priority was given, however, to securing the vast oil reserves of the Dutch East Indies and the British possessions further south, striking a knockout blow at British imperialism and the taking of Singapore, then the world's largest communication switching station and the centre of British naval power defending interests in the region. Ultimately, Japan sought to eject the Royal Navy from the Indian Ocean by taking out its base on the island of Ceylon (now Sri Lanka). Thus it was that Yamamoto planned to split his forces, dispatching the Kidō Butai with its six carriers, together with escorting warships, to an operation against Pearl Harbor, and sending the Second and the Third fleets south to support land invasions against the British. He intended to retain the First Fleet in home waters as a strategic reserve, and base the Fifth Fleet at Truk in position to defend operations in the Central Pacific, while the Sixth Fleet defended northern Japanese waters.

Yamamoto sold the idea to the Naval General Staff, highlighting the military advantage they had, in the form of six carriers and 414 combat aircraft, which could be used to neutralize the ability of the US Navy to respond to land invasions in South-east Asia. But Yamamoto's strategy differed from that of the Kidō Butai, which wanted to destroy the carriers rather than the battleships. Yamamoto saw

Photographed from one of the attacking aircraft, Japanese bombers hit the US naval base at Pearl Harbor, 7 December 1941, bringing the United States into the war. US Navy

the attack not only as a disabling strike against the US Navy but also as a way of dealing a demoralizing blow to the American political leadership, believing that their isolationist policy would prevent US intervention in the region. To do that he felt that they should attack the battleships and other warships, which were valued more highly by the Americans than the carriers, thereby imposing Japan's prioritization of carriers on US thinking. The Naval General Staff decided to go with Yamamoto's plan, and on 7 December 1941 some 350 Japanese combat aircraft took part in a succession of raids on the US fleet in the harbour.

The first wave began at 7.48 am and involved 183 aircraft in three groups. These included 49 Nakajima B5N bombers equipped with 1,760 lb armour-piercing bombs, which were dropped from 10,000 ft; and 40 B5N bombers equipped with torpedoes. The second group hit Ford Island and Wheeler Field with 51 Aichi D3A dive-bombers, each releasing a 500 lb general-purpose bomb. The third group comprised 43 Mitsubishi A6M Zero fighters, which were present to control the skies and conduct strafing of ground targets. Ironically, the first wave had been picked up by the USA on radar at a distance of 156 miles but, thinking them to be anticipated Boeing B-17s arriving from the US mainland, they were ignored.

The second wave also consisted of three groups of aircraft, the first comprising 54 B5Ns with 550 lb and 132 lb general-purpose bombs, the second of 78 D3As with 550 lb bombs, and the third with 35 Zero fighters.

In an action that lasted barely 90 minutes, 2,403 Americans were killed and 1,178 wounded. Four battleships were sunk, four damaged and nine other ships were extensively damaged. The USA lost 188 aircraft with a further 159 damaged. The Japanese side of the balance sheet saw 64 dead with the loss of 29 aircraft and 74 damaged, five midget submarines lost and the crewmember of one captured.

A third strike aimed specifically at fuel and munitions dumps was also considered. Due to the consolidated nature of the base and its vital importance to US Pacific operations, this could in fact have dealt a much more debilitating blow than did the losses caused by the first two waves. However, although logical, a third strike would have taken considerable time to mount, given the refuelling and rearming of aircraft on the carriers that would have been involved. What's more, the fuel situation for the Japanese ships was quite critical, and US resistance to the second wave had been considerable. Both of these factors undermined the argument for a third strike, which would have left both carriers and aircraft vulnerable to a US counter-attack. Adm Chuichi Nagumo, in command of Kidō Butai, therefore chose to withdraw the fleet and in so doing provided an opportunity for the Americans to respond quickly.

For the USA, the attack could have been very much worse. At the time, eight of the nine US battleships assigned to the Pacific Fleet were moored in the harbour, but the three carriers – USS *Saratoga*, USS *Lexington* and USS *Enterprise* – were out at sea on previously planned operations. The carriers *Yorktown*, *Ranger*, *Hornet*, *Long Island* and *Wasp* were also absent, in various deployments in the Atlantic Ocean or off the eastern seaboard. If any of those had been in Pearl Harbor they would likely have been destroyed too. As it was, all the carriers were intact and undamaged. This fact alone helped to energize an American response and resulted in showdowns at the Battle of the Coral Sea in May 1942 and the Battle of Midway the following month, both of which struck a decisive blow at the Imperial Japanese Navy and its massive air fleet.

In the meantime, after the attack on Pearl Harbor the Japanese Navy divided its campaign into two distinct operational phases: the first involved the seizure of key objectives, including the Philippines, British Malaya, Borneo, Burma, Rabaul and the Dutch East Indies; the second was to take control of vast swathes of the Pacific, including occupation of New Guinea, New Britain, Fiji, Samoa and the area around Australasia, such as the Solomon Islands. The first phase went according to plan and the Japanese occupied Guam on 8 December, the Gilbert Islands on 9–10 December and Wake Island on 22 December. As the Japanese Army surged south supported by its bombers, Singapore fell on 15 February, putting an end to the dominant presence of British influence across South-east Asia.

Throughout these offensives, air power played a decisive role, and land that was occupied went on to be defended with vigour equal to that with which it was taken. In its final major attack as part of the first operational phase, in April 1942 the Japanese sent heavy cruisers into the Indian Ocean. Here, the carriers supported a major naval campaign that saw attacks on Colombo and Trincomalee on Ceylon. However, although naval carrier planes sank the British carrier HMS *Hermes*, the mauling the Japanese fleet received from the Royal Navy diminished the forces it would have available for the Battle of the Coral Sea in May.

To support the second phase of its objectives, the Japanese naval forces swept into the Coral Sea, an area south-west of the Solomon Islands in the South Pacific, using carriers from the Kidō Butai. The operation involved a landing on Tulagi, which was achieved on 3 May, and a planned landing on Port Moresby, which was scheduled for seven days later. The overall plan was complex, intricate in its detail and called for precise sequences laid out in a tableau of over-sophisticated manoeuvres. It involved 60 ships led by the carriers *Shōkaku* and *Zuikaku* with several warships and a force of 250 aircraft, of which 140 were on the two primary carriers and the light carrier *Shōhō*. However, having been redeployed chasing down the Imperial fleet, the US carrier *Yorktown* showed up and hit the strike force as both US and Japanese carriers milled around trying to find each other.

On 7 May, the carrier forces clashed. Each side prematurely dispatched aircraft, the Americans sinking the *Shōhō* but the Japanese missing their targets. The following day, with each side fully aware of the position of the other's forces, 69 aircraft from the Japanese carriers found and sank the *Lexington* and damaged *Yorktown*. On the Japanese side, the *Shōkaku* was severely damaged and while *Zuikaku* escaped unscathed, its aircraft losses were high – a fact that caused the Japanese to pull back and abort plans to land on Port Moresby.

Having already been depleted by the clash with the British Navy in the Indian Ocean, the Japanese forces were now severely damaged. This was to have consequences that would only become evident later. In fact, this was the last time the Kidō Butai operated as a single strike unit. Its dispersal gave America brief breathing space for the next encounter, which would prove decisive.

A DECISIVE BLOW

These actions in the Pacific and Indian Oceans were the first air battles fought between carriers at sea. This shifted the strategic role of the naval flagship from the battleships, which for 40 years had held pre-eminence in naval power, to aircraft carriers engaging each other directly. The ways of waging aerial war at sea were very different to operations between air forces based on land. Success with naval 'flattops' depended to a large degree on the robust capabilities of two components: the carrier and the aircraft it operated. In the case of the Coral Sea engagement, *Shōkaku* was disabled as a fighting vessel and the air fleet of *Zuikaku* was decimated, leaving neither carrier fit for action. This meant that they were unable to support engagements at the Battle of Midway – arguably the seminal example of how naval air power had grown and supplanted the role of the big capital ships.

Both sides recognized the role Midway would have on the future of the war in the Pacific Ocean. For the Japanese, it was an attempt to destroy US naval power in the region for all time and give them total control of the Pacific Ocean. For the Americans, it was a crucial battle for preventing further expansion of Japanese forces by defeating its navy and preventing its air power from savaging US forces. But here, again, Japanese tactics were marred by over-complication, as well as the fact that they relied on a depleted force of only four carriers from the Kidō Butai to soften US defences and land 5,000 troops.

Hoping to neutralize Midway's air defences through a surprise attack, as they had at Pearl Harbor, Japan's fate again came down to available air power, the use of the aircraft involved and the way the offensive was managed.

The urgency of their objective of dealing a death-blow to the US presence had been exacerbated by a daring air raid on Tokyo under the command of Lt-Col James Doolittle, which was carried out on 18 April 1942. Outraged by the pre-emptive attack on Pearl Harbor and upon hearing that it would take several months to bring US forces up to an offensive posture, President Roosevelt ordered a shock raid – dubbed the 'Doolittle Raid' – on the Japanese capital city using US B-25 Mitchell bombers launched from a carrier. Stripped bare of all essential equipment, including defensive armament, and with twice the usual fuel load, the plan was to convey these land-based aircraft to within range of Japan and send them off on a one-way mission; the intention was that they would land in China after flying on beyond Japan, since it was not possible to recover the B-25s back on the USS *Hornet*. Fifteen of the 16 aircraft dispatched duly bombed targets in Tokyo and flew on some 13 hours after taking off, having flown 2,590 miles. One aircraft went off course and landed in the Soviet Union.

Initially, Yamamoto preferred the idea of conducting a knockout blow to the Americans by returning to Pearl Harbor, but the increased deployment of land-based aircraft there after the initial attack made this plan altogether too risky to attempt. Instead, he decided to establish an outer perimeter defence line through Midway Island. Situated 1,300 miles north-west of Pearl Harbor, the Midway Islands were just over 2,500 miles from Tokyo. Not quite appreciating the unique nature of the Doolittle Raid performed at the very limits of capability and unlikely to be continued, Yamamoto worried that if Midway were not taken, land-based aircraft could again strike Japan. In any event, Midway was the only logical place at which to hold the line.

Believing that he could lure the Americans into a trap, Yamamoto sought to impose the maximum psychological damage by simultaneously taking two of the Aleutian Islands. Since he didn't want the Americans to divert naval resources to defending those northern islands between Russia and Alaska, that operation was to be a surprise. Yamamoto was confident that he could attract all the primary US assets in the Pacific Ocean to a single location and deliver one destructive blow at Midway. However, in the event, the numbers were not on Yamamoto's side, as two Japanese carriers, six cruisers and 12 destroyers were assigned to the Aleutians, 1,400 miles to the north, thereby diluting the Japanese forces available for Midway.

The Americans had 26 ships, including three carriers (*Enterprise*, *Hornet* and *Yorktown*), and 233 aircraft, supplemented by a further 115 on Midway itself. Yamamoto's Kidō Butai, by contrast, mustered 20 ships, including four carriers (*Kaga*, *Akagi*, *Hiryū* and *Sōryū*), and their 248 aircraft. Due to the events at the Battle of the Coral Sea, only one of the flagship Japanese carriers (*Akagi*) was available.

The battle engaged before dawn on 4 June when Adm Nagumo launched 108 aircraft, of which 72 were D3A and B5N bombers and the balance Zero fighters. These attacked Midway Island itself but failed to destroy the defences. US aircraft based on Midway took off one hour after the Japanese launched their aircraft, followed into the air by 116 carrier-based aircraft on their way to attack the Japanese fleet. The US land-based aircraft failed to hit anything but Nagumo decided to recover his own aircraft and prepare for an attack on the US carriers.

This was the first flaw in Nagumo's plan. The US dive-bombers were already in the air and heading his way, which meant that when the three Japanese carriers were hit they had aboard fuelled and bombed-up aircraft, which quickly became raging infernos. Only the *Hiryū* remained active and able to launch a counter-attack, which put the *Yorktown* out of action. Later that afternoon, the *Hiryū* was also sunk by US carrier-launched bombers.

The plan to invade Midway was duly abandoned and Yamamoto withdrew. In addition to the four fleet carriers that had been sunk, the Japanese lost a heavy cruiser, another was severely damaged and 248 aircraft were destroyed with 3,057 men killed. In addition to the *Yorktown*, the Americans lost one destroyer, 150 aircraft and 307 killed.

THE US AIRCRAFT

In the Battle of Midway, the TBD *Devastator* and the SBD *Dauntless* were crucial in the destruction of the four Japanese carriers and fleet ships engaged by the US task forces. Both built by Douglas, these aircraft remained the mainstay of the US Navy, the *Devastator* as a torpedo-bomber and the *Dauntless* as a conventional bomber.

The *Devastator* made its first flight in April 1935 and adopted a conventional low-wing monoplane configuration with retractable undercarriage and a three-man crew located in tandem enclosed by a 'glasshouse' canopy. Powered by a single 900 hp Pratt & Whitney R-1830-64 radial engine, it had a maximum speed of 206 mph and a range of just over 700 miles with a 1,000 lb bomb. Defensive armament comprised two 0.30 in machine guns, one fixed firing forwards and one moveable in a dorsal position.

The *Dauntless* had been designed and developed by Northrop but that firm subsequently became a subsidiary of Douglas. A little bigger and heavier than the *Devastator*, the *Dauntless* was powered by a single 1,200 hp R-1820-60 engine, which provided a top speed of 245 mph and achieved a range of 1,100 miles. It had the capacity for carrying a 1,600 lb load under the fuselage, or 325 lb under each wing. Defensive armament comprised two fixed forward-firing 0.50 in guns and two 0.30 in guns in a flexible dorsal mounting. Robust, strong and capable of absorbing damage, the *Dauntless* was one of the most celebrated types used by the US Navy.

Decidedly inauspicious at its first outing at Midway, the Grumman TBF-1 Avenger was ordered two years before it was introduced operationally, designed and built by a company with a credible reputation for floatplanes and a line of naval fighter types. However, Grumman had never produced a dive-bomber. The Avenger took shape as a mid-wing monoplane with an appearance similar to the *Dauntless*. Powered by a single 1,700 hp Wright R-2600-8 radial engine, the Avenger had a top speed of 276 mph, a range of 1,215 miles and could carry a 1,600 lb load in its single bomb bay. It had a single forward-firing 0.30 in machine gun, one 0.30 in ventral gun and a single 0.50 in gun in a dorsal turret. At Midway, six Avengers were sent up but only one returned – an appalling debut. However, the use of the aircraft was vindicated throughout the Pacific war by the succession of credible achievements that followed, which gained it a high reputation.

The primary air defence fighter taken to sea for the Pacific wars was the Grumman F4F-4 Wildcat, the first monoplane from this manufacturer. It was also the precursor to the F6F Hellcat, the latter becoming one of the most outstanding fighters of all time at sea or on land. The Wildcat emerged in 1935 from an initial biplane concept that changed when another aircraft, the Brewster Buffalo, demonstrated clear advantages for the monoplane. However, despite having a high performance, the Buffalo never did show promise and saw only limited service. Nevertheless, the Wildcat took some lessons from the Buffalo and despite being a contemporary of that type – the first monoplane in Navy service – it excelled in terms of performance and operational capability.

Powered by a 1,200 hp P&W R-1830-86 radial engine, the Wildcat had a maximum speed of 330 mph and a range of 900 miles. In addition to two forward-firing 0.50 in guns it could carry a modest 250 lb bomb load and had provision for six 5 in rockets under the wings. In service at the same time as the Japanese Zero, to which it was inferior in performance, it stood up well to its competitor in combat and proved its worth from the outset, entering Navy service in 1940. In the early stages of the Pacific war, the Wildcat was the sole Navy fighter and in 1942 demonstrated a victory/loss ratio of 5.9:1.

From the Wildcat grew the Hellcat, the most successful US Navy fighter of the war, which was ordered into production at the end of July 1941. A series of developments evolved as the Hellcat became the prime aircraft in its class, entering service with the US Navy in August 1943. Powered by a 2,000 hp P&W R-2800-10W radial engine, the F6F-5 had a top speed of 380 mph and a range of 945 miles, carrying six forward-firing 0.50 in guns, with an option to replace two of those with 20 mm cannon. Replacement of Wildcats occurred quickly as the capabilities of the Navy carrier groups expanded and the requirement grew with the intensity of operations in the Pacific theatre.

The statistics for the Hellcat are legendary. By the time production ended in November 1945, 12,275 had been built. Several examples in private collections can still be flown today, preserved for air displays and set-piece simulations of classic World War II air battles. Surprisingly, very few modifications were applied to the Hellcat, so perfect was the fit between its design and the mission requirement. In the service of the US Navy and Marine Corps and with the Royal Navy's Fleet Air Arm in which it also served, it is credited with 75 per cent of all Japanese aircraft shot down by the US Navy throughout the conflict – a total of 5,223.

One other aircraft that deserves special mention is the Vought F4U Corsair carrier-based fighter, which went into combat in February 1943 at Bougainville in the Solomon Islands. Used initially from land bases, the Corsair had been specified in 1938 but did not make its first flight before May 1940. Characteristically possessing an inverted gull wing, the aircraft was powered by a 2,000 hp P&W XR-2800-4 radial engine. This was a massive unit comprising two banks of nine cylinders positioned one behind the other, which provided some variants of the Corsair with a top speed of 470 mph and a range of more than 1,000 miles. With folded wings to allow carrier deployment, at first the type was not considered suitable for operations at sea but that quickly changed and the Corsair went to war with great success. It was attributed with having a success/loss ratio of 11:1. The flexible operational standard of this fighter made it unequivocally the finest carrier-based aircraft of its type during the war and it easily deserves its high reputation. This type, like the Hellcat, survives in 21st century skies in the hands of collectors and private owners.

THE ROLE OF CARRIERS

Both Japan and the USA learned early in the development of the aeroplane and aerial warfare that naval aviation would be vital in any future conflict. Indeed, the Americans recognized the role that carrier-based forces could best fill and developed the aircraft to support that, seeing the carrier as a floating airfield rather than playing a supporting role to the traditional warship. This was in part because Japan and America shared the common dilemma of having strategic interests situated across vast tracts of water and therefore did much to pioneer the new science of carrier-to-carrier warfare, frequently with the ships out of sight of each other.

For the British, however, obsessed with a land-based air force and having long been stuck on the idea of long-range strategic bombing as a mechanism for defeating an enemy, naval aviation had been a poor cousin. It was therefore ill-equipped, starved of funds and never accorded the aircraft it should have acquired during the admittedly cash-strapped interwar years. Yet, paradoxically, it was the British who were at the forefront of carrier design and technology, which they developed for the air war at sea – concepts that were adopted by all the world's navies that used carriers.

END RUN

For all that the detail of the Battle of Midway was complex and interwoven with fast-changing situations and decisions, the outcome revealed both the importance and the vulnerability of the carrier and its complement of bombers, dive-bombers, fighters and reconnaissance aircraft. After the battles in the south-west Pacific Ocean, the expansion of US naval air power gradually began to tilt the balance away from the Japanese initiative and towards a protracted slog across to islands that would later be used by the land-based US air forces to pound Japanese cities.

In the meantime, on 7 August 1942, US forces backed by naval air power landed on the islands of Guadalcanal and Tulagi in the Solomon Islands, pushing the Imperial Japanese Navy on to the defensive for the first time. In response, V-Adm Gun'ichi Mikawa gathered five cruisers, two light cruisers and a destroyer from the new 8th Fleet and ordered an attack that cost four Allied heavy cruisers.

However, in failing to attack the unguarded transport ships he left the door open for US consolidation of the bridgehead on Guadalcanal. Slow to respond to what they interpreted as merely a reconnaissance expedition on the part of the Americans, the Japanese Navy lost the chance of annihilating the US enclave. In fact, it wasn't until 24–25 August that Japan deployed a force of four battleships, five aircraft carriers and 30 destroyers to remove the Americans. This became known as the Battle of the Solomon Islands, the third carrier battle of the war.

Guadalcanal lies at the south-easternmost tip of a string of islands stretching about 650 miles in a north-westerly direction, and is situated about 700 miles due east of New Guinea. Strategically, this was a vital access point to Australia and New Zealand. In seeking to push the Japanese back from that area, the Allies sought to protect against any further southward expansion of Japanese occupation. It proved to be a long, hard battle of attrition that would last until the Japanese surrendered in 1945, and engaged opposing forces including warships and aircraft carriers, embracing naval and land-based aircraft.

By the end of the war, the Japanese had lost 86,000 men killed, more than 50 ships sunk and about 1,500 aircraft destroyed in the air and on the ground in this protracted campaign for possession of the Solomons. The Allies – with forces assembled from Britain, Australia, New Zealand, Fiji, Tonga and the Solomon Islands themselves – lost 10,600 men killed, more than 40 ships and 800 aircraft.

In mid-1942, however, the USA was now beginning to influence air warfare in other areas, far removed from the Pacific Ocean. And that would lead to the defeat of Nazi Germany in a very different type of aerial warfare.

CHAPTER 13
The Combined Bomber Offensive

RAF BOMBER Command in mid-1942 was on the cusp of change, replacing its first generation of bombers to go to war with a new range of 'heavies': four-engine aircraft that could dramatically increase the load of bombs carried to targets in Germany. By this stage in the war, the USA was on board and was prepared to energize the might of its war machine through unprecedented production levels and munitions output. This would eventually overwhelm the Axis; the tripartite pact that had been signed by Germany, Italy and Japan on 27 September 1940 had created a cabal of totalitarian countries intent on global domination, but the collective production capacity of the Axis was significantly below that of the USA alone, let alone that of the British too.

Immediately after the attack on Pearl Harbor on 7 December 1941, President Roosevelt announced that the war against Nazi Germany would take precedence over the war with Japan. At the time this made a lot of sense, despite it appearing somewhat paradoxical, given that it was the Japanese who had first attacked the USA. At the end of 1941, the German war machine was still on the ascendant, having extended the frontline to within sight of Moscow. In fact, the whole of the Continent was now in Hitler's grasp and the British were seemingly incapable of mounting a serious military threat in Europe. What's more, with the Italians now supported by the Afrika Korps under the erstwhile command of Gen Erwin Rommel, North Africa was also under threat. Roosevelt knew that if Russia fell, the full might of the Wehrmacht could strike Britain and leave America without a foothold for mounting a campaign against Hitler's armed forces.

The issue of the US justification for going to war with Germany was settled in the end just four days after the attack on Pearl Harbor, when Hitler declared war on the USA. The US plan was to unhinge German forces from their illegal occupation of sovereign states across Europe while using existing naval, and some land-based air, power to push the Japanese back and prevent their further expansion across the Pacific Ocean. The question was, how best was America to integrate itself into the existing war with Germany? That matter was resolved when Winston Churchill arrived in the USA with his chiefs-of-staff on 22 December for the Arcadia Conference to discuss strategy for a 'Grand Alliance'. Lasting until 14 January 1942, it endorsed the president's view that air power could make a decisive difference and shift the balance while most of the German forces were tied up in Russia, far to the east.

The proposed operation would use both American and British air power in a co-ordinated campaign to support a ground operation that would see British and American troops jump across the Channel, land in western Europe and sweep the Germans aside. Seeing the English Channel as no more of an obstacle than the Mississippi River, the Americans underestimated the amount of men and materiel that would require, the resistance they would meet on landing and the appalling loss of life that would ensue. Roosevelt's chief military adviser, Gen Marshall, was all for 'smacking it to 'em' and was only dissuaded by all the persuasive might of the British prime minister and his military advisers, who were able to recount in detail the difficulty they knew the Germans had faced when anticipating a cross-Channel leap of their own.

Without any battle experience on the ground or in the air, the only logical plan was for American air power, such as it was, to join in a combined operation with the RAF (only later formally known as the Combined Bomber Offensive) in attacking Germany's industrial heartland, the specifics of which were to be ironed out later, and to support a combined landing on the north-west coast of Africa in Morocco and Tunisia. Known as Operation *Torch*, this would put pressure on the Germans by driving east along the coast of North Africa to come into a pincer action against the British driving west from Egypt. Bordered to the north by the Mediterranean Sea and to the south by the Sahara Desert, the Germans would be either destroyed when the two Allied forces met in the middle, or the Afrika Korps would be pushed up through Sicily into Italy; there was no other route to escape through. This action would provide operational experience with co-ordinated invasion activity, give the American GIs experience against German troops and provide a dummy run for a later invasion against north-west Europe as a main assault.

THE LEND-LEASE BILL

Although Roosevelt had fought against isolationist policies of non-intervention beyond the territorial borders of the USA, there was considerable support at the White House, and among US citizens, for sending American aid to help stem the tide of Nazism in Germany and Fascism in Italy. However, there were laws under neutrality acts that prohibited the USA from supplying military aid to belligerents without a declaration of war. These were circumvented when Roosevelt signed the Lend-Lease bill, which entered into law on 11 March 1941. This enabled direct leasing (export) of machines and equipment to the Allies in return for the use of foreign territories by the USA as and when they needed them. Thus began the universal presence of US influence in many countries that formed the Allied alliance, and that would prevail more extensively after the war and fuel the globalization of American culture.

Overall, the USA provided $50.1 billion (equivalent to $600 billion in 2020) to the Allies – a figure that amounted to 17 per cent of the money spent by the USA on war funds between 1941 and 1945. The UK received 63 per cent of that leased value, 6 per cent going to the Soviet Union and 3 per cent to China, with the balance provided to other Allied nations. Apart from some ships, none of this equipment was returned by the recipients, nor was it required. The agreement ended in August 1945 and equipment that was delivered after that date was charged at a greatly discounted $1.075 billion, paid for by loans from the USA.

GETTING READY

Excited by these plans, on 3 January Roosevelt ordered a production quota of 60,000 aircraft in 1942 and 131,000 in 1943 for both the Army and the Navy. Most essential were trainers to prepare a new contingent of pilots and air crew, required now in vast numbers on an unprecedented scale. The Navy, meanwhile, was said to require 10,220 aircraft in 1942 and 21,790 the following year. But the cost would be staggering. As the design requirements grew and the technology improved, the prices went up, which would drive government defence spending to levels unseen before or since. Yet money alone would not provide the means of defeating the Axis. Organization, planning and the administrative management of both civil and military operations would, as the British had proven, be essential to fighting the war and producing the equipment needed to win.

Previously known as the Army Air Service, the organization, management and operation of US air power had been under the Army Air Corps since 2 July 1926. On 20 June 1941 it became the Army Air Forces (AAF) within the Corps and would remain so for the duration of the war. Unlike the RAF – which in 1936 had formed the several Commands (Fighter, Bomber, Coastal, Training), each dedicated to a particular role or function – the AAF consisted of a series of numbered air forces, the first four of which were defined by geographic area in the USA: Northeast, Northwest, Southeast and Southwest air districts. Each was considered responsible for the air defence of their sector and supported with a complement of all different types, as though each were a national air force in its own right.

After the Japanese attack on Pearl Harbor, these air forces were numbered 1, 2, 3 and 4 respectively and would remain permanently based in the USA. Over time, others were added: the 5th, 6th, 7th, 13th, 14th and 20th Air Forces served in the Asia-Pacific theatre while the 8th, 9th, 12th and 15th Air Forces were attached to the European and African theatres, and the 6th was assigned to the Panama Canal Zone. Not until after the war would the USAAFs be united in a single and separate force from the Army, named as the United States Air Force on 18 September 1947. This joined the US Army, Navy and Marine Corps as the fourth military service, all of which were administered from the Pentagon and the Department of Defense, which in 1947 replaced the Department of War (also known as the War Office). But if the structure of the air forces were important, the men and the materiel would be vital. And that meant building a lot of aircraft – quickly.

Recognizing that America would soon have to fight, on 29 December 1940 – a year before the USA declared war on Germany – Roosevelt delivered a speech in a radio broadcast that acknowledged the 'arsenal of democracy' required to defeat political extremism. However, the demands of the civilian consumer market were very different to those of a nation at war, where all the country's resources would be focused on supplying the machinery of conflict. Roosevelt called on William Signius Knudsen, from General Motors' Chevrolet division, and Henry Kaiser, supremo on giant projects and the builder of the Hoover dam, to mobilize an industry capable of outproducing the enemy's factories. Capacity was a real challenge, not only because of the greater production quota demanded but also because the aircraft were getting much more complicated.

Educated at Tuskegee University, Alabama, and known as the Tuskegee Airmen, a group of Afro-Americans volunteered for combat duty, flying with the 332nd Fighter Group and the 477th Bombardment Group. USAF

As an example, the Consolidated B-24 Liberator bomber, which had been designed in 1939 and was in service two years later, was a big advance over the smaller Boeing B-17 Fortress, which first flew in 1936. Powered by four 1,200 hp, P&W R-1830-33 engines, designed around a high-wing, twin-vertical tail configuration, the B-24 could carry an 8,800 lb bomb load. It had a top speed of around 300 mph and a range of 2,200 miles. Developed into a variety of marks and variants, most carried 10 x 0.50 in guns in nose, tail and dorsal turrets and two side mountings in the centre fuselage. As a bomber, it was formidable in capability and performance, seeing service in all theatres of war, but as a large and complicated aircraft it was a manufacturing challenge.

It took more than 488,000 individual parts assembled into 30,000 components together with more than 140,000 man-hours to produce a B-24. At the factory, it required 54 separate work stations with at least six hours of work at each before it could be moved to the next one in line, eventually to emerge as an assembled aircraft. A noted industrialist, Charles Sorensen, was brought in to conceptualize a completely new way of producing aircraft – reliably and quickly. Based on his overall outline, Sorenson employed architect Albert Kahn to design what amounted to the largest single building in the world – a production line under one roof that was more than a mile long. Overhead cranes delivered elements of the B-24 directly to work stations, which meant that the aircraft didn't have to be pushed around. Under this method of production, from this one facility alone, Consolidated turned out more than three B-24s a day and in all built more than 19,000 for the war effort at various plants.

ROSIE THE RIVETER

Between 1941 and 1945, the voracious appetite for munitions was greater than it had been at any time, anywhere, in peace or war. US production capacity therefore went into hyper-drive, transforming the lives of ordinary people and triggering a social revolution, the impact of which resounds down through the decades to the present.

At the beginning of 1942, women made up only 20 per cent of the work force – mostly unmarried women aged 20 or 21. Within six months, that had risen to 33 per cent on the back of a massive recruiting drive that saw women flock in droves to sign on and get working. Contrary to what previously had been culturally unacceptable, married women were also encouraged to get out of the house and join the expanding force of female workers. Appointed to her position in April 1942 as director of the Women's Bureau, Mary Anderson reported that 2.8 million women were in paid war work.

Because it was assessed that women had a better eye for detail than men, they were favoured by the aviation industry for jobs as riveters, each capable of completing 1,000 fixtures a day versus 660 for a man. Indeed, companies specifically requested women over men, for their speed, accuracy and commitment. So encouraged were these workers that they were proud to take on the role of 'Rosie the Riveter' – the cultural icon associated with women doing these jobs – believing themselves capable of doing anything in industry that had traditionally been the preserve of the male employee, except, of course, physically demanding tasks calling for great strength.

Within two years, 475,000 women worked in the aircraft industry and by 1944 at least 50 per cent of women of employable age laboured for the war effort, with all but 13 per cent in permanent jobs. For the first time in history, more married women were in work than their unmarried contemporaries. This broke down social barriers and gave women a greater

Women played a significant role in wartime munitions production and were vital workers on assembly plants across the United States. Department of Defense

say on the shop floor as well as at the drills, jigs and machine tools they operated with dexterity and professionalism. It is a matter of record that almost all the aircraft manufacturers quietly polled preferred women workers to men if only because of their drive and tenacity.

There was, however, a balance to be struck between existing designs – aircraft that could be produced to a sure design, and quickly – and new types with untested lineage and new, largely unproven, technology. Between 1941 and 1943, the USA went to war with essentially the same aircraft, but from mid-1943 a transitional shift began to equip the US air forces with a truly intercontinental bomber, the B-29; new long-range escort fighters, the P-47 and P-51; and design of types that would not appear before the end of the war but that would provide an intermediate range of aircraft for the Cold War era.

For immediate application as the USA went to war in 1942, the Army Air Force had the Boeing B-17, a four-engine aircraft powered by the Wright R-1820 radial engine. The B-17E had a top speed of 317 mph, a cruising speed of 224 mph and a range of 2,000 miles with a 4,000 lb bomb load. Designed in the mid-1930s, it adopted the concept of the self-defending bomber and bristled with defensive armament, the B-17E sporting eight 0.50 in and one 0.30 in gun in nose, dorsal, ventral and fuselage positions. Later, the B-17G was equipped with a chin turret under the extreme forward nose of the fuselage and carried up to thirteen 0.50

in guns and 6,000 lb bomb load with a range of 2,000 miles. All this came with a significantly reduced speed and climb capability, which was acceptable in the European theatre in which this version primarily operated from the end of 1943.

Together with the B-17, the Consolidated B-24 formed the mainstay in the conflict in Europe for the duration of the war. By contrast, the next sequential bomber, the B-29, was employed exclusively in the Pacific theatre of operations. This was an entirely different aircraft in that it foreshadowed the introduction of the very heavy bomber category. With a pressurized cabin providing much greater crew comfort, obviating the need to continuously wear face masks for oxygen at high altitude, the B-29 was appropriately named 'Superfortress'.

Designed to a specified requirement for an aircraft to carry a 2,000 lb bomb load a distance of 5,333 miles at 400 mph, the B-29 was equipped with self-sealing fuel tanks so that they would survive all but the most destructive gunfire. Heavy defensive armament would protect it from hostile attack. It also had to be capable of carrying a 16,000 lb bomb load over less distance and to have the capacity for operating off standard airfields. Inevitably compromises were made as expectation outpaced the available technology, and the B-29 made its first flight in December 1942. When it entered service in June 1943, it was still some months away from carrying out bombing missions, yet the decision was made to use it exclusively against Japan.

The B-29 was a formidable demonstration of how far air power and the technology of aerial warfare had come. Technologically, it was far in advance of the B-17s and B-24s that carried much of the air offensive to German-occupied Europe. With four 2,200 hp Wright R-3350 engines, it had a characteristically bulbous nose into which glazing was set a bomb-aimer's window and equipment for what then passed for pinpoint bombing. There were two separate pressurized sections in the fuselage: one in the nose area for some of the crew and a second in the aft centre section of the fuselage for controlling some of the defensive armament.

Specially designed and built by Sperry, four remote-controlled gun barbettes were installed – two in the top of the fuselage and two in the lower fuselage, each with two 0.50 in guns – together with one 20 mm or three 0.50 in guns in a remotely operated tail turret. This form of armament was new and had integrated radar-controlled gun sights – a precursor to post-war concepts that went on to be adopted for future aircraft.

When it appeared in service, the B-29 had a maximum bomb capacity of 20,000 lb and a theoretical maximum speed of 357 mph. It could maintain a cruising speed of 220 mph. Operational range was about 3,250 miles, depending

on the weight of bomb carried, with a service ceiling of more than 31,000 ft –
considerably more than the B-24 at 28,000 ft.

With a new generation of technology and more advanced aero-engineering,
costs of production inevitably increased. The resilient B-25 used by Col Doolittle
to carry out his audacious raid on Tokyo from the deck of the USS *Hornet* cost less
than $117,000 per aircraft while the B-17, which was the mainstay of the European
bombing campaign, cost $187,000, despite the volume of production of this type
exceeding that of the B-25. Each B-24, although more capable and with a better
performance, cost the government $215,000. The considerably more advanced
B-29 came in at $509,000. Moreover, the B-17 had a crew of ten while the B-24 and
the B-29 had a crew of 11. Every crew member went through the same basic flying
training and familiarization, which added further to the value in each individual
aircraft, while the significant increase in bomb load added cost to a single mission.

A similar story can be found with the fighter aircraft used by the Americans
during the war. In 1941, the Curtiss P-40 Warhawk cost $44,000, the more capable
P-51 came in at $51,000 and the P-47 Thunderbolt had a price tag of $88,000.

THE AMERICANS ARRIVE IN BRITAIN

US air forces began their move to England under the codename 'Bolero'. This
saw the 8th Air Force begin initial deployment on 20 February 1942 in order to
plan the mass migration of units in preparation for a major air offensive against
Germany. To start with, there were only six people, including Gen Ira C. Eaker.
On 25 February, they went to RAF Bomber Command at High Wycombe in
Berkshire to set in motion the wheels of the offensive. Lacking the ability to
conduct precision bombing of targets in enemy-occupied Europe, just 11 days
earlier Bomber Command had received instructions to begin a campaign of 'area
bombing' with 'priority over all other commitments'.

As the Americans began to find their feet in a country with which they were
largely unfamiliar, a considerable swathe of planning and organization was
required. They would rely heavily on the British for supporting the infrastructure
– from planning where to set their bases and helping to co-ordinate everything
from personnel to selecting targets, to establishing a ferry route for the bombers
deployed from the US to the UK. They even needed assistance getting to grips
with the weather, relying initially on the British to provide meteorological services.

As the personnel began to arrive, each was given a booklet advising them to
act respectfully, courteously and to tone down any gung-ho attitude that may
have gone down well in America but that would be looked upon with contempt

by the one country that had stopped the Wehrmacht in its tracks and dealt a near-crippling blow to the Luftwaffe. Personnel arriving in the UK were instructed in British customs, how certain approaches were unwelcome and how not to assume that they would be welcome everywhere.

EAGLE SQUADRONS

On an individual level, Americans had been involved from the very outset of hostilities, represented by volunteers who changed their nationality to Canadian so that they could fight for Britain and its allies; US law prohibited American citizens from joining the armed forces of another nation. As Canadian citizens, 11 American pilots flew in the RAF during the Battle of Britain.

The first of three 'Eagle' squadrons (Nos 71, 121 and 133) was formed on 19 September 1940 and although 6,700 individuals applied, only 244 were recruited to these units. A memorial to the contribution made by pilots of the Eagle Squadrons can be found in Grosvenor Square, London, opposite a statue of President Franklin D. Roosevelt.

American pilots of No. 71 'Eagle' Squadron who volunteered to fly with the RAF after taking Canadian citizenship to legalize their contribution before America entered the war. David Baker Archive

They need not have worried. The cultural habits of these new arrivals took hold quickly in an austere atmosphere where shortages through rationing were an everyday part of life for the majority of British people. From the outset, the warmth and inclusivity with which the Americans were welcomed in most homes adjacent to camps and bases was reciprocated with frequent parties for local children, weekend dances and Christmas parcels for homeless families. The distribution of rations and provisions flown over for their own use brought respect from a nation that had literally nothing to spare and little to give, save for the basic essentials of life. In sharing their own rations with the public in a country already weary of war and suffering from frequent bombing, for the most part the Americans were met with respect and gratitude.

Thanks to the decision at the Arcadia Conference that the Americans would be independent in terms of support, facilities and equipment, they were allocated an area of East Anglia in which to deploy their forces. RAF Bomber Command could retain their airfields and camps in Lincolnshire and Yorkshire. This would ensure separate and unified chains of command and control both in deployment of the large number of air crew and in the operation of aircraft. RAF Fighter Command would maintain its occupation of airfields in the south and the south-east of England and retain the division of the various groups as they had been established before the Battle of Britain.

Initially, the British earmarked 15 airfields for the Americans – eight in England, two in Scotland and five in Northern Ireland – but the primary cluster was around Cambridge by the time US aircraft began arriving in June 1942. These included B-17s and B-24s, which were flown across the Atlantic via Greenland and into Prestwick, Scotland, from where they deployed down to East Anglia.

Unlike the RAF, which separated bombers from fighters, the Americans insisted on retaining their convention of equipping each Air Force with its own distribution of these types, both to act as escorts for the bombers and to protect the bases from attack. Whereas the British assigned approximately 16 aircraft to a squadron, three squadrons to a wing and six or seven wings to a group, the Americans set up 8–15 aircraft to a squadron, three or four squadrons to a group and two or more groups to a combat wing.

Further to these preparations, several assembly depots were built for aircraft arriving in parts by ship, the US manufacturers setting up assembly plants at several locations across the west of the UK for transatlantic convoys arriving at Liverpool. The movement of US personnel began with the first shipment arriving on 11 May 1942 after a two-week voyage from the USA. The liner *Queen Elizabeth* was converted to troop carrying, as were a number of other ships suitable for carrying large numbers of personnel. As the numbers grew, they were supplemented by troops assembling in the UK for the cross-Channel assault on mainland Europe. By March 1943, some 1.15 million Americans had made the crossing, of which 232,000 were with the Army Air Forces.

The initial plans for accommodating the Americans fell far short of what was actually required. During 1942, it was anticipated that the 8th Air Force would grow to 137 air combat groups, including 74 bombardment, 32 fighter, 12 observation, 15 transport, 4 photographic and 1 mapping. To support them, the British planned 127 airfields dedicated to the US Army Air Forces. However, the planning for Operation *Torch* threw this into disarray and not before the spring of 1943 was it operating between two and six groups, barely able to put up more than 100 aircraft operational at any one time. And then there were increasing demands for raids on U-boat pens and German-occupied ports on the west coast of Europe as the expanded convoys and flow of merchant goods increased – events that raised the submarine war to new heights. The Americans were learning the painful consequences of hubristic assertions as they toned down their expectations of the impact they could make.

THE GENESIS OF COMBINED BOMBER OFFENSIVE

While the Americans obtained all their intelligence data and targeting information from the British and recognized the need to work in close co-operation with their ally, there was a determination to maintain an independent stance and not to be subsumed into operations dictated by the RAF. Although the work of co-operative forces was frequently referred to as the Combined Bomber Offensive, in reality this was a long time coming, not officially getting under way until June 1943. It began with a directive named Point Blank, which specifically focused both the USAAF and the RAF on an intensive operation to clear the skies of German fighters over Nazi-occupied Europe.

THOUSAND-BOMBER RAIDS

For its part, RAF Bomber Command was taking advantage of the new four-engine 'heavies', which were opening the possibility of a considerable increase in scale, both in the number of aircraft involved in a single raid and in the tonnage of bombs dropped.

When last we left Bomber Command, the RAF was on the cusp of receiving this new capability. This, and the provision of equipment and the technological changes such as Gee, inspired Air V-Mshl Harris, resulting in a plan for a 1,000-bomber raid on industrial targets in the Ruhr. This confidence was endorsed, in principle, by two particularly successful raids: one on Lübeck and the second on Rostock, both on the Baltic coast of north Germany.

On the night of 28/29 March 1942, a force of 234 aircraft – including Wellingtons, Hampdens, Stirlings and Manchesters – achieved what was later credited as the first major success for Bomber Command when they struck the old town of Lübeck. The RAF lost 12 aircraft (5 per cent) of the force but almost 300 crews claimed to have hit the target with 400 tons of bombs, destroying 30 per cent of the built-up area, including many of the historic buildings that dated back to the medieval age. More than 300 people were killed. The town was largely left alone after this, since the RAF was advised that the port was a focus for the shipment of Red Cross supplies.

On four successive nights beginning 23/24 April, Rostock was bombed by the RAF using essentially the same tactic that had been practised against Lübeck: a concentrated incendiary attack to start fires and overwhelm the fire services, followed by high explosives in an area bombing raid. On the first night, 161 aircraft were sent out to bomb the town, together with the Heinkel factory. The second night, 125 aircraft were focused on attacking the town itself and on the third night 128 bombers hit the town again, starting many fires. In the fourth raid, just over 100 bombers were sent for what the official history describes as 'the masterpiece'. In all, almost 2,300 buildings were destroyed or seriously damaged across 130 acres – some 60 per cent of the town. Had the residents not fled into the countryside after the first night, the overall total of 204 killed and 89 injured would have been considerably higher.

The intention of mustering 1,000 bombers for a single raid became obsessive and focused the leadership of Bomber Command, igniting the enthusiasm of both the Marshal of the RAF, Sir Charles Portal, and Winston Churchill. The latter, it should be noted, was having qualms about the moral turpitude of extensive city bombing and certainly, a little later, of the extensive use of firestorm raids created to destroy as much property and kill as many people as possible. In an uncharacteristically less-than-flowery reference to consequences, Churchill said later that if the Allies failed to defeat Hitler, 'we will all be hung as war criminals'.

To effectively deploy 1,000 aircraft across one target it was necessary to decrease the amount of time the aircraft were exposed to flak and to night fighters. It was routinely taken that a raid by 100 aircraft would require four hours over the target, and two hours for a concentration of just over 200 aircraft. But for 1,000 aircraft, Air Chf Mshl Harris wanted 90 minutes, which exposed crews to losses from aircraft colliding. On the plus side, this would so overwhelm the anti-aircraft batteries that individual aircraft would have a reduced probability of being hit by enemy fire. Moreover, it would swamp the fighter defences and again increase the probability of survival. In short, for any one individual airman, going in a stream of 1,000 aircraft meant that you had a greater chance of getting home again.

Harris planned the first of these 'thousand bomber' raids for 26 May 1943, the night of a full moon, and selected Hamburg as the target. However, the weather was unfavourable, delaying the attack by three days, so the target was shifted to Cologne. The raid took place on 30/31 May, when 1,047 aircraft were sent up – a force consisting of 602 Wellingtons, 88 Stirlings, 131 Halifaxes, 28 Whitleys, 73 Lancasters, 46 Manchesters and 73 Hampdens.

Approximately 1,455 tons of bombs were dropped by the estimated 898 aircraft that bombed the target, starting 2,300 fires. Of these, 1,700 were rated as 'large' by the local German fire service. The attack rendered 45,132 people homeless, killed almost 500 people and injured a further 5,000. Of the 700,000 citizens of Cologne, an estimated 145,000 fled into the safety of the neighbouring countryside. The RAF lost 41 aircraft (of which two had collided) – more than the attrition rate of any other raid to date – but the percentage was an acceptable 3.9 per cent of the force dispatched. An interesting factor was revealed by the evolution of the loss rate across the three waves – 4.8 per cent, 4.1 per cent and 1.9 per cent respectively – which appeared to show that the defences were progressively overwhelmed by exhaustion and smoke as the attacks progressed.

Throughout the next several months, the RAF kept up its usual rate of bombing, and further thousand-bomber raids were also mounted. These began with Essen two nights after the raid on Cologne. On that occasion, the raid totalled 956 aircraft with a 3.2 per cent loss rate, including four of the 74 Lancasters that set out. The usual sequence of nightly raids, involving 150–300 aircraft, followed as Harris set up Bremen as the third of his thousand-bomber targets.

The raid on Bremen was carried out on the night of 25/26 June. It involved 960 aircraft, this time with 96 Lancasters as the balance shifted from the older types to the newer 'heavies'. Getting to this number required the pulling in of every available aircraft, with the usual reliance on the training squadrons and some aircraft from Coastal Command. Tactical changes cut the raid time to 65 minutes over the target, calling for an intense and totally overwhelming use of force. Later, changes to the way the raids were carried out would progressively shrink the time over the target until, ultimately, the RAF was able to put 700–800 aircraft over the target within 20 minutes.

This use of extreme force did not completely achieve its end objective – the destruction of the Focke-Wulf factory at Bremen. Moreover, with a 5 per cent loss rate, the stress on Bomber Command was too great to continue with these thousand-bomber operations. Churchill therefore intervened to prevent further scavenging of Coastal Command just to put a five-figure number over Germany. After Bremen, the front line units persisted with a high level of activity, but without bringing in aircraft from the Operational Training Units, which generally were equipped with aircraft that had been retired from front line service and were not intended to take part in fully operational raids over enemy territory.

The last four months of 1942 saw several changes in Bomber Command, not least those brought about by the challenges that resulted from the increasing capacity of the German defences to knock down the bombers. Day raids were still sustained, but the main force of activity concentrated on night bombing as one further method of evading detection. Crews who had proven themselves adept at finding their targets in the dark were selected out and used as leaders on successive raids so that they could guide following streams more accurately. But this was only a stopgap measure.

Since late 1941, the Air Ministry had been toying with using a 'Target Finding Force', which was essentially what had evolved in 1942 with the use of these lead crews. However, Air Chf Mshl Harris was opposed to what he perceived to be an 'elite' force of elevated crews being moved out into special roles, preferring to keep these experienced crews embedded within the squadrons for purposes of morale. Nevertheless, the logic of the idea prevailed and the concept of a Pathfinder Force emerged. These used specially adapted munitions, which, on exploding on the ground, would emit a coloured light to serve as a beacon for the bombers behind. Harris was duly won over and the Pathfinder Force grew to become a critically important part of the formations making up a heavy night raid.

A major challenge for the second half of 1942 was morale. In general, particularly with the first of the thousand-bomber raids, air crew were surprisingly enthusiastic about their job. Despite heavy casualties, they were buoyed up by the strident leadership of Bomber Harris. During 1942, though, as the intensity of the raids grew and the demands on air crew became greater with the bigger and more capable 'heavies', an individual would be required to fly 30 operations on his first tour of duty, followed by a rest and then a second tour of 20 operations. It was not expected that a crewman would continue to fly in Bomber Command after 50 operations over enemy territory but quite a number did – beyond the time that it was wise for them to continue. At a loss rate of 1 per cent, an average crewmember could expect a 60 per cent chance of surviving 50 operations; at a 2 per cent loss rate, only a 30 per cent chance; and with a 4 per cent loss rate, only a 15 per cent chance of making it through alive. When the Pathfinder operations got under way, losses were at 4.6 per cent.

THE FRAGILE MIND

With increasing numbers of personnel entering RAF Bomber Command without experience, replacing those killed on operations, it became more and more difficult to maintain the same level of standards and morale as the inevitable erosion of the will to go on took its toll.

Mindful of this, and with losses soon to give bomber crews only a 50:50 chance of surviving a full dual tour of 50 operations, squadron commanders worked with trained medical personnel to watch for the signs of fatigue and extreme stress. These were of the kind that no other soldier of war felt, simply because there was no other arm of a fighting service anywhere in the world that lost such a high number of personnel on a routine basis.

In one particular case, as a typical example, a young rear gunner (who asked to remain anonymous) was pulled out of line after more than two tours and approached by his commanding officer with an order to take a train to an airfield in Scotland. Puzzled as to the reason, he was given a travel voucher and off he went. On arriving at this remote location he was met by a corporal and a truck, which delivered him to the airfield. Here, he was shown to quarters, where he had a room all to himself. Imagining that he had been selected for some highly dangerous operation, he waited until a knock came on the door and a junior officer requested him to 'pop along to the CO's office when he had settled in'.

The mystery deepened – COs never 'requested' anything! Smartening himself up, he went along and met the commanding officer, who invited him in. As he stood to attention he was told that his station commander had been advised that the young gunner should rest a while, away from the destructive mayhem of war. Upon hearing this news, the pilot collapsed on the floor and sobbed his heart out.

He never remembered exactly how long he stayed in what was not an airfield but a hospital, for those who had survived physically but suffered dreadful mental damage. This particular pilot had been saved from the brink of mental destruction, but only just in time.

His experience was one among many. Countless other individuals were driven almost to insanity by the invisible spectre of death stalking them, along with the rest of the crew, as they climbed nightly into what could all too readily become their coffin. In the dark, bouncing around under the intense barrage of anti-aircraft guns, the intense beam of a searchlight and the sudden rat-a-tat-tat of an enemy fighter's machine guns, the end would not always be sudden. But for this one individual, thanks to this intervention, there was now a future.

A YEAR OF EXPANSION

Many of the raids carried out by Bomber Command were against targets in occupied countries, pressed into service for the Nazi regime. One such was a raid against the Le Creusot factory in France. Long viewed as the equivalent of the giant Krupps munitions industry based in Essen, Germany, it had made a great name for itself as the manufacturer of heavy guns, locomotives, tanks and armoured vehicles. Contravening an earlier embargo on daylight raiding, justified on account of it being heavily defended, Harris sent 94 Lancasters out during the day on 17 October 1942. The majority were instructed to hit the factory complex as well as a large accommodation block at one end of the facility.

It was to be a low-level attack not dissimilar to one against the munitions factory at Augsburg in the previous April, when seven out of 12 Lancasters had been shot down. Almost 140 tons of bombs were dropped from 2,500–7,500 ft, with little opposition, and only one aircraft was lost when it flew so low while attacking a transformer station that it hit one of the buildings. Post-attack damage assessment showed that most of the bombs had fallen short and of the ones that reached the target, most struck the accommodation block.

Another attack, on 6 December – this time against the Phillips radio and valve factory in Eindhoven in the Netherlands – involved a variety of aircraft, including 47 Lockheed Venturas, 36 Bostons and 10 Mosquitoes. Conducted at low level, in clear weather and without escort, 14 of the 93 aircraft were lost and 23 of the rest were damaged by bird strikes during the 70-mile flight inland from the sea. Eindhoven was largely deserted on this Sunday, yet 138 Dutch people were killed in a raid that did little damage to the factories.

Accurate bombing was still a desire rather than a capability. Despite the use of Gee as a navigation and bombing aid, it fell far short of a total solution. Because of the somewhat dubious value of bombing deep into enemy territory, notwithstanding the increased chance of losses due to enemy defences, other wartime demands kept Bomber Command from realizing its full strategic potential. These included tasks supporting the needs of Coastal Command and tactical bombing supporting other operations, some of which were requested by the Navy.

Late in 1942, some welcome assistance arrived in the form of Oboe, a blind bombing system that was based on two radio transmitters in England sending signals to a transponder on each suitably equipped aircraft. When measured as a function of the time it took for the coded signal to return, the lapse in time provided information that could be used to calculate the distance of the aircraft from the source. The use of Oboe depended on a direct line of sight and it was found that the Mosquito, with its operating altitude in excess of 30,000 ft, was the ideal carrier. This was demonstrated when it was first tested under operational conditions on the night of 20/21 December 1942 during a raid on the small Dutch town of Lutterade. Despite furious efforts, German scientists were never able to effectively silence Oboe, which continued to be used where appropriate until the end of the war.

Aside from the fact that it only operated when it was in a direct line with the receiving aircraft, the principal handicap with Oboe was its inability to work unless the two beams could intersect – a requirement that severely limited the range at which it was effective. Overall, both Gee and Oboe had a maximum operating range of 220 miles. Fortunately, there now emerged a more productive solution to the need for accurate bombing in all weathers and even in the dark – one that was researched and developed during 1942. Known as H2S, it was an adaptation of the Air-to-Surface Vessel (ASV) radar. It featured a steerable radar beam, which had been used by the Navy to search for submarines from the air. Taking advantage of the fact that a 9.1 cm cavity magnetron could power a radar to show reflections on a cathode ray tube that were indicative of surface features, when used in conjunction with a topographic map it could penetrate cloud to identify the signature features of the ground below.

On hearing about delays brought on by disagreement about whether it was worth developing H2S, on 3 July 1942 Churchill ordered high-level production of the radar. Clearly, the Pathfinder force was ideally placed to use H2S; during 1943, these aircraft were pioneers in introducing radar-guided bomber fleets. During 1944, there were sufficient numbers of sets to equip all Bomber Command's aircraft.

For much of the time, 1942 had been a year of consolidation, of trialling operations with the new generation of 'heavies' and experimenting with a swathe of scientific and technical developments promising more effective navigation and targeted bombing. Yet Bomber Command still had its intentions diverted by the constant demands for aircraft deployments to North Africa and in support of the anti-submarine campaign, the latter through requests that they bomb coastal harbours and U-boat pens on the Atlantic coast.

By early 1943, the Axis forces were being driven out of North Africa and Italy would soon surrender and string up its Fascist leader, Benito Mussolini, on a meat hook in public view of a populace thoroughly tired of being dragged through the agonies of total war. Operation *Torch* had delivered the first American troops to the west North African coast and, with Gen Montgomery's Eighth Army pushing Rommel's Afrika Korps back along the coast to meet them, evacuation through Sicily evicted Axis forces from Africa. The German and Italian forces in North Africa duly surrendered on 13 May 1943 and the Allies took 275,000 prisoners.

For much of the preceding three years, the air war over the Middle East and North Africa had been driven by the contested lands that the Axis believed could win them the war. They intended to do this by controlling the Mediterranean, through routes into the underbelly of Russia from Asia Minor, and by expanding east to threaten British interests. These aerial conflicts had been at times decisive; a great proportion of the Luftwaffe's transport fleet had been decimated trying to consolidate Axis forces on the east North African coast from across the Mediterranean out of their bases in the Balkans. So, in several ways, the eviction of enemy forces from Africa secured a platform for pushing German forces back up from the boot of Italy all the way to the Alps.

A RETURN TO STRATEGIC BOMBING

With these victories in Africa secured, the RAF looked to resume its major bombing campaign on German cities and industries supporting the Nazi war effort. But the threat from German submarines was never far from the debate about which resources to use where. And, on 14 January 1943, a chilling directive from the War Cabinet ordered Bomber Command to forthwith conduct 'a policy of area bombing against the U-boat operational bases on the west coast of France'.

For some time, German engineers had been constructing massive concrete shelters for U-boats at Lorient, Saint-Nazaire, Brest and La Pallice. Bomber Command paid little attention to these works when they were in a vulnerable phase of construction, when the exposed nature of the work would have meant they could have been destroyed fairly easily. Instead, by early 1943, the U-boat pens and associated construction had been finished, meaning that the Germans now had virtually bombproof U-boat shelters. What's more, general and technical personnel could now be housed either in specially protected buildings and bunkers or in dispersed locations in the countryside. The result was that when the RAF was required to area bomb French towns, the effect had little significant military value. A lot of French people died and wide swathes of populated areas were brought to ruin in the fruitless attempt to destroy the U-boat pens and help win the war in the Battle of the Atlantic.

Nevertheless, by early 1943, Bomber Command was free to resume its strategic bombing campaign – and with expanding capacity. On 13/14 February, 466 aircraft dropped more than 1,000 tons of bombs on Lorient, shifting from the propaganda assemblage of 1,000 aircraft made up from reserves and training units to one comprised of fully operational squadrons. From early March to late July, Bomber Command executed what it termed the Battle of the Ruhr. This consisted of 43 major operations across a wide range of targets throughout occupied Europe. Concentration on specific areas would have too easily alerted German defences and consolidated their anti-air and fighter forces. It was therefore necessary to mix targets and dates so as not to demonstrate a predictable pattern. In addition to causing damage, a major advantage of the bomber offensive was that it tied up increasing numbers of German military personnel in air defences.

For the first time, the extended range of the Stirling, Halifax and Lancaster bombers opened targets as dispersed as Stettin (Poland), Pilsen (Czechoslovakia), Munich (Germany) and Turin (Italy), hitting major industrial facilities and conurbations housing their respective workforces. Self-evident too was the increasing strength of Bomber Command. While the monthly average availability of all bombers during 1942 hardly fluctuated above 400, by the end of 1943 that availability had risen to an average of more than 800. And as a measure of the increased numbers of aircraft coming through to the squadrons, more than compensating for the losses, the average bomb lift per month for all types of bomber increased from 824 tons at the end of 1942 to more than 2,100 tons by May 1943 and just short of 3,000 tons by the end of the year.

OPERATION *CHASTISE* – AKA THE DAMBUSTERS RAID

Yet for all the activities of what was referred to as Main Force, there were some unusual assignments, none perhaps more famous than the celebrated Dambusters – a unique operation immortalized through celluloid and the 1955 film of the same name. And nothing did more for morale at home in Britain, despite the operation being of significantly less value to the war effort than was proclaimed at the time – and perhaps, as remembered since, both in film and in books.

The origin of the raid harked back to the pre war determination that in the event of conflict with Germany, the Ruhr and its industrial might should be the focus for attention. It was noted that its dams, with their ability to keep the power switched on through hydro-electric energy generated by the controlled flow of water, were prime targets. The question was therefore not so much where to attack, but how. The means lay in the ingenuity of Dr Barnes Wallis, the inventor of the geodetic structural frame used for the Vickers Wellington bomber.

At first, Wallis believed that a 10 ton bomb dropped from a height of 40,000 ft could do the job of breaching a dam wall, releasing the water, flooding the local area and cutting the power supply that kept the factories working. However, calculations indicated that this would be almost impossible to achieve. With only primitive test equipment, Wallis calculated that a 4.1 ton bomb packed in a drum-shaped cylinder and released after having been given a 500 rpm backspin would, if dropped against the dam, hug the wall as it fell through the water. If it was equipped with a hydrostatic fuse set to go off at a pre-calculated depth, the explosion would conduct all the energy of the charge through the drum case and on to the dam wall, to which it was firmly pressed due to the effect of the backspin. That, he deduced correctly, would carry sufficient energy to crack the dam, allowing the enormous pressure of water to split the wall and release a flood.

The problem was that the bomb could not be dropped in the conventional manner; the drum containing the explosive would have to be released from a maximum height of 60 ft above the water and at a precise speed of 240 mph. What's more, the aircraft would have to fly in a straight line over a heavily defended target at night. There would be high risk, to valuable aircraft and to an even more valuable crew. This was multiplied due to the fact that the intention was to hit several dams during a co-ordinated raid over the Ruhr.

Initially, there was strong opposition to the operation, which would call for precision flying by an expert and highly experienced set of crews as well as the diversion of Lancaster bombers and the establishment of a special squadron to carry out the operation. As head of Bomber Command, Air Chf Mshl Harris saw this proposal as just another diversion from the remorseless nightly hammer blows he imposed across German industry as a whole. Meanwhile, Air V-Mshl Francis Linnell, at the Ministry of Aircraft Production, believed that the work would take Wallis away from his primary job of developing a new aircraft called the Windsor. Pressured by Linnell, the chairman of Vickers-Armstrong, Sir Charles Worthington-Green, forced Wallis to resign over the issue.

After exhaustive trials against scale models of dams and at a real dam in Wales, Portal overruled opposition and, with the backing of Churchill, ordered the raid to go ahead. Known as Operation *Chastise*, it was targeted against the Möhne and Sorpe dams that feed directly into the Ruhr industrial area, and the Eder dam that feeds into the Weser river. To conduct the operation, special crews were selected from No. 5 Group and sent to train under Wing Commander (Wg Cdr) Guy

Gibson at RAF Scampton, north of Lincoln. In a highly secret programme, 21 bomber crews were assigned to what was then known as Squadron X – it had yet to receive its official number, 617 Squadron.

The raid took place on 16/17 May 1943. It involved specially modified Lancaster Mk III bombers, which had been stripped of armament and most of the armour, and each modified to carry a single bomb, named 'Upkeep', which was attached to a device for imparting backspin before it was released. Nineteen Lancasters were sent off in three waves carrying the 'bouncing bomb' as it was dubbed. One aircraft had to return when it struck the sea crossing to the Continent, tearing off the bomb. Five more were shot down or crashed and one was badly hit by anti-aircraft fire and had to turn back. With 12 aircraft remaining for the attack, Gibson's crew and four other aircraft hit the Möhne dam and breached it, while three hit the Eder dam and this too was breached. Two others hit the Sorpe dam and a secondary target, the Schwelm dam, but without result.

Of the 19 aircraft that set out, eight were lost and of the 56 crew members, 53 were killed. However, in breaching the two dams, the raid achieved a significant part of its objective and most of its purpose. The release of the 330 million tons of water contained in the Möhne dam caused flooding and general disruption of transport networks and communication links, and the output from the Ruhr steel production plants was cut by about 75 per cent. The breaching of the Eder dam caused major damage to the city of Kassel when the resulting tidal wave struck. Two major power stations were destroyed and a further seven were put out of action for a while. Regrettably, of the 1,650 people killed, half that number were prisoners of war and forced labourers, mainly from Russia, who were being contained in various work camps across the surrounding area.

Overall, the disruption to German war production was minimal. Co-ordinated planning for follow-up raids using conventional high explosive dropped in the usual way could have done considerably more to disrupt power and resources, not least the many workers required to clean and repair the dams. Harris had no heart for such an effort, though, and the attentions of Bomber Command quickly refocused on destroying large industrial plants and cities through area bombing. And by this time, the American Air Force was beginning to display capabilities that really would endorse the expectations of the agreement defining the Combined Bomber Offensive.

CHAPTER 14
Firestorms and Learning Curves

ON THE night of 10–11 September 1939, ten RAF aircraft flew over Hamburg for the first time and dropped propaganda leaflets imploring the Germans to stop their attack on Poland. The next visit to Hamburg took place on 17/18 May 1940, when 48 Hampdens bombed the oil installations in this strategic industrial port. From then on, this ancient city, free port and major industrial and maritime centre on the north-west coast of Germany was repeatedly hit with increasing numbers of aircraft.

During the period known as the Battle of the Ruhr, from March to July 1943, Air V-Mshl Harris decided to hit Hamburg hard. On 3/4 March 1943, for instance, 417 aircraft hit the port installations and the nearby town of Wedel, causing much damage. Harris also chose this city as the first target for a combined operation planned with the US 8th Air Force. As Europe's largest port and the second largest city in Germany, he felt that its relative proximity to the UK would render it a highly suitable target for this initial endeavour to focus both British and American air forces on one objective. The directive ordering this operation, codenamed 'Gomorrah' (after the biblical story of the city destroyed by God for its wickedness, related in Genesis 19:24), was signed off by Harris on 27 May.

The plan involved the RAF flying a night operation followed by two days of US daylight bombing missions, followed by a second RAF operation against Hamburg. It did not quite work out that way. The 8th Air Force was assigned to targets on or close to Hamburg, such as Kiel, but intense smoke from the night raid encountered by the B-17s caused the Americans to withdraw from the plan. Harris next mounted three major raids on Hamburg in the space of six days but they were not planned as anything exceptional.

A countermeasure to confuse the Würzburg early-warning radar controlling the anti-aircraft guns and the Lichtenstein radar used by night fighters was introduced on the first of these raids. Known as 'Window', it consisted of small strips of aluminium foil secured by adhesive to pieces of thin paper. If these were dropped in large numbers by bombers the radar would be totally saturated by the false reflections of several hundred thousand individual strips. Bomber Command also employed H2S for this sequence of raids on Hamburg, in addition to visual navigation.

The first of the three raids took place on the night of 24/25 July 1943 when 791 aircraft – including 347 Lancasters, 246 Halifaxes and 125 Stirlings – set out. Of these, 728 aircraft dropped 2,284 tons of bombs over a period of 50 minutes. The bombs fell a little off-centre from the optimized target, creeping back (where the footprint of bombs dropped begins to retreat back out of the city) 6 miles. Nevertheless, great damage was caused to government buildings, including the main police station, the local authority offices and industrial facilities, as well as to the zoo, where 140 animals were killed. In all, 1,500 people died in the raid and in the conflagrations that followed, made worse and more enduring by the destruction of the telephone system, which rendered the city's 40,000 firemen unable to co-ordinate their activities.

Late in the afternoon of the following day, with dense smoke roiling over the entire city and adjacent districts, 123 B-17s of the 1st Bombardment Wing, US 8th Air Force, took off to bomb Hamburg as planned. However, visibility was appalling and the mission was called off. At the same time of day, the 4th Bombardment Wing put up 141 B-17s to attack the submarine yards at Kiel, about 50 miles due north of Hamburg. Of these, 118 aircraft reached the target, although they were still unable to achieve their primary objective. The intention had never been to merge air forces for a single operation but rather to co-ordinate strikes to maximize the disruption; sustained bombing round-the-clock would prevent fire crews, rescue teams and civilians from recovering.

The RAF went out for the second night on 27/28 July, when 787 aircraft were dispatched to Hamburg, including 353 Lancasters, 244 Halifaxes and 116 Stirlings. All the Pathfinder work was done using H2S, and the target creep-back that had been noted two nights earlier was only marginal. In all, 729 aircraft dropped 2,326 tons of bombs, which were placed much more precisely than they had previously within a concentrated zone. To put this in perspective, to this date the greatest tonnage dropped in a single raid had been 44 tons on Guernica on 26 April 1937, 100 tons on Rotterdam on 14 May 1940, 711 tons on London on 10 May 1941 and 1,455 tons on Cologne on 30 May 1942.

It was estimated with some certainty that on the raid this night some 500–600 bombs fell within a 2 square mile area. What ensued was unique to this date: the creation of a firestorm. This was due to several factors, most importantly the unusual meteorological conditions. The weather was hot and lacked humidity, and there had been a violent thunderstorms over the North Sea on the previous night, which had caused an earlier bombing raid on Hamburg to be cancelled. On 27–28 July, the temperature was a stifling 30° C (86° F) with humidity down around 30 per cent, whereas normally for this time of year it would be up to 50 per cent.

Hamburg had not seen rain for a long time, which meant that the entire place was tinder-dry. As the bombs fell, a great number of major fires began to break out throughout the districts where blue-collar workers lived. The balance of bomb loads carried contained a mixture of approximately 50 per cent incendiaries and the rest in a variety of different high explosives. There was nothing intrinsically unique about the distribution of bomb types, yet what was to ensue was different to anything that had been experienced in warfare of any kind. It was in effect a true firestorm in that the weather and the fires created by the bombing blended and merged to ignite the very air itself. That had not been seen before, anywhere.

With the majority of fire crews occupied in the western parts of the city, trying to dampen down fires that had started three nights previously, any movement from area to area was hampered and in some cases totally prevented by the agglomerations of rubble and building falling into the streets. As the fires in the Hammerbrook area began to merge together about halfway through the raid itself they developed into a funnel of upwardly accelerating air currents – a vortex of fire and burning materials hurtling upwards to great altitude. Reliable accounts speak of adults, children, animals and furniture being drawn up into the flaming column as if an atmospheric vacuum cleaner on an incomprehensibly gigantic scale were hovering over Hamburg and sucking everything upwards.

As the air itself ignited it sucked the oxygen out of the lower levels and drew more in from the surrounding area, causing tornadoes of fire that raced at great speed inwards to the vortex. People were asphyxiated. Many panicked and fled makeshift shelters in their homes, only to be sucked up through the air, carried high over the heads of their horrified neighbours with all the appearance of flaming candles. Others raced for any exposed water, particularly the regions of the Alster

The aftermath of the raid on Hamburg reveals the devastation caused by the fire raids on a scale never experienced before. USAF

waterway, and were trapped in temperatures at boiling point. Several eyewitness reports spoke of horses in flames fleeing from the Hertz haulage business.

A great number of the estimated 42,000 people killed that night (equivalent to all the British killed to this date in German air raids since the war began) were asphyxiated in pockets of carbon monoxide, many in basement shelters with exits blocked by debris. Some 16,000 multi-storey apartment buildings, homes for 450,000 people with a collective frontage of 133 miles were destroyed as an area of 4 square miles was completely burned out by the central vortex of the firestorm. A total of 12 square miles was devastated, with the destruction of 24 hospitals, 277 schools and 257 government buildings.

Looking down from his aircraft, one crew member said afterwards: 'The blaze was unimaginable. I remember saying to the navigator, who was engrossed with his charts: "For Christ's sake, Smithy, come and see this. You'll never see the like of it again!" But Hamburg raised for me for the first time the ethics of bombing. I took the view so-called civilians were part of the German war machine ... the only ones you are left with were the children ... they were not involved, so you were left with a terrible feeling about them.'

Other air crews testified that they could feel the heat from the fires, reporting soot on their aircraft and being able to smell the awful aroma of roasting flesh. Many were deeply affected by what they saw that night and much later would express having felt doubts that remained with them for the rest of the war, and beyond. Of the 1.7 million Germans in the city, 1.2 million were evacuated by the authorities but it shook the Nazi hierarchy to the core; even propaganda minister Joseph Goebbels wrote in his diary about a 'Sword of Damocles' hanging over the country.

Two nights later, Bomber Command was back. On the night of 29/30 July, 777 aircraft set off – including 344 Lancasters, 244 Halifaxes and 119 Stirlings – and again H2S was used for marking the target. This time, the formations were to approach the city from the north and north-east to attack areas that had been left relatively unscathed. But the markers were 2 miles too far to the east and identified an area just to the south of the earlier firestorm. As the creep-back migrated up 4 miles, it intruded again into the devastated zone and eventually rained bombs down on a new residential area. In all, 707 aircraft dropped a further 2,318 tonnes of bombs, mainly on workers' houses. This time, there was no firestorm but the separate fires raged on. In one tragic incident, 370 people who sought refuge in the basement of a department store were asphyxiated by the carbon monoxide when the exits were blocked with rubble and falling masonry.

As if in some mock response, when Bomber Command sent out another 740 aircraft to raid Hamburg on the night of 2/3 August, many had to turn back. Fierce and intense thunderstorms beat back the raiding bombers, turning the attempt into a fiasco. Thirty aircraft were lost to extreme and violent turbulence, and to lightning strikes and to icing on the wings and control surfaces bringing them down.

For the rest of the year, Bomber Command resumed its attacks on industrial and strategic targets such as factories and manufacturing plants for war machinery, and there were three raids on Berlin between late August and early September. This came at a price; reaching out so far across the Continent exposed the bombers to anti-aircraft fire and to higher levels of attrition, loss rates climbing to 7.5 per cent. What's more, summer months were never good for deep-penetration raids, but as winter began to lengthen the nights, the safety of the dark was comforting for the crews. However, this was somewhat undermined by the fact that the Germans were developing ever-more sophisticated means of locating the bombers.

Changes in the structure of the force level saw the retirement of the Wellington bomber, replaced completely now by the 'heavies' coming off the production lines in increasing numbers. Some changes were also made in the modernization of aircraft equipment and in more capable technology, including G-H, which would replace Oboe in 1944 as a navigation aid for up to 80 aircraft at a time, instead of a single one with the older system. There was also a proactive disruption effort called Corona, the name for a ground-based listening system that picked up communications between German night fighters.

On the ground in England, men and women fluent in German would mimic Luftwaffe flight controllers and give the enemy fighter pilots incorrect information about the location and position of the RAF bombers, sending them far away from the incoming formations. The most sophisticated use of Corona was to put an additional German-speaking crew member into individual bombers to disrupt the communications. Codenamed 'Airborne Cigar', this proved particularly effective. In other attempts to confuse the Luftwaffe, fast-flying Mosquitoes conducted diversion raids, though these did little to distract the enemy. Only when small forces of larger bombers repeated the same practice would the German defences take notice and begin directing defensive fighters to the decoy intrusion, leaving the primary force relatively clear.

SPECIAL ATTENTION

Since the mid-1930s, long before the war began in September 1939, a secret group of scientists and engineers under the leadership of German Army Gen Walter Dornberger had been working on a project to develop a rocket-powered ballistic missile capable of propelling a 1 ton warhead over a range of 200 miles. Known as the A4 (*Aggregate 4*), and eventually renamed by the German propaganda ministry the V-2 ('revenge weapon No 2') it was developed and tested on the island of Peenemünde in the Baltic, just off the north German coast. Beginning slightly later and also on Peenemünde, the Luftwaffe, too, had been developing a similarly secret weapon: the Fieseler Fi-103, which would be dubbed the V-1 (since it was the first to be used operationally).

Whereas the V-2 was a rocket – flying an arched trajectory that would exit the atmosphere and reach the fringe of space before curving back down to strike its target faster than the speed of sound – the V-1 was purely subsonic. Powered by a pulse-jet engine it too carried a 1 ton warhead a distance of 200 miles but would fly to its target like an aeroplane, albeit one without a propeller and powered solely by its reaction engine. There could be some defence against the V-1 but nothing could combat the V-2.

Having received some snippets of intelligence information about these rockets, the War Ministry ordered photographic reconnaissance of Peenemünde.

The pictures were not conclusive, however, and there was debate about what these strange-looking objects were. Lying on its side and taking the form of an elongated cigar, the A4 was assumed to be a rocket, though opinion was divided as to whether the Germans could have produced something so advanced. Once again, Dr R.V. Jones of the intelligence section of the Air Ministry was called in to examine the evidence. He came down firmly on the side of those who believed it to be a rocket, despite Lord Cherwell claiming that it was nothing more than a spoof to deceive the British and had about as much warlike potential as the inflatable sausage-shaped balloon it appeared to be!

Nevertheless, Churchill ordered Chairman of the War Cabinet Duncan Sandys to form a special committee. This was ordered to examine all the evidence – the Germans had been testing the V-2 out across the Baltic and, although shrouded in secrecy, word about this activity had reached British intelligence long before any photographic evidence from high-flying aircraft had been obtained – and to reach science-based conclusions. It was then tasked with organizing a raid to demolish the facility where several thousand workers were employed, and destroying the laboratories, workshops and launch pads.

On the night of 17/18 August 1943, therefore, Bomber Command sent 596 aircraft – comprising 324 Lancasters, 318 Halifaxes and 54 Stirlings – on a special raid to Peenemünde. Regrettably, the initial marker had the first bombs fall on a labour camp for forced workers about 1½ miles from the aim point. However, the master bomber system subsequently brought the main force back on target and 560 aircraft dropped almost 1,800 tons of bombs, of which 82 per cent was high explosive, so as to smash up the extensive facilities across the site.

MASTER BOMBER

The master bomber concept involved high-frequency radio equipment installed in certain aircraft. It allowed crew members in different aircraft to communicate with each other and in this way respond to instructions from the lead crew. First tested on the night of 20/21 June 1943 in a raid on the electronic works at Friedrichshafen, the attack on Peenemünde was the first major operation in which it was employed.

On the night of the raid, 500–600 captive workers were killed, along with 180 Germans, and there was extensive damage to the laboratories and test facilities, including some of the launch pads and associated equipment for supplying the fuels and fluids used in these exotic devices under development there. The RAF lost 40 aircraft, a high 6.7 per cent of the raiding force. It was on this operation that the bombers first encountered the Schräge Musik – twin upward-firing cannon installed in the upper forward fuselage of specially converted Luftwaffe Bf-110 fighters that were designed to rake the underside of the bombers with high-velocity 20 mm shells. Named after the German word for out-of-tune music, it was widely adopted as the Luftwaffe sought any means by which to stem the tide of Allied bombing and strafing incursions across occupied Europe.

The long-term consequences of the raid for the V-2 programme were minimal, however, the Germans moving their test operations to newly constructed launch sites in Blizna, Poland, while retaining drawing offices and administrative operations at Peenemünde. It would be a year before the V-2s began falling on targets in south-east England, preceded by some months by the V-1 'flying bomb' (or 'doodlebug' as it was known in Britain).

AN AMERICAN JOURNEY

For the remainder of 1943, RAF Bomber Command exerted sustained pressure on German cities and industrial towns, testing the defences by continuous operations and planning a significant increase in both scale and capability for 1944. During this period, the Americans reached new heights with their gradually evolving plans for sustained daylight bombing, integrating with the RAF only in the specifics of what they were bombing and where. Sustained daytime bombing had been a long time coming and had taken the Army Air Forces far longer than they expected to reach peak performance.

Since mid-1942, the 8th Air Force had been shadowing RAF operations as they got to grips with an enemy so very close across the shallow North Sea. The first American to drop bombs on enemy soil was Capt Charles C. Kegelman, who flew one of 12 Bostons on 29 June 1942 against the Hazebrouck marshalling yard in northern France. However, it was not until 17 August that year that the USAAF flew its first independent mission. This saw Col Frank A. Armstrong lead 12 B-17s from Polebrook, Northamptonshire, to attack the Rouen-Sotteville marshalling yards in France. This mission achieved good results and got away with light casualties. On returning to their base, Air Mshl Tedder, commanding air operations in the Middle East, sent a message to the crew: 'Yankee Doodle certainly went to town and can stick yet another well-deserved feather in his cap.'

The first US raid carried out by the 8th Air Force on a target in Germany occurred on 27 January 1943 when 53 B-17s out of 91 that set off found their

THE BATTLE OVER MALTA

The Americans were not just based in the UK. On 28 June, Gen Brereton had arrived in Egypt to take command of US air operations in that sector and would command the Middle East Air Force, which was to prove a vital element in support for the RAF Desert Force as it pushed the Axis out of North Africa. Persistent attacks on enemy facilities and in direct confrontation of Luftwaffe airborne forces had played a pivotal role in driving back the German and Italian forces. Fiercely contested, the survival of the island of Malta midway along the Mediterranean became a legendary story of heroic air battles, first by ageing Gloster Gladiator biplanes and then by Spitfires delivered by aircraft carrier, resounding through history as playing a critical role in preventing the Axis from achieving their objective – to overwhelm and invade Malta and to turn the entire Mediterranean Sea into an Axis lake.

target; all the B-24s dispatched lost their way and returned without result. Frustration followed on 2 February when 61 B-17s and 22 B-24s from all six operational bombardment groups tried to find the marshalling yards at Hamm but failed due to poor weather. The next raid on 14 February resulted in all 74 bombers turning back, again in poor conditions.

Longer and more extended missions into hostile air space posed severe problems, especially for the vulnerable B-17s, which to this date had not yet received the chin turrets that provided effective defence from frontal attacks. Only limited protection was afforded to the American bombers – tightly packed formations of 18 aircraft were envisaged and tested in a combat box, stacking two or three aircraft vertically in a single combat wing. What's more, there were difficulties – operationally, administratively and culturally – between the two air forces at command level (the air crews got on remarkably well). And these would prove far more difficult to resolve than anyone had anticipated.

Some frustration had been embedded when President Roosevelt and his military adviser George C. Marshall had been irritated by not receiving British endorsement for their plan to push on across the English Channel in 1942. Considering the Germans to have remained as they had observed them in 1917 – an enemy entrenched behind heavily defended fortifications on a fixed front – it seemed logical to invade Europe and engage the enemy on the ground. This had inbuilt flaws. Nevertheless, it worried Roosevelt that he was having to placate an increasingly impatient Congress, and the American public, and explain why more than a million US troops and airmen were sitting in billets and barracks in England waiting for the word to go. His predecessor in that earlier war, Woodrow Wilson, had faced the same problem, answering to an electorate and a legislature that had only limited patience with inactive Americans abroad, seemingly unable to make a difference.

The absence of real change was made all the more palpable by the fact that only 79 missions had been flown in 1942, and none with 80 or more aircraft, although some relief was felt in the second half of 1943 when there was a US campaign to support a long slog up the spine of Italy as part of the action in the Middle East and the Mediterranean. The expectation that the B-17s and the B-24 could defend themselves was also undermined by the reality of the situation. The war against the Luftwaffe was very different to the one that these aircraft had been designed for, and there was thus an increasingly strident call for escort fighters.

When the Americans arrived in the UK, the only competent escort fighter was the Lockheed P-38, a twin-engine, twin-tail-boom aircraft with a maximum speed of more than 400 mph and a range of 450 miles. Designed in 1937 and having made its first flight in September 1940, the P-38 Lightning was used effectively in the Pacific War and in Europe but it lacked range. Not until 24 December 1942 did the first Republic P-47 Thunderbolt fighters arrive in Britain to support 8th Air Force operations.

Competing as a potential escort fighter, the P-47 had made its first flight in May 1941. Although it was advertised with a range of 530 miles, capable of escorting bombers out to a distance of 270 miles, it lacked the drop tanks – fuel tanks carried under the fuselage or wings which were dropped off when empty to return the aircraft to its usual handling qualities – and in reality could not be relied upon to stay with the raiders for more than 175 miles. Moreover, it had poor acceleration getting from the cruising speed of the bombers to the pace of attacking fighters. It was therefore suggested that the P-47 should fly top cover and pounce on Luftwaffe predators rather than staying with the bombers and trying to engage the incoming fighters.

The P-51, by contrast, evolved into a credible escort fighter. The type had first been requested by the British when in January 1940 they went to the USA in search of aircraft to order for the RAF. North American Aviation took just 117 days to design the P-51 and flew the prototype for the first time in October that year. Powered by a 1,100 hp Allison V-1710-F3R engine, it had been authorized on the basis that two prototypes would be supplied to the US Amy so that they could evaluate it for possible production and domestic use. The first employed by the (then) Army Air Corps failed to impress, although the British did order a batch, the first of which flew in May 1942 as the Mustang.

Poor performance was eventually alleviated by the adoption of the Rolls-Royce Merlin engine. Flight tests with the type followed in November 1942, which showed a 50 mph increase in speed, pushing it to more than 400 mph in a full-throttle burst. This was achieved when Stanley Hooker of Rolls-Royce designed a two-stage supercharger with intercooler for the Merlin 61 engine, which also raised the service ceiling to an incredible 41,000 ft. There was also an additional fuel tank behind the pilot's seat.

Finally, the USAAF had an outstanding escort fighter. They flew their first combat mission in December 1943 and on 15 January 1944, they provided escort across the German border. Two months later, they escorted B-17s and B-24s all the way to Berlin and back.

US BOMBING MISSIONS

The build-up to peak performance occurred rapidly during the second half of 1943. In January, the 8th Air Force had 80 B-17s and B-24s operational, compared to an assigned paper inventory of 225, with 85 crews available. By the middle of the year, those respective totals had grown to 378 aircraft of 800 assigned and 315 crews. In January 1944, 842 aircraft were available for operations from a paper assignment of 1,630 with 1,113 crews listed. Those totals would continue to increase.

What was more important was the increasing number of aircraft available for operations compared to the assigned number: 35.5 per cent in January 1943, 47 per cent in July and 52 per cent six months later. Yet, despite the long, slow climb in capability, the Americans were anxious to play a part in destroying vital production facilities supporting the German war effort and therefore planned a series of raids on the ball-bearing factory at Regensburg.

On 17 August 1943, a force of 188 aircraft penetrated deep into Germany and hit the Regensburg facility. Some 127 then went on to the Schweinfurt factory, where 50 per cent of all German fighter production was focused. Since this target was 100 miles further on, those bombers had to fly south to land in Tunisia rather than attempting to make the return flight across heavily defended Germany.

It was a rough mission. No sooner had the US aircraft crossed the Continent on the way out than the waiting Luftwaffe pounced, putting up a sustained attack that lasted 90 minutes, hitting the Regensburg bombers that were up ahead of those going for Schweinfurt.

Luftwaffe controllers positioned fighters from as far away as the Baltic, and aircraft employed as spotter planes far from the vicinity of the approaching bombers maintained a running commentary on their location. In so doing, the Luftwaffe displayed a new level of attack, and tactics that had not been seen before. By this time, the already legendary Adolf Galland was in overall charge of the fighter units – the Jagdwaffe – and the procedures followed by its pilots.

Attacking in groups of two or three, the Jagdwaffe pilots used a javelin formation in packs of up to 25 aircraft, slicing across the bombers' nose positions in groups of 7–15 aircraft simultaneously. As directed by Galland, they dived straight down almost vertically right through the bomber formations, aiming their guns at the mid-upper turrets of the bombers, using rockets with proximity fuses set to detonate close to but not directly on the surfaces of the bombers, so that the shrapnel would damage various parts of each aircraft simultaneously, with crippling effect. There were also trials with parachute-retarded bombs that were dropped directly on top of individual bombers. These didn't always produce the expected effect as controlling the descent of a parachute under such dynamic conditions was virtually impossible.

The intensity of the attacks on the encroaching bombers was greater than any that had been experienced to date. During the initial engagement, 24 of the 127 bombers that made it through to the target were shot down. The remaining US aircraft, however, dropped 299 tons of bombs on the factories. The Schweinfurt raiders coming on behind were more than three hours later than planned due to bad weather leaving England and were depleted by technical trouble and navigational errors. This meant that only 188 of the 230 that set out made it to their target. This time lag allowed the Jagdwaffe to land their fighters, refuel and re-arm and get back in the air. Only 152 bombers survived the day, 36 being shot down for a loss rate of 19 per cent on each raid.

Nevertheless, the mission was successful in that damage at the ball-bearing factories reduced production from 169 tons to 50 tons and there was a delay of three months in restoring output to any semblance of normality.

Despite the losses, the 8th Air Force was back on 14 October 1943. Two-hundred-and-ninety-one B-17s and 29 B-24s set out, with additional fuel tanks in the Boeing bombers, since the target was in excess of their usual range. However, the B-24s were unable to form up quickly enough to depart as part of the prime formations of B-77s and instead made for the diversionary target of Emden, leaving 196 escorting P-47s behind over Aachen, 240 miles from the British coast. The Jagdwaffe responded by attacking with new ways and means of downing their aerial prey. Single-engine fighters – Bf-109s and Fw-190s – sliced right through the bomber formations, which had to remain fixed within their boxes to avoid collisions, strafing them with 20 mm cannon fire. These were followed by twin-engine Bf-110s, which launched rockets from about 3,000 ft and from the rear.

Despite the mauling they received from the active fighters, 229 bombers dropped 395 tons of high explosive and 88 tons of incendiaries over the target, Schweinfurt. But it had been carnage. Sixty aircraft had been shot down, a quarter of all those that had reached the target. When counting those badly damaged and others that could eventually be repaired, this left only 31 B-17s of the 229 that set out available for immediate reassignment. As a result, this catastrophic day saw a halt to daylight operations until special drop tanks had been made available for the P-38s, which extended their range out to 520 miles, or 585 miles with two tanks each from February 1944. These supplemented the P-51s, which had yet to arrive in sufficient numbers.

A BLOW TO MORALE

In addition to the loss of aircraft and men, US pilots suffered further knocks to their confidence. There had been a sense of protection that came from the bombers being tightly packed, which made the pilots feel that it was probably going to be someone adjacent who got the attention of the incoming fighters, but in reality it was all too easy for a minor technical problem in just one engine to cause an individual aircraft to gradually lose his place in the box and slip slowly behind. Thus isolated, he would receive the full attention of the Jagdwaffe hunting down stray and wounded bombers.

Other problems, too, bore down on the nerves of the crews, and not always from the Luftwaffe, the anti-aircraft fire or the probing radar. There was a tendency for the mid-upper turret to suddenly catch fire and burn off a considerable part of the centre section of the upper fuselage. It transpired that the rotation of the turret, necessary for the gunner to bring his guns to bear on an enemy, was chafing electrical wiring around the ring that operated the turret, fraying and setting light to combustible materials on the inside – where the gunner sat.

THE GERMANS STEP IT UP A GEAR

The terrifying duplicity of the Luftwaffe's assault heralded a new level of sophistication practised by the defenders: concentrations of fighters picking off one formation after another and individual fighters then finishing off the lame ducks and stragglers.

Added to this was the increased number of German fighters that became available after the collapse of Axis operations in North Africa and the Mediterranean, when they were redirected back to northern Europe. Moreover, under the newly appointed armaments minister Albert Speer, the manufacturing output of the German war machine appeared to increase commensurate with the increase in day and night bombing by the Combined Bomber Offensive. Counter-intuitively, the more the Allies bombed the factories, the more aircraft the Germans produced! This is evident from the figures. Production increased from 12,400 aircraft in 1941 to 15,400 in 1942 and 24,800 in 1943. The following year, German industry would turn out an amazing 30,781 aircraft. There had also been a determined shift in bomber production from 28 per cent of all output in 1941 to 19 per cent in 1942, while fighter production increased from 34 per cent in 1941 to 44 per cent in 1942 and 57 per cent in 1943. In 1944, fighters accounted for 76 per cent of all types.

One of the reasons for the overall increase in war production – which did of course also include ground equipment such as tanks, armoured fighting vehicles, guns and artillery pieces as well as submarines and naval vessels – was due largely to the dispersal of factories and manufacturing plants. Just as Russia had begun to draw its own manufacturing capability away from the frontline and back toward the Urals, so too did the Germans seek ways of diversifying the construction and assembly plants.

During 1944, this would extend to hiding small workshops and manufacturing in woods and country locations that were difficult to spot from the air. Construction workers also began building massive facilities that looked like giant bunkers. These were situated partly underground and were protected by layers of concrete with sloping sides several tens of feet thick – so thick that no known bomb could crack them open. Most of these facilities were built using slave labour from concentration camps where some of the 7 million citizens of occupied countries were brought to be worked to death on production lines deep inside horizontal mine shafts, or in these specially built facilities.

To put to work slave labourers drawn from across the Continent, skilled prisoners were kept in cages inside major factories. Openings in the cages allowed components and parts for aircraft and tanks to pass through. Prisoners would work on these before assembled units were moved across and out of the cage at the other end. Germans working in these factories could see the prisoners and daily witnessed the atrocious conditions that people from all over mainland

Europe were forced to endure during their last days producing war machinery for the Third Reich. On the part of the slave workers, wherever they could, they would try to sabotage in subtle ways small components manufactured for aircraft, which would only be discovered when the aircraft were delivered to operational units. Even just an oily rag hidden deep inside an engine could cause a fire.

WOMEN'S ORGANIZATIONS IN WORLD WAR II

The Woman's Auxiliary Air Force (WAAF) was formed on 28 June 1939. Operational at airfields and RAF stations across the UK, the WAAF provided an invaluable service in a wide range of supplementary and administrative functions, including packing parachutes, operating the barrage balloons, working on analysis and interpretation of reconnaissance photographs, and in cyber-warfare. Some uniformed officers also worked on code-breaking and intelligence operations at Bletchley Park, where the Enigma codes were interpreted. At peak strength, in 1943 more than 180,000 women were registered in the WAAF.

Established on 15 February 1940, the Air Transport Auxiliary was a civilian organization that recruited women pilots to ferry aircraft from manufacturers to various units; deliver repaired aircraft back to squadrons; and move aircraft from factories to various maintenance facilities for the installation of ordnance, guns and ammunition. This freed up men to be recruited into combat squadrons for fighting in the air. Many women logged a wide range of aircraft in the course of these duties – from Spitfires and Hurricanes to 'heavies' such as the Lancaster, Stirling and Halifax. In all, the ATS delivered 309,000 aircraft of 147 different types. There were instances where the women, on coming across enemy aircraft loitering in the skies, set about them with guns blazing!

The equivalent in the US Army Air Forces was the Women's Auxiliary Ferrying Squadron, formed in September 1942. This had a brief life: on 15 August 1943, the Women Airforce Service Pilots (WASP) organization was set up for women pilots to carry out ferry and transport duties, test new aircraft, deliver others and carry out gun practice, tow targets for live practice and fly cargo missions. In all, 1,074 women were accepted for training and 38 lost their lives on duty.

In the Soviet Union, 800,000 women joined the Russian combat units. While they too played their part in ferrying aircraft and delivering supplies in transport planes, there was little inhibition about putting them to work as combat air crew. In fact, great numbers of women flew with fighter forces as pilots or gunners and many stories of heroism and outstanding bravery are on record in the Russian archives. Indeed, the Russian women built a formidable reputation for their outstanding bravery and sustained and persistent determination to help save their country. These included three women in particular, who together flew more than 4,400 combat missions.

It is a sad reflection on the attitude of the time that many women of all nationalities suffered discrimination both during and after the war, the men in uniform frequently resenting their participation. After the war, men lobbied their governments in Britain and the USA for the women to be disbanded – and they were. This was because many men in the RAF and the USAAF saw women as a threat to their jobs and openly resisted their continued presence within the ranks.

Women pilots made a major contribution to the war effort by ferrying aircraft large and small from factories and between airfields, sometimes flying big four-engine 'heavies' across the Atlantic either from the US or from factories in Canada. USAF

Chapter 15
Blitzing the Axis

THE SCHWEINFURT and Regensburg raids in August and October 1943 raised interesting questions about the strategy used in this kind of so-called precision bombing, and there was a degree of uncertainty about its accuracy and effectiveness. It also raised issues regarding the night-time area bombing strategy conducted by the RAF compared with the more surgical selection of targets and the desire for precision espoused by the US Air Forces. As Air V-Mshl Harris' equivalent, Gen Ira Eaker had been single-minded in supporting precision bombing.

What's more, there were differences at the highest level not only in the RAF – about the priority placed on area bombing – but also within Bomber Command itself. Air Cdre S.O. Bufton, Director of Bombing Operations, strongly advocated a follow-up to the American raids in the summer of 1943, urging that: 'If both operations are successful, German resistance might be broken and the war ended sooner than could be possible in any other way.' However, Harris was firmly committed to the nightly area bombing and would not be persuaded to divert Bomber Command resources to backing up the Regensburg and Schweinfurt raids.

Moreover, just as the 8th Air Force was getting into its stride during the late summer of 1943, the 9th Air Force launched attacks on the Rumanian oil fields from the Mediterranean, now free of Axis contest. It was here that the respective air forces of the three Allied powers (Britain, the USA and Russia) set the seal on the way the war would end, just as the events of 1940–42 had determined the ultimate fate of Nazi Germany by Hitler's uncompromising dash for territory that was beyond his ability to hold.

On the Russian front, the Russians had crushed all hopes of a German victory at Stalingrad over the winter of 1942–43. More than 2 million men and women fought for the life of their respective countries, resulting in almost 2 million dead and the total defeat of the German 6th Army under Generalfeldmarschall von Paulus at Stalingrad. At this one city, the Luftwaffe also lost more than 1,600 aircraft, of which 900 were destroyed and the rest captured. The Luftwaffe therefore had to draw heavily on reserves, and German bombers pounded the city into rubble, creating ideal pockets of resistance. Meanwhile, Russian aircraft production from factories withdrawn deep behind the lines had turned the tide of defeat into hopes of a Soviet victory, and from early 1943 it was a long, bitter and tough fight all the way to Berlin two years later.

The collapse of confidence within the Luftwaffe hierarchy was taking its toll too. For example, on 18 August 1943, the Luftwaffe chief-of-staff, Jeschonnek, blew his brains out – a direct result of the massive raids on Schweinfurt the previous day and the attack on Peenemünde that night. For the Luftwaffe, the rates of attrition for aircraft engaged in the air war were climbing, reaching almost 14 per cent for all types between January and July that year. For combat aircraft, the rate was an unsustainable 16 per cent and for fighters alone, almost 20 per cent. The aircraft could be replaced faster than the pilots, and as the percentage of experienced crewmembers fell, the efficiency of the Jagdwaffe began to suffer.

By late 1943, the odds were shortening against the ability of the Jagdwaffe to stem the increasingly intense tide of bombers raiding the Reich. The errors of the preceding years – in not mobilizing a sufficiently robust production programme, in leaving it too late to address the problem of pilot retention during expanded periods of attrition and the lack of adequate attention to non-combat losses – was building up. Between February and the end of August 1943, availability of fighters authorized declined from 80.5 per cent to 71 per cent, while availability of bombers fell from 71 per cent of authorized strength to 56 per cent.

Surprisingly, after 1940, the training standards of the Luftwaffe had begun to decline, too, and increasingly the experienced instructors were replaced by others new to the requirements of the job. This had repercussions. Between 1941 and 1944, 40–45 per cent of all losses were through non-combat accidents, a situation to which the senior leadership seemed oblivious. However, this is not an uncommon statistic. In 1943, for instance, the US Army Air Forces lost just over 5,600 air crew in 20,389 accidents unrelated to combat. The following year there were modest improvements in the record but here too there were 16,128 major accidents with the loss of almost 5,000 air crew.

'BIG WEEK'

For their part, not before the end of 1943 did the Americans gain an effective fighting force for aerial warfare over Germany, fully two years after the attack on Pearl Harbor. This was due entirely to the need for adequate equipment, the requirement for which only became evident after the initial failure with pre-conceived bombing strategies, notably the belief in self-defending bombers; the availability of escort fighters (known as 'little friends' to the bomber crews) transformed the situation. With the decision to schedule a cross-Channel attack on Nazi-occupied Europe around the middle of 1944, defeat of the Luftwaffe was a prerequisite for any chance of success. Even massive troop concentrations on the landing beaches would not ensure survival against intense attack from the air.

In planning the destruction of the Luftwaffe, or at least the elimination of its effective fighting potential, the concentrated effort of both the RAF and the USAAF was essential. British participation was forced upon a reluctant Harris in a memorandum from Charles Portal, chief of the RAF. Still reluctant to divert his bombers from attacks on the cities, Harris was forced to submit to this bigger objective and thus commit increasing numbers of his aircraft to what would be referred to as D-Day (the 'D' was an alliterative designation for the commencement of ground operations, following on from letters A–C, which were preliminary steps to that event).

In preparation for D-Day, raids against German aircraft production would be followed by attacks on the oil industry in order to deny the Luftwaffe its vital fuel. Next, a concentrated counter-force attack on German fighters and the organization that controlled operations would complete the campaign. Weather forced a delay in the first phase, known as 'Argument' until what would become known as 'Big Week'.

Big Week began on 20 February 1944, and over the course of seven days the 8th Air Force completed 6,200 sorties, hitting 18 aircraft assembly plants and two ball-bearing factories. On the first day, losses were only 15 bombers out of the 880 that hit their targets, an acceptable loss rate of 1.7 per cent including four fighters. As the Luftwaffe became aware of the pattern, however, the losses mounted. Over the week, 248 Allied aircraft were lost, of which just 28 were US fighters. But production quotas were finally catching up fast, the number of P-51 Mustangs available at the end of Big Week being 90 per cent higher than it had been at the start. The effect was enormous: the Luftwaffe lost 20 per cent of its full complement of fighter pilots including one-third each of all Bf-109 and Fw-190 pilots.

But Big Week was not an exclusively US affair. RAF Bomber Command flew support raids, including a massive operation to the Messerschmitt works at Augsburg on the night of 25/26 February, where 1,070 aircraft were sent out. Of that total, 734 split into attacks on Schweinfurt two hours apart, suffering losses of 5.6 per cent and 3.2 per cent. This indicated that the first wave had drawn the Jagdwaffe into an initial attack against the incomers but had been unable to regroup back into the air for the second wave.

NEW STRATEGIES

Part of the strategy had been to unlock the escort fighters from staying close around the bombers to protect them. Just as Galland had wanted to free the fighters from close-in bomber escort in the Battle of Britain, so the Americans unleashed their fighters to go after the German defenders. The Army Air Forces finally had a production level and the ability to impose an attrition rate on the enemy that would rapidly erode the capability of the Luftwaffe to respond. Hitting hard and incessantly, predating upon the German fighters that were on the defensive, the Jagdwaffe was taking a beating from which it could not recover – which was the plan.

The nature of the big air battles that developed over Germany during this period was a reaction to the combat box formation adopted by the USAAF in October 1943, and that in turn was a direct response to lessons learned over the folly of self-defensive tactics. The combat box consisted of three groups of 12 bombers in tight formation aligning themselves to create a 36-plane combat box. This was staggered in various positions so as to concentrate the collective defensive firepower of more than one hundred 0.50 calibre guns. The conventionally armed versions of the Bf-109 and Fw-190 were inadequate for withstanding the firepower of the combat box, but the Fw-190 was the ideal aircraft for an upgrade. In addition to the two machine guns carried in the nose and two cannon in the wing roots, two more guns were mounted in cannon pods attached to the underside of the wings, giving the Fw-190 A-6 derivative two machine guns and four cannon. Several derivations subsequently evolved according to operational experience for what became known as the *Sturmböcke* bomber-destroyers.

By far the most effective change in American tactics was to free the escorts to conduct 'fighter sweeps' far ahead of the bombers, with the idea of clearing the skies of the enemy for the raiders coming through. All these changes, mostly improvements, occurred after Lt Gen James Doolittle took over command of the 8th Air Force from January 1944. Famed for the 'Doolittle raid' on Tokyo

Tight combat boxes of aircraft often resulted in those below getting in the way of bombers above releasing their load, with devastating results as here with this raid on Berlin, 19 May 1944. USAF

in 1942, Doolittle had skipped the rank of full colonel and jumped straight to brigadier general and then to major general, reaching the rank of lieutenant general in March 1944.

Changes in tactics and operating procedures were not solely the prerogative of the air combat arena over Continental Europe. The Luftwaffe had maintained periodic bombing of targets in Britain, and in the first of 1944 a significant new offensive began. Known as Operation *Steinbock*, initially the Luftwaffe mobilized 474 medium bombers for what would be dubbed the 'Baby Blitz', primarily against London but also some other cities, between 21 January and 29 May 1944. The aircraft employed were developed versions of the same types used during the Blitz of 1940: the Junkers Ju-88 was improved into the Ju-188 while the Dornier Do-17 was adapted into the bigger and better Do-217. The Luftwaffe had also taken delivery of the Messerschmitt Me 410 Hornisse Schnellbomber, which would be used for attacks on Britain. During this operation, lost aircraft were replaced as necessary to maintain the numbers.

But these were changed times: the night-fighter defences had become highly sophisticated, aided by advanced technical devices including radar and new armaments such as air-to-air rockets. The Luftwaffe bomber crews used for *Steinbock* were inexperienced and lacked the confidence displayed by their predecessors more than three years earlier. Over this four-month period, the Germans lost 525 aircraft to the British 28, and 1,556 British civilians were killed.

There had been a precedent for this four-monthly campaign in the so-called 'Baedecker Blitz' of April and May 1942. Named after the German tour guides that had become essential reading for British visitors going to European sites and for Europeans visiting Britain, these attacks targeted the cultural centres of Britain. However, while this blitz is known as the primary attack on historic places and sites of great cultural value, in reality the Luftwaffe never really did let up on attacking the heart of what it felt defined the very essence of Britain.

SUPPORT AT NORMANDY

By 1944, the RAF had shown considerable expansion since 1941 and nowhere was that more evident than in the strength and strike potential of Bomber Command. We saw earlier that by the end of 1943, Bomber Command had at its disposal more than 800 bombers capable of delivering a bomb lift of almost 3,000 tons. During 1944, Bomber Command would expand to boast more than 1,500 aircraft available at any one time, with a deliverable load of more than 6,500 tons of bombs. This unprecedented expansion stands in marked contrast to the scant force it was in 1939.

In preparation for the D-Day landings, the United States Strategic Air Forces (USSTAF) had been formed on 23 February 1944. As a point of interest, on the previous day, VIII Bomber Command had officially become the 8th Air Force, despite it having been referred to as such from its inception. The strategic planning staff remained intact and held authority over the 9th Air Force and the British 2nd Tactical Air Force, which were the operational arms of the Allied Expeditionary Air Forces (AEAF). To some degree, the operations of the 12th and 15th Air Forces were also embraced by USSTAF and VIII Bomber Command was inactivated, at least on paper.

The primary objectives of the USSTAF was threefold: to isolate the assault area on the Normandy beaches and to neutralize the enemy positions along that coastline, as well as preventing reconsolidation; to denude the area of enemy air operations and prevent any reinforcements from moving into the area at adjacent camps and airfields; and to destroy coastal facilities that could aid the enemy, detect Allied invasion forces or help move Wehrmacht units back into the region. In the sustained campaign that ensued, the Allied air forces dropped 76,000 tons of bombs on French railroads, with the attacks on bridges proving so effective that the 2nd TAF (Tactical Air Force) and fighter-bombers of the 9th Air Force readily took up the challenge.

It was the 9th Air Force that bore the brunt of the responsibilities for air support for the invasion plan and for attacking rail installations, airfields and coastal batteries. The plan was that IX Fighter Command, functioning through IX Tactical Air Command until the US Third Army was on shore and operating autonomously, would fly escort on bombers, carry out reconnaissance and conduct offensive sweeps over France. During the actual assault phase, five P-47 groups and four groups of 8th Air Force P-38 Lightnings would maintain full daylight patrol over the beaches to clear the skies of enemy aircraft. Two other P-38 groups and four P-47 groups would bomb enemy gun batteries at H-hour (the time of the landings) and directly support landing forces coming ashore. Gen Brereton would note that the tactical air plan alone was written in 847,000 words on 1,376 pages!

Supporting the actual landings, about two or three days before the invasion, the 8th Air Force was to have sent 60 per cent of its bombers into the Reich and the remaining 40 per cent to carpet-bomb the Pas-de-Calais area in order to deceive the Germans into thinking that this was the location of the long-anticipated invasion. However, the real attention would focus on the Normandy beaches where, on D-Day itself, the RAF was to drop 6,000 tons of bombs in the hours before dawn. In the last 30 minutes before the landings, naval guns would place 2,500 tons of shells on the beaches, while 500 tons of bombs would be supplied by medium bombers and 4,800 tons from the 8th Air Force, involving 1,200 B-17s and B-24s.

To assemble in time for the concentrated attack, the three 8th Air Force bombardment divisions would have to converge in the sky up to 100 miles from their bases and head south, approaching beaches at right angles straight in from the sea. They would then withdraw via the Cotentin Peninsula to land back in the western counties of England. Throughout the day of the landings, tactical air power was to be used to block transportation nodes and chokepoints, bomb bridges and generally seal the area to inhibit the movement of German forces into the area.

The 9th Air Force was fully committed to its strategic role until it was redirected to the pre-invasion operations beginning on 10 March 1944, while the USSTAF sustained its priorities to erode the Jagdwaffe and clear the skies. From that date, the 9th was assigned 30 targets in Belgium and north central France. Tactical air power saw a blending of fighter-bombers with the medium bombers, some 101 chunky P-47 'Jug' aircraft supporting 163 B-26 Marauders dropping 263 tons of bombs on 8 April by discharging one-hundred-and-twenty 250 lb bombs in diving attacks. A fierce attack by 48 P-47s the following day halted troop trains and freight cars being moved south, damaging rail yards in Namur and Charleroi. On 10 April, 148 Marauders from the 9th Air Force dropped 184 tons on Namur while the RAF bombed Charleroi, followed a day later by 193 Marauders dropping 173 tons on Charleroi and 138 tons around the general area.

This level of intense bombardment was maintained in the coming weeks. In order to minimize civilian casualties and confuse the enemy while opening up air space for greater accuracy by individual aircraft, the formations were broken up into smaller numbers. However, despite the remorseless pounding of pre-invasion targets, the desired level of collapse in the German transportation routes had still not been achieved, even though the goal of dropping 45,000 tons of bombs on railways by 1 June had been far exceeded. Elsewhere, there were outstanding results from other sectors of the pre-invasion bombing campaign. Allied aircraft had dropped 71,000 tons of bombs on rail centres, 4,400 tons on bridges and 800 tons on open railway lines. Rail traffic movements in France had been reduced dramatically between 19 May and the weeks after the invasion. Even by mid-July, five weeks later, rail traffic across northern France was virtually non-existent.

For the German part, captured documents revealed that Luftwaffe establishment levels were failing to be maintained. In May 1944, against an establishment inventory of 2,680 fighters there were only 1,729, of which only 1,195 were operational. And whereas a figure of 1,052 night fighters existed on paper, only 644 were on strength, with only 434 fit to engage in combat. Thus, for the Luftwaffe, there were insufficient bombers to carry the attack to the enemy in Britain, for example – as the Allies had to the German population in their towns and cities. What's more, against a fighter establishment of 1,824 in May there were 1,259, of which a mere 801 were serviceable. However, soon the Germans would have V-1 buzz bombs and V-2 rockets and would be able to recommence the bombardment of London and the Home Counties. For now, though, there were an estimated 900 aircraft, half of them bombers, which the Luftwaffe just might be able to throw against the invasion forces.

To swing the probability of success towards the Allies, deception tactics were used – and would prove to be a trump card. Not only were there diversionary raids, but also deployments of mocked-up tanks and vehicles made of plywood and compressed cardboard, which were set up at locations all across the south-east of England. These were intended to make it appear as though a major concentration of armour was waiting to spring across the English Channel at its narrowest point, from Rye in East Sussex to Dover. What could not be mocked up, however, was the total lack of harbours and large ports in that area from which to set an invasion force loose upon the region of the Pas-de-Calais, despite the German High Command believing that this was the place from which the invasion would come.

These diversions aside, there were very specific requirements imposed by the Allied Expeditionary Air Forces, commanded by Air Chf Mshl Trafford Leigh-Mallory. The Luftwaffe had about 350 airfields within a 100-mile radius of the Normandy shore from which it could operate, although in early 1944 most of those were unused, and only a few were well equipped and fully operational. While not pushing too enthusiastically to destroy these targets, thus running the risk of giving the game away as to the location of the landings, B-26 Marauders flew strikes against the more critical of these airfields. In addition to causing considerable damage, this allowed the pilots to garner experience and knowledge about their location so that a more concentrated focus on rendering them completely unusable could be made immediately after D-Day.

The airfield destruction programme plan was completed by Leigh-Mallory at the end of April and included all the airfields and usable landing grounds in an arc of 150 miles around Caen, which was dedicated Area I. Eight airfields and landing grounds were assigned to the RAF, 12 to the AEAF and 20 to the 8th Air Force. Area II reached out to Germany and the Netherlands, where 59 airfields and landing grounds were to be bombed by the B-17s and B-24s of the 8th and 15th Air Forces. That campaign started on 11 May with the 9th Air Force dropping the greatest weight of bombs in Area I. The 8th Air Force committed its heavies to the D-Day preparation plan with two mighty raids on 9 and 23 May, with 400 bombers attacking airfields clustered around Paris on 24 May, followed by other airfields as far north as Brussels on the following day.

By D-Day on 6 June, airfields in Area I had received 6,717 tons of bombs, of which 3,197 tons were dropped by the 9th, 2,638 tons by the 8th and 882 tons by the RAF. However, only four of the 32 Area I targets were in Category A, indicating total and complete destruction, and German aircraft were noticed to be still operating out of others that had been considered possibly unusable on reconnaissance photographs. However, it was believed by the RAF that the reason why enemy opposition was so light was due to the strategic role sustained by the heavies on their industrial targets in the Reich, which kept the Jagdwaffe committed to air defence where the raids were most threatening to industrial output.

On 5 June, the day before D-Day, 5,904 tons of bombs had been dropped and four-hundred-and-ninety-five 60 lb rocket projectiles had been fired at coastal batteries. A further 17,190 tons had been dropped on batteries outside the invasion sector. As D-Day approached, photographic reconnaissance operations were stepped up and across the armed services an integrated use and application was introduced on a completely new scale, in which co-operation between the separate fighting services had never been tighter.

To a great extent, the USAAF had been lagging behind in this area. However, by early 1944 it had established photographic units that were at least as good as the best the British could provide. And because of the longer and more sustained need for pictures of enemy targets, the infrastructure in the UK was quite capable of satisfying the requirements of the American air units without the need to bring over heavy and cumbersome processing equipment from the USA. The 10th Reconnaissance Group of the 9th Air Force was assigned to this dangerous duty and received a Distinguished Unit Citation for carrying out a complete beach survey covering the area from Blankenberge to Dunkirk and from Le Touquet to Saint-Vaast-la-Hougue from 6 to 20 May. They flew from Chalgrove, Oxfordshire, which had been a USAAF station (AAF-465) since 1 November 1942.

As D-Day approached, it was photographic assignments rather than tactical reconnaissance that became more important. These included very low, wave-height runs up the beaches to provide invasion commanders in the initial assault with detailed photographs of what the beaches would look like from several miles out, at 1,500 yards and at the shoreline. But even that was not good enough. The boat commanders needed to know what lay just beneath the waves, so photographs were taken by photo-reconnaissance aircraft flying as low as 15 ft to get pictures of underwater obstacles.

INVASION

Originally scheduled for 5 June but delayed a day to secure a window in the weather, the long-awaited invasion of the Normandy beaches began in the early hours of 6 June, supported by what was the largest aerial fleet ever assembled in support of a single objective. For weeks, the operational readiness of squadrons had been a top priority, the response of the enemy uncertain, resistance to the landings largely unknown and the outcome in doubt for several days after the first waves of soldiers had walked ashore and the initial parachute drops had been made.

It was as though everything that had been discussed and planned for the last several years had been geared towards this one great time of test, one day short of 30 months since reaction to Pearl Harbor mobilized the mighty resources of the USA and energized its people to one all-defining purpose: the defeat of Nazi Germany and the forces of Imperial Japan. To this end, more than 4,000 aircraft with the 8th Air Force were made ready for action this day, with an equal number plus 1,300 troop-carrying aircraft at the disposal of Gen Brereton's 9th Air Force. In all, more than 10,000 aircraft, of which 2,200 were American, British and Canadian bombers, attacked targets along the coast and further inland.

French civilians suffered huge losses as villages and towns were flattened to prevent German reinforcements reaching the advancing Allied forces, and roads and coastal areas were strafed and bombed to destroy all infrastructure that could be of use to a defending force. France had already suffered greatly; throughout the five years of German occupation and attacks by British and American air forces, some 68,000 French civilians had been killed by bombing alone – more than had been killed in the British Isles during the same period. In addition, more than 100,000 had been injured and 432,000 houses completely destroyed in air raids.

Yet there was no other way of achieving the ultimate objective, and the bombing had only just begun. Despite the destruction, the vast majority of the French people welcomed the liberators with warm hearts, open arms and tear-filled eyes of relief that an end was in sight after years of fear, torture and subjugation of a proud and generous people. For their part, most American soldiers – who had been shocked at the strictures placed upon the British people to ensure their own survival – were overjoyed to finally be over there to help free an occupied country.

While most missions flown from the UK by the USAAF in its first two years had been bombing and offensive attacks, D-Day needed a major airlift of paratroops and glider towing. In the largest troop carrier operation in history, the 8nd and 101st Airborne Divisions of the US Army took off from airfields as far apart as Devon and Lincolnshire, heading for locations behind Utah beachhead. The plan was for 17,000 men and equipment to be placed in this area, and involved 900 aircraft and 100 gliders of IX Troop Carrier Command. These were assembled after dark on 5 June while RAF Stirling bombers dropped 'Window', the strips of aluminium used to confuse enemy radar screens described earlier.

The main drops were made straight after midnight in the first four hours of 6 June, but ground obstructions and heavy anti-aircraft fire made this a challenging task. Yet only 41 sorties out of 1,606 on 6/7 June were failures, with just nine gliders out of 512 lost to enemy action. This figure was far lower than the most optimistic projections by the Supreme Allied Commander, Gen Eisenhower, and even the sceptical RAF had to congratulate the Americans on what many had projected would be a catastrophic and suicidal mission.

Most astonishing of all was the almost total lack of enemy air activity to counter the invasion; only three Fw-190 fighters were chased off and 22 Luftwaffe aircraft attacked the shipping after nightfall. Moreover, VIII Fighter Command had been unable to make contact with enemy aircraft in the air during an early morning offensive sweep. This was fortunate, for there would have been plenty of target opportunity had the Jagdwaffe been in a position to take advantage of the day.

A massive predawn raid by 1,361 B-17s and B-24s dropped 2,944 tons of bombs on the coastal batteries and shore defences. Most of these were dropped through the heavy overcast skies using radar, the last bombs being dropped ten minutes before the first waves of Allied soldiers went ashore. Most fuses were set to detonate on contact, thereby reducing the number of craters that could impede the anticipated advance of Allied soldiers.

Throughout the first day, several hundred medium bombers attacked peripheral areas to seal off defensive units of the German Army, hitting roads and transport links outside the area immediately accessed by the Allied troops coming ashore, and carrying our harrying attacks on roads and camps. The major pre-invasion raids quickly changed to tactical air action on the day itself, 528 heavy bombers being dispatched to hit chokepoints in Thury, Harcourt, Saint-Lô and Caen. Heavy cloud prevented all but three groups returning home. Nevertheless, 566 B-24s destroyed all of Caen except for a single bridge, which seriously delayed the 21st Panzer Division.

In addition to these operations by the USAAF, on the night of 5/6 June the RAF flew 1,211 sorties, with 1,012 aircraft attacking ten artillery batteries covering the invasion beaches, flattening wide areas of the immediate inland zones. A major contribution from the RAF involving 483 bombers on the night of 8/9 June saw the first use of the 12,000 lb Tallboy bomb against the Saumur railway tunnel, which effectively sealed off a major access route for the German Army, bringing down 10,000 tons of earth in the process.

US ARMY AIR FORCE PERSONNEL   US COMBAT AIRCRAFT

Year	Personnel	Year	Aircraft
1940	51,165	1939	1,269
1941	152,125	1940	1,356
1942	764,415	1941	4,002
1943	2,197,114	1942	11,139
1944	2,372,292	1943	26,734
1945	2,282,259	1944	40,157
		1945	39,192

Chapter 16
Victory in Europe

IN ALL, 11,950 aircraft of the USAAF and the RAF were directly involved in the Normandy landings, of which 7,722 were dispatched by the 8th and 9th Air Forces alone. Losses came to 71 aircraft, brought down by flak and anti-aircraft fire. What was needed over the next days and weeks was support through tactical air strikes by the combined air forces and a resumption, specifically by RAF Bomber Command, of the strategic assault on German towns and cities while the 8th Air Force got back to targeting the industrial heartland of the Reich.

In the period 6 June to 31 July, the RAF and the 8th and 9th Air Forces dropped 35,500 tons of bombs, carrying out 15,000 sorties on freight yards alone, while 16,000 sorties and 24,500 tons of bombs were directed exclusively against bridge targets. This amounted to an average of more than 1,000 tons a day. By just mid-July, these raids had successfully reduced the volume of German freight traffic by 57 per cent.

However, despite this success, the difficulties that the Allied ground forces were experiencing resulted in a rethink about the way the war would progress to its end; reminiscent of optimism expressed in the first weeks of World War I that the conflict would be over by Christmas 1914, such optimism was echoed in 1944. It would not be over by Christmas, and the struggle to defeat the German forces would slog on into 1945. To speed up the breakout from the Normandy region, which was proving particularly difficult, the combined Allied air power therefore focused on Operation *Cobra* – the use of overwhelming force to smash all opposition.

H-hour came on 25 July, when 1,507 B-17s and B-24s, plus more than 380 medium bombers and 559 fighter-bombers, dropped a total of 4,169 tons of bombs in an all-out effort at dislodging the Wehrmacht. German resistance built up now, following a sluggish response after D-Day when Hitler refused to accept that the Normandy landings were anything other than a distraction effort. As intelligence information began to come in, including from German prisoners, it was clear that while the casualties were relatively light for the amount of tonnage dropped, the impact on morale had been severe and the ability of the Wehrmacht to resist had been considerably reduced.

In August and September, the Allied forces pushed 400 miles eastwards and the pace now became a matter of logistical supply – new supply routes for gasoline and maintaining the requirement for munitions. Day-to-day supplies required for the ground troops also limited the rate of progress as the front line advanced up towards Paris. By mid-September, the US 3rd Army could advance only at the pace of the supply chain and was regulated by that factor alone. German forces were being overwhelmed at an increasing rate but, dangerously short on gasoline, the Allied forces were brought to a halt along the Moselle river and by the old German Siegfried Line defences. The Siegfried Line had been built during the late 1930s along a defensive position 390 miles long opposite the French Maginot Line. It had almost 20,000 defensive positions including machine gun posts, tunnels for high explosives and tank traps. It had been built primarily as defence against by the French and would later form an obstacle to Allied troops moving into Germany.

Surprisingly to their crews, as they were not intended as tactical targets supporting the Allied push, some of the bombing effort had translated into tactical support, while a significant number of aircraft had been converted into transports to deliver much-needed supplies. As the logistics situation improved and the balance was restored, a determined effort to smash up the German war machine meant that the priority was once again the destruction of German industry, factories and marshalling yards. What was now planned was, for the first time in the war, more than just an integration of objectives, defined by the Combined Bombing Offensive, but a systematic onslaught unlike anything experienced by the Germans prior to D-Day. With a total of 4,400 operational heavy bombers available to the 8th and 15th Air Forces and RAF Bomber Command, by mid-summer 1944 it was possible to put that force into action. Whereas the American bombers, preoccupied with D-Day, had been free to drop only 2,842 tons on strategic targets in June, they would drop 7,398 tons in July and 8,442 tons in August.

The strategic air offensive had prompted the Luftwaffe to assign almost exclusively to the defence of the Reich the fighters that were being built in the dispersed facilities. And this in spite of Allied raids on production facilities and oil supplies. Output from German factories had shifted to fighters in an effort to stem the round-the-clock bombing and by this date they constituted 54 per cent of all German aircraft production. By January 1945, that figure would be 81 per cent. However, during early June 1944, the German Air Fleet in the west, Luftflotte 3, had only 500 serviceable aircraft, of which only 150 were day fighters and 50 were night fighters. Of the 400 bombers on strength, only 158 were serviceable.

Although it seemed counter-intuitive at the time, German aircraft production had seemingly increased at the same rate as the proportion of bombs dropped on the factories and assembly plants, and the statistics appeared to confirm that. Away from the Normandy area, USAAF aircraft were reporting increased opposition. Fighter production provided the Luftwaffe with 2,177 single-seater fighters in June, 2,627 in July, 2,779 in August and 3,031 in September, or 4,103 if fighters of all types were included. For comparison, as recently as February that year, they had received only 1,016 aircraft of this type.

What was not fully appreciated at the time – due to a lack of intelligence, which fuelled much debate among American air units – was that the entire German aircraft manufacturing industry was in the process of being dispersed even further, to small, concealed units scattered throughout south-west and south-east Germany. Here, components were being produced and distributed to assembly facilities hidden deep inside woods, forests, caves and even tunnels, many of which had been excavated for an entirely different purpose. The work was done by the 7 million workers from the occupied countries who had been brought in as an impressed labour force to replace factory employees who had been killed by the carpet-bombing or called up to fight on the Eastern Front.

Unaware of all this, and determined to demonstrate that strategic bombing would play a major role in the outcome of the war to the satisfaction of the Allies, American Army Air Force planners began to set up a series of major air raids to crush what were believed to be the remaining industrial areas of production, which were in reality a decreasingly important set of targets. But for the immediate aftermath of D-Day, air units were required to continue their support for the invasion forces, which had priority.

Although there had been only a sluggish movement of ground forces out of the Normandy region, through the Bocage country and on to the 'breakout' drive south, east and north-east, IX Engineer Command had managed to complete the construction of an emergency landing strip on D-Day. Throughout the next several days, the 9th Air Force went all out to deploy its fighter units on French soil. Remarkably, that was achieved as early as 13 June, when the first fighters flew in. By 31 July, all but one of its 18 fighter-bomber groups was in France. The breakout itself was supported on 25 July by a saturation bombing raid with 1,503 heavy bombers and 561 fighters, from which only seven aircraft were lost.

THREATS

Yet another distraction frustrated the best efforts of Commander of Strategic Air Forces Gen Spaatz to return his air forces to the strategic objectives: a series of new weapons, which appeared that summer. On 13 June, the first Fieseler Fi-103 flying bomb, dubbed V-1 by the German propaganda ministry, was fired against England, with a further 1,000 launched over the next eight days. On 8 September, the first A4 (V-2) rockets were launched against Paris and London. Gen Eisenhower was so concerned about their capabilities that he believed the Allied invasion of Europe might have been 'impossible' had these weapons been available to the Germans six months earlier.

However, these futuristic weapons were not the only threat to expectations of an early end to the war in Europe. In August, the first Messerschmitt Me-163 Komet rocket-propelled interceptor had been declared operational, followed in October by the first Me-262 twin-jet fighters. These posed a threat to Allied bomber formations even though the Luftwaffe was struggling to make operational sense of the new technology. In just four months, the new age of the jet-powered aircraft and the rocket-propelled missile had become portents of a future arms race that was to have far-reaching consequences.

This was a window to the future that was not exclusively in the hands of the Germans. Unknown to all but a very few people in the USA and England, a team of scientists were working to build the world's first atom bomb, which would come to dominate strategic thinking in the post-war decades.

For the present, only the new Messerschmitt fighters challenged the increasing ascendancy of Allied air power, divided by necessity between strategic and tactical assignments. To counter this threat, on 19 July, aircraft factories in the Munich vicinity were hit by raids from 400 heavy bombers, adding further damage to ruinous attacks by the 8th Air Force on 11, 12 and 13 July. Five days later, 500 heavies from the 15th Air Force raided a complex of factories at Friedrichshafen. In response, the Luftwaffe sent up almost 300 fighters and lost more than 45 when 200 B-24s bombed the jet fighter assembly works. In all, these factory raids deprived the Germans of 950 aircraft.

Then, on 19 July, while the 15th Air Force was attacking Munich, the 8th Air Force put 1,082 heavy bombers on a mission to fan out right across the area and place 2,780 tons of bombs on a variety of targets. They were protected by 670 fighters from VIII Fighter Command.

And so it went on, day after day. Very often, targets would be switched on the day of the raid when weather intervened, as it did on 21 July, when 1,110 heavy bombers were sent to carpet-bomb Saint-Lô in order to clear a path for the US First Army. When cloud covered the prime target, the bombers and almost 800 fighters instead headed for southern Germany, where the B-17s and B-24s dropped a total 2,415 tons on airfields, factories and the Regensburg and Schweinfurt plants.

These attacks were becoming costly for the Allies, especially ones against heavily defended targets – locations calling for low-level strikes by aircraft designed to bomb from 20,000 ft – but they seemed to be working. Further concentrated raids against the oil refineries at Ploești, just outside Bucharest, Rumania, brought down oil production to 10 per cent of its previous level. Overall, the 15th Air Force took 59,834 airmen over this one target during the course of the war, dropping a total of 13,469 tons of bombs, for the loss of 350 heavy bombers.

The campaign came to an abrupt end in 1944 when Rumania changed sides and repatriated American airmen. Several tales emerged from this time. One related how how an airman squeezed himself into the radio compartment of a Bf-109 that had been hurriedly plastered with the stars and stripes and was flown by a Rumanian pilot to a friendly airfield in Italy. On hearing about the situation in that war-ravaged location, airmen of the 15th Air Force converted 56 B-17s into transports and flew to Ploești to bring back the former American prisoners-of-war – 1,162 of them in three days.

Not such a happy conclusion was experienced when Bulgaria surrendered the following month. Hoping to repeat the exercise, the 15th set off again to bring more ex-prisoners-of-war home but the Bulgarians had already put them on trains and sent them to Turkey, whence they were delivered to Aleppo and on to Cairo, from where the 15th finally managed to fly them out. Their sick and emaciated bodies were a shock to the airmen of the 15th, who heard at first hand about the beatings, imposed starvation and virtually non-existent medical treatment. But with the men rescued and their condition improving daily, the 15th could now turn their attention to the remaining oil resources.

In one of the most concentrated raids carried out, on 24 August almost 2,000 heavy bombers from the 8th and 15th Air Forces attacked synthetic oil plants at Merseburg-Leuna, Ruhland, Brüx and Freital, and aircraft plants at Brunswick and

Hannover. At least 30 enemy fighters were shot down. There were minimal losses to the AAF groups. The size of these raids was not uncommon; frequently massed formations of more than a thousand heavy bombers had been flying out each day, added to which were extraordinary totals contributed by night from RAF Bomber Command bases in England. From 19,635 RAF sorties in the first quarter of 1944, the intensity had grown to 37,215 in the second quarter and 54,153 in the third.

Tonnage dropped by the 8th Air Force had grown, too, increasing from 36,000 in May to 60,000 in June, 45,000 in July, 49,000 in August and 40,000 in September. Losses were increasing with the advanced intensity of operations, although loss rates per raid were now well down. Nevertheless, the 8th Air Force was losing around 300 heavies and 3,000 air crew per month, in addition to a monthly average of 150–280 fighters. For their part, the 15th Air Force experienced much heavier losses; in August, Gen Eaker estimated that 30 per cent of the 15th Air Force's air crew who had been involved in enemy engagement had been brought down on hostile territory. But if the human losses were great, so too were the achievements of the Army Air Forces, whose efforts had brought oil production in German territories down to 23 per cent of previous levels, and gasoline production somewhat less than that.

As events began to stabilize, during the late summer of 1944 priorities began to even out, the first given to the land campaign, the second to the destruction of the oil and gasoline facilities, and the third to counter-air operations. By now, the intensity of air activity was beginning to challenge the productive output of America's supply of bombs and munitions, most of which being dropped by the USAAF had to be brought over in ships. There were also some challenges regarding fuel for the aircraft, although the shortages never reached a level where they constrained operations.

Responding to the diminishing number of Luftwaffe fighters encountered, formations became smaller, fanning out so as to reduce exposure to anti-aircraft fire. Fighters would roam around instead of remaining so close to the bombers, hunting down their prey before the bombers could be attacked. With experience of flying the heavies themselves, bomber pilots were put in fighters, which would fly just ahead of the bombers and guide them round bad storms or on flight paths to cut down on condensation trails – which could act as tell-tale markers for enemy fighters some distance away.

The better summer weather, combined with an increasingly experienced cadre of air crew, allowed a significant increase in the accuracy of bomb placement. For example, the number of bombs falling within a 1,000 ft radius of the target point (known in the post-war missile era as the 'circular error probability', or CEP) grew from 18 per cent in April to 32 per cent in June and 50 per cent in August, for the 15th Air Force, and slightly less than that for the 8th Air Force. Increased value also accrued through the use of pathfinder forces and the adoption of H2X, the renamed Mk 6 version of the H2S radar system adapted by the 8th Air Force and known as 'Mickey'. Pioneered by the RAF, the system allowed 'blind bombing' accuracy to reach these improved levels and its application grew with the influx of Magnetrons shipped from America, which ran at 3 cm wavelength.

SHUTTLE RAIDING

During the summer months of 1944, a scheme pondered in the early days after Pearl Harbor was implemented, albeit for a brief period. It had occurred to the senior AAF leadership in 1942, when the Wehrmacht was at the gates of Moscow, that targets in Eastern Europe could be hit by bombers flying from England and carrying on to land in Russian-held territory. This shuttle bombing would afford access to targets that would otherwise be beyond the reach of aircraft, which had to be able to fly back to the UK, while avoiding running a second time into defensive fighter screens in western Europe. It was a concept that had been tested successfully in 1943 with flights from England to North Africa, when targets in lower Bavaria had been bombed on the way through. It would also have the advantage of inducing the Germans to spread out more thinly the air defences of the Reich and therefore minimize to some extent the vulnerability of any one raid.

In October 1943, approval was granted to approach the Russians about this idea, codenamed 'Frantic', but it received a less than enthusiastic response. The matter was raised at a higher level at the Tehran Conference in December 1943 but only on 2 February 1944 did Soviet premier Joseph Stalin agree to accommodate 200 aircraft at six bases, initially. In reality, only three airfields became available: Poltava, Mirgorod and Piryatin, not far from Kiev in Ukraine. Throughout April and May, work went on at a fast pace to transform thoroughly inadequate airfields into fully operational bases, American style, with resources pouring in through Murmansk and the Persian Gulf Command. About 1,200 US support staff moved in, despite ponderous Russian bureaucracy, and set up a new Eastern Command under USSTAF.

The expectation was that missions would fly from Italy to targets that could not normally be reached, such as the Heinkel aircraft works at Riga and at Mielec, a town near Lwów in Poland. When informed of these targets, the Russians objected, the inference being that they feared attracting attention to preparations for a ground offensive that they were building up in the area. Gen Spaatz was authorized to 'inform' the Russians rather than request approval, which seemed to work, although the desired targets were left alone for a while.

On 2 June 1944, four battle-hardened groups of 130 B-17s from the 15th Air Force and a P-51 group of 70 fighters from the 306th Wing, all led personally by Gen Eaker, flew out to bomb marshalling yards and rolling stock at Debrecen on their way to the assigned airfields in Russia. On their arrival, the Russians provided a small reception committee of local dignitaries and were most cordial in welcoming the Americans.

From their Russian bases, the Americans next launched an additional raid on 6 June, the day of the Normandy invasion, and then got stuck behind a weather front, which kept Gen Eaker grounded. The airmen were allowed to wander around the devastated and blitzed communities close by the airfields, receiving cordial friendship from the local Russians. A general sense of shared purpose infused the gatherings and hospitality was shared generously with the Americans. Finally, on 11 June, they returned to their base in Italy, bombing more targets in Rumania on the way.

However, disaster ensued after a raid on Berlin when the 8th Air Force flew on to the Russian bases. A lone Heinkel He-177 shadowed the formation and several hours later a large force of German bombers arrived overhead, dropping 110 tons of demolition bombs, incendiaries and fragmentation devices. These destroyed 43 B-17s and 15 P-51s and damaged 26 heavy bombers. The incendiaries set light to 450,000 gallons of fuel, which had been brought into Russia with meticulous care. The next night, the Germans returned again but the Americans had flown their aircraft out from Mirgorod before the raids had begun.

The event disrupted plans to place American fighter units on the bases, the Russians believing that this would only exacerbate the situation and endorse to the Germans the strategic importance of the locations. Without protection, the Americans were reluctant to relocate three heavy bomber groups to Russia. On 26 June, the surviving force of 71 Fortresses and 55 Mustangs left Russia, bombing German targets as they went on their way to Italy. Determined not to let their bombers remain more than one night in Russian bases, on several occasions over the next month mass raids by fighter bombers struck Rumanian airfields, oil plants and transport facilities. The last shuttle bombing mission took place on 11 September, departing two days later to land back in Italy.

There was one postscript to Operation *Frantic*. When a patriotic force of Poles in Warsaw rose up against the Germans, as they believed they had been urged to do by Moscow, Soviet armies who were approaching the city to fight the Germans came to a halt 6 miles from the outskirts. As the Germans set about the systematic destruction of Warsaw, the Russians remained at a distance while the British flew in relief missions, dropping supplies by night to replenish depleted stocks for the beleaguered Poles. Despite direct appeals from Washington, for reasons of their own, the Russians refused to budge. In consequence, and so as not to upset the Russians, the resupply flights ceased.

Finally, the Russians gave their approval for the drops to continue on 11 September, almost six weeks after the resistance to defend Warsaw had begun. Two days later, 107 B-17s duly dropped 1,284 containers packed with guns, small-arms ammunition, grenades, incendiaries, explosives, food and medical supplies. All but 150 containers fell directly into the hands of the Germans. No further drops took place and no bombing raids on the German lines were launched. By the end of the first week in October, the Germans had completed the eradication of the Polish Warsaw 'army', having killed 250,000 Poles in that one city. The Russians moved in in January 1945. Only long after the war did it become clear why this was so: the group who had instigated the uprising were not the one the Russians wanted in control of Poland after the Germans were evicted, and it did not serve their purpose to save them.

NEW TARGETS

Having landed on the mainland of southern Europe on 3 September 1943, and on the beaches of Normandy on 6 June 1944, the invasion of the south of France took place in and around the coastal town of Marseille on 15 August. For several weeks, a massive campaign of aerial support was organized, involving both the USAAF and the RAF. This further stretched resources in what was becoming a slog, making progress at a much less effective pace than had been planned. The breakout from the Caen area was still going much more slowly than expected and Italy was proving to be harder to liberate, now that the Italian people had taken their future in their own hands and deposed the Fascist regime.

During the thrust across France, the 9th Air Force supported the operations of Lt Gen Omar N. Bradley's 12th Army Group with IX Fighter Command, providing 1,500 P-47s, P-51s and P-38s, which were divided among the 18 groups. Command of the 9th switched from Gen Brereton to Maj Gen Hoyt S. Vandenberg during the course of the campaign. It fell to the 9th Air Force to do most of the tactical air support for the advancing American armies. By the time they reached France's eastern border it had brought over to Continental Europe the command structure and logistics bases and had begun to build the

241 airfields that would eventually support the Allied offensive against Germany itself. In a contested attempt by Gen Montgomery to spring north, capture vital bridges across the Rhine at Arnhem and charge into Germany across the north European plains, outflanking the main defences of the Ruhr, on 17 September the Allied air forces flew 1,500 transport aircraft and 500 gliders, protected by more than 1,300 fighters, across the North Sea to land 20,000 troops by parachute and glider. Supporting this, the 8th Air Force had 'softened up' the area the day before when 821 B-17s dropped 3,139 tons of bombs, supported by 644 fighters. In direct support of the Arnhem operation, 248 B-24s dropped freight for land forces, protected by 575 fighters, which also carried out ground strafing.

The Arnhem landings were not successful, despite heroic efforts by the troops and airmen involved, and as winter set in the German position was getting increasingly perilous. In October, there were 56 Allied divisions on mainland Europe, in November 69 and by February there would be 81. A major change in command and control of British and American units came on 15 October when the headquarters of the Allied Expeditionary Air Forces was disbanded and all air power was moved to the direct control of Gen Eisenhower in his role as Supreme Commander, with Air Chf Mshl Sir Arthur Tedder as his deputy.

Completely unknown to the Allies, the Germans had been preparing for an offensive through the Ardennes region in a desperate bid to reach the coast and split the Allies, in what would become famous as the Battle of the Bulge. Indeed, just 18 hours before the Germans struck, briefing air commanders, Eisenhower's team dismissed the Ardennes as 'nothing to report'. However, in the early morning hours of 16 December, the Sixth Panzer Army launched an all-out offensive on a 25-mile front and while Luftwaffe operations were quiet that day, on 17 December the Jagdwaffe flew in great strength. These were countered by the AAF flying 647 sorties.

Hampered by exceptionally bad weather – fog and low cloud – all air operations were restricted to sporadic engagement, until the weather cleared on 23 December as a high-pressure area drifted west and for five days completely cleared away all the murk and mist. Tactical support for the ground forces, halting and reversing the Wehrmacht's westward surge, which had been achieved only as a result of inclement weather, was expanded.

The biggest bombing operation in the history of the war took place on Christmas Eve 1944 when 2,046 heavy bombers took off, escorted by 853 fighters, to attack strategic targets. The 1,884 bombers effective over their separate targets dropped 5,052 tons of bombs. Losses amounted to 12 bombers and twin fighters, on a day when IX Troop Carrier Command sent 160 aircraft to drop 319,412 lb of essential supplies to Allied forces in the Bastogne area.

The following day, 25 December, the 9th Air Force flew 1,920 sorties, including 1,100 fighter-bombers, the medium bombers dropping 1,237 tons of munitions to disrupt enemy rail movements and road operations within this base area. By the following day, the German ground forces were unable to resist the remorseless attacks from the US Third Army and the march to the Rhine resumed, the 2nd Panzer Division completely smashed, the roads so scarred that even motorcycles found it difficult to travel.

NEW CONCERNS

On 4 December, war leaders had gathered at Supreme Headquarters Allied Expeditionary Force, Bushey Park, just outside London, to discuss the way the war could be brought to a swift conclusion. The general consensus was that it could drag on for most of 1945, if not longer, and this despite extraordinary resources, outstanding performance from the AAF and almost unlimited opportunities. But still German resistance was solid and seemingly unbreakable. Assistant Secretary of War for Air Robert A. Lovett asked Gen Arnold whether the American armed forces had not been trying to do too much too soon. The Germans were fighting a total war on their own borders with shortened lines of communication and had excelled in several new types of weapon.

A few weeks later, in January 1945, the sombre mood persisted at Supreme Headquarters Allied Expeditionary Forces and at USSTAF, with Gen Arnold writing to Gen Spaatz that: 'We have a superiority of at least 5 to 1 now against Germany and yet, in spite of all our hopes, anticipations, dreams and plans, we have as yet not been able to capitalise to the extent which we should.' But great lessons were being learned through the melancholy overview, fuelled by a misjudgement about the true level of remaining German military capabilities.

At face value, German jet fighter production was accelerating, new classes of weapons were appearing in ever-greater numbers and there was a belief that a new wonder-weapon, a V-3, might be deployed at any time. In reality, the Germans were in a worse condition than anyone realized. Despite this, the inventory of German single-engine fighters increased from 1,260 in September to 1,700 in November and 2,040 in December, while a massive retraining programme put bomber pilots in fighters to replenish units. The diversified production plan orchestrated by Minister of Production Albert Speer largely dispersed 27 primary manufacturing and assembly facilities into 729 smaller units in remote locations.

With the full scale of German production diversification unknown to the Allies, about three-quarters of the USSTAF effort was committed to tactical targets, together with a similar proportion of RAF Bomber Command. And, despite the relatively small commitment to strategic targets, this was effective at reducing the oil output and gasoline production – even though poor weather conditions generally hampered the air war throughout January. When the Combined Chiefs of Staff met in Malta on 30 January 1945 – just prior to the Yalta Conference between Roosevelt, Churchill and Stalin – the ground forces, with air support, had reversed the German surge into the Ardenne, reached the River Rhine and heard that Russian armies were advancing into German Silesia and Upper Prussia.

It was thereupon agreed that the might of strategic air power would be unleashed to support the campaign in the East. This decision covered air operations by the 8th Air Force and RAF Bomber Command and would result in a major effort being mounted against cities such as Berlin, Leipzig and Dresden (the latter being specifically requested by the Russians). This requirement was urged upon the British and American air planners so as to break up armoured resistance in and around the big urban agglomerations ahead of the advancing Red Army.

After several weeks of little bombing effort against the German capital, on 3 February 1945 the 8th Air Force sent up nearly 1,500 heavy bombers and 948 fighters to Berlin. Of these, 1,370 bombers were effective, dropping nearly 3,300 tons of bombs. Most of the city was free of cloud, ensuring accurate bombing and bringing extremely high levels of civilian casualties. This in itself brought questions in high places since the senior leadership of the AAF had been unanimously opposed to the indiscriminate bombing of city areas with its attendant loss of civilian life. Operational commanders explained that targets were in fact transportation facilities. This ruminating dialogue continued while the 8th Air Force and RAF Bomber Command were laying waste to large areas of Dresden, Cottbus, Magdeburg and Chemnitz.

Concern for the lives of air crew had worried US Army leaders in World War I, when Gen Pershing had wanted to replace piloted bombers with unmanned radio-controlled aircraft to deliver bombloads on enemy positions. Some 20 years later, in 1944, a similar plan was proposed. This involved using 'war-weary' B-17s stripped of armour and guns and loaded with 20,000 lb of explosives. Guided into the air by a pilot who would then bail out, the unmanned projectile would be controlled by radio signal from a 'mother' ship close by. By 1 January 1945, six missions had been carried out. None of them had been successful.

During February, the 8th and 9th Air Forces hammered away at mainly strategic targets, with 234,800 tons of bombs going on the oil campaign. By now, the Russians had liberated large areas of Poland, Hungary and Silesia, where the Germans had synthetic plants. These raids also helped erode the production of jet and rocket fighters and the attention paid by the RAF to German cities finally brought an end to the economic life of the Third Reich, immobilizing millions of workers, together with impressed foreign labourers, and freezing Germany's once efficient rail network.

As Austria was overrun, the 15th Air Force turned on the German jets – something Gen Eaker had long itched to do – and bombed the facilities at Regensburg where the type was being built. With pressure now building towards a crescendo of activity, Operation *Clarion* was put into play. This saw all available Anglo-American air power being put into the sky to strike a major blow against German communications, hitting at both economic life and the tactical requirements of the war. This operation came out of the planned Operation *Hurricane*, which proposed a mighty assault on the German people themselves, but which had been outlawed by the leadership on grounds that it was tantamount to terror bombing.

Despite this ruling and averred avoidance of terror bombing, one city in particular – the ancient and historic Dresden – was subjected to four devastating raids between 13 and 15 February. These would forever epitomize the dilemma facing those who advocated the area bombing of cities in the hope of ending the war. The raid occurred at a pivotal point after the Wehrmacht had lost the Battle of the Bulge and the Russians were within 45 miles of Berlin. Indisputably, the Germans had already lost the war; what was not clear was just when a formal surrender might take place. The Germans had already been told in a statement from President Roosevelt in 1943 that there could be no conditional surrender. Only total, unconditional surrender implying the full occupation of Germany by Allied forces was possible.

Alone within the Nazi hierarchy, Hitler refused to pursue any form of surrender. If Hitler had been assassinated in July 1944 by the unsuccessful bomb plot orchestrated by some in senior social, military and political circles, and replaced as head of state, there is little doubt that the leadership may have considered a conditional surrender to prevent total occupation of their country. But that did not happen. So, late in January 1945 the RAF was called upon to conduct a bombing raid on Dresden, which at the time was a defended city – meaning it was a garrison for the Wehrmacht as well as containing many industrial facilities, 110 factories operating for the war effort and 50,000 workers in that industry.

At the turn of the year, intelligence decoded at Bletchley Park had revealed that the Wehrmacht was moving large numbers of troops into eastern Germany and consolidating the military presence around the city. The Russians saw this as a potential obstacle to their fight to reach Berlin and requested that the British and the Americans destroy the city to prevent consolidation of German forces. Moreover, an intelligence assessment delivered to Churchill indicated that if the Germans did consolidate on the East, they could hold the Western Allies at the Rhine and continue the fight with the Russians until at least November. Fearing that the dash for Berlin could stall, it was therefore decided to assist the Russians in any way that would prevent that.

The raids on Dresden were the only activation of a plan known as Operation *Thunderclap*, considered in summer 1944 but cancelled that August due to it being too severe and counter-productive. As conceived, *Thunderclap* would have brought US and British air power to converge on several major German cities, starting with Berlin, in a co-ordinated series of raids that aimed to totally and completely destroy all physical remains of those urban areas.

To explain the thinking behind this proposal, it has to be remembered that so horrified were the Allies at the physical destruction and human suffering meted out by the Nazis that political groups in the USA were calling for the complete post-war deindustrialization of Germany, forever consigning them to a village and agrarian lifestyle. The political economist Henry Morgenthau convinced Roosevelt to write to Secretary of State Cordell Hull and Secretary of War Henry Stimson affirming a policy after the war of having the Germans 'fed three times a day with soup from Army soup kitchens' so that they would 'remember that experience for the rest of their lives'.

In response, Roosevelt said, 'We either have to castrate the German people or treat them in such a manner that they can't go on reproducing people who want to continue [to behave] as they have in the past.' This was a prevalent view – something that has been lost to many historians now, long after those events – and it helps to explain what motivated the destructive bombing of cities. In balance, when told that such an operation could result in the death of 40 per cent of the German population, Roosevelt recanted his extreme view.

In this context, the implementation of the raids on 13–15 February appear not so unusual, given the military imperative and the uncertainties of the time. Nevertheless, in those raids the Allies dropped 2,900 tons of high explosives and incendiaries on a city that was crammed with civilians, military personnel and munitions workers. In the first raid, the RAF dropped 500 lb and 4,000 lb 'cookies' – high explosives used to blast walls and blow out doors and windows to create oxygen funnels to allow the passage of fire and flame from the incendiaries. In a period of just 15 minutes, the Lancasters released 881 tons of bombs on an area measuring merely 1.25 miles by 1.75 miles. Estimates of the casualties vary but it is probable that at least 25,000 people were killed in Dresden, for the loss of seven aircraft.

Elsewhere, there had been a near revolt among Polish air crew who had learned that night about the decision at the Yalta Conference that Russia was to have vast swathes of Poland after the war. Many of them threatened to rebel, so their British officers removed their side arms. However, in the end the Poles responded to a plea from the Polish government in exile for them to do their duty, which they did.

END GAME

On 22–23 February, an intensive and sustained bombing and strafing assault was conducted by the 8th and 9th Air Forces against all forms of communications. USAAF fighter pilots were told to strafe fleeing escapees on the ground in order to heighten confusion and chaps – the Germans reported that very few incidents of this nature were reported. Few too were the German fighters now seen in the sky. This meant that the bombers were able to drop their loads from 10,000 ft due to the reduced level of anti-aircraft fire, which allowed them to attack in small groups. These were so successful that the heavy bombers were able to switch from tactical attacks and return to their strategic targets.

In March, the AAF briefly experienced the potential of the Germans' jets and rocket planes as Me-262s and Me-163s attacked in force, seeming to play with the P-51s until the latter got the better of them and began to shoot them down. The Me-262 was fast and nimble but power levels in the early jet engines were not conducive to rapid thrust changes and the aircraft had little low-speed performance. This left them vulnerable when coming in to land, providing opportunities for ambush that were seized by the P-51s.

All the while, the RAF kept up its nightly raids on industrial and urban areas, on 11 March dropping the largest ever weight of bombs on a single target when 1,079 aircraft put down 4,738 tons on Essen, exceeded the day after when 4,899 tons were dropped on Dortmund. Meanwhile, the 15th Air Force was expending two-thirds of its efforts on transportation raids and the rest on the oil campaign.

Throughout the month, the heavies kept up an unremitting assault on towns and cities that had already been bombed, preventing clearance and reconstitution in order to maintain total paralysis and disruption to normal life. In the closing weeks of the war, the ferocity increased to a height not seen before – a determination driven on by the intensity of German military resistance.

The assault on the Rhine began on 21 March when 2,000 bombers from the 8th Air Force, the 9th AAir Forces and RAF Bomber Command hit German defensive positions, followed by further raids of similar size on the following day. Three days later, the RAF bombed Wesel, now almost abandoned by the civilian population, and the Army subjected it to an intensive artillery bombardment. Eyewitnesses told of the ground heaving up and down like a trampoline under the shockwaves from the bombs and shells pounding the land.

After providing support for the crossing of the Rhine by Allied forces, the 8th Air Force resumed its attacks on the already dwindling number of strategic targets. Each day, more than a thousand bombers were assigned to ports around Wilhelmshaven and Hamburg and oil and industrial facilities. During the last days of March, RAF Bomber Command exceeded its own previous weekly record by dropping 67,365 tons of bombs, the final onslaught affecting Hannover, Paderborn, Münster, Hamburg and Osnabrück. Elsewhere, in mid-April the 8th Air Force sent more than 1,200 bombers to drop incendiaries, napalm and 2,000 lb demolition bombs on garrisons still holding out in the Bordeaux area.

The incessant raids in support of the ground campaign achieved consistent results despite the dwindling list of targets for industrial demolition from the air. Most of the tactical support operations in the final weeks of the war were carried out by the 9th Air Force. The intensity of the bombing campaign had been growing and had reached a peak. Of all the bombs dropped on Germany during the war, 72 per cent had been dropped after 1 July 1944.

Proselytized by Hollywood film-makers and popular literature, it was claimed that it was the American Army Air Forces who liberated Europe from Nazi tyranny; largely, it is often said, by US bombers pounding the heart out of Germany's industrial war machine. The statistics tell a very different story. Of more than 68,000 tons of bombs dropped on Berlin, the RAF delivered two-thirds; of the 48,000 tons dropped on Cologne, Bomber Command was accountable for 72 per cent; and of the 38,300 tons dropped on Hamburg, 59 per cent were courtesy of the RAF. Bomber Command was responsible for 99 per cent of the bombs dropped on the vast industrial city of Essen, with its massive Krupps works, 98 per cent on Duisberg and 56 per cent on Kiel and Frankfurt.

The extensive bombing had driven the majority of the German population from their homes and their cities, with the mass movement of civilians reaching a peak of 25 million people – all looking for homes, adult relatives, their friends and in many cases their children. It is impossible to know the precise number of German civilians killed by the Allied bombing but a reasonably safe figure is about 650,000 – tenfold the number of British civilians killed during the war.

Of the remaining urban areas, the cities were hollow shells, not just in terms of smashed buildings and crushed rubble but also in the human vacuum created by the majority who fled.

By May 1945, just 20,000 people remained in Cologne of a prewar population exceeding 770,000. The population of Essen, Dusseldorf and Frankfurt shrank to less than half while Munich lost 41 per cent, Berlin 40 per cent and Hamburg 35 per cent. The bombs were impersonal in that the dead and mortally wounded were an indiscriminate distribution of civilians, prisoners-of-war, slave labourers and uniformed officials, not counting military personnel. In November 1944 alone, bombing in Germany killed 17,440 of which 84 per cent were civilians.

Elsewhere, French towns, villages and a few cities were bombed in order to suppress Nazi activity and to destroy munitions factories, marshalling yards and camps carrying out work for the Germans under the agreement signed by the Vichy government. Between the invasion of France and the end of the war, 53,601 French civilians died as a result of these activities, 85,316 buildings had been destroyed and a further 183,103 seriously damaged. There had been debate among the Allies about the bombing of French targets, a not inconsiderable level of opposition being raised. In the end, like the war itself, the bombing had taken on a life of its own, seemingly unstoppable by mere mortals.

But the air war had been about a lot more than the attacking bombers and the defending fighters. As the pendulum swung in favour of the Allies, evolved versions of aircraft that first saw combat at the start of the war joined new types that had been developed since the conflict began, on raiding flights across the western corner of Nazi-occupied Europe. Aircraft such as the Typhoon and the later marks of Spitfire, with infinitely greater performance and fighting capability, created havoc on roads, railways, marshalling yards, airfields, military barracks and a host of specialized targets.

On 30 April 1945, Hitler committed suicide and on 8 May the war was over. Between these dates, during the first week of May, the 8th Air Force flew 4,147.1 tons of emergency food, dropped to the starving populations of distressed and famine-stricken Netherlands and surrounding areas. With the war technically still going on, the Germans acquiesced to this humanitarian assistance, and together with the RAF, US air forces dropped in total some 11,000 tons of food rations.

As a final mark of gratitude for the work they had done to keep the bombers armed and flying and the air crew equipped and fed, around 30,000 RAF ground personnel were taken on sightseeing tours by air of the targets they had sent the aircraft to bomb. These tours aroused mixed emotions; the sheer scale of destruction was hard to convey in words and many came back deeply affected by what they had seen, all awed by the intensity of the strategic and tactical air offensive against Nazi Germany.

THE TENACIOUS MOSQUITO

One aircraft in particular, the de Havilland Mosquito, stands out for its high performance and flexibility. For daylight attack, low-level operations and sheer carrying capacity for its size, the Mosquito outperformed many other types. With the range to attack Berlin, to serve as a pathfinder for bomber streams and to carry a miniaturized version of Barnes Wallis' dambusting bomb, it also served as a highly effective night fighter and photo-reconnaissance aircraft, identifying many places that became high-priority targets due to their importance.

Amid many tales of derring-do, there is one raid that stands out. Conducted from a height only marginally above the line of trees and telegraph poles, the attack on the Amiens prison on 18 February 1944 was notable in its audacity, bravery and success. It involved nine Mosquitoes, which blew a hole in the wall surrounding a containment area for French resistance workers and political prisoners incarcerated for interrogation, torture and execution. It had been learned that more than 100 were to have been shot on the following day. The breach allowed 255 prisoners to escape with the loss of four air crew. Regrettably, 182 were eventually recaptured and the Germans killed 260 in reprisals. It is often claimed that the French resistance asked for the raid, but that is not so. In what is still a classified operation, the Secret Intelligence Service requested what was, even for the RAF, a highly skilled operation. We may never know the real reason for the request.

Although referring to the airmen and ground crew of RAF Bomber Command, Sir Arthur Harris was well aware of the contribution made by all air crew of the Allied air forces who, by night and by day, had put themselves in harm's way to achieve the defeat of a totalitarian power and to liberate occupied Europe when he poignantly addressed the contribution made by both the RAF and the US Army Air Forces: 'It is to them and their kind that Britain today is not a mere slave market in a Nazi Empire. That was the Plan. Never forget it.'

Following the end of the war, political judgement lifted its gaze to a more reflective and distant horizon and was more visionary, full of relief and a sense of opportunity; having survived five awful years of war and carnage, nothing would deny the surviving generation a better future. Winston Churchill, as eloquent as ever, put it in words that were read in the US Congress on 16 August 1945: 'When we look back on all the perils we have laid low and all the dark designs we have frustrated, why should we fear for our future? We have come safely through the worst.'

Yet even as the aftermath of war in Europe was emerging, the forces of a new confrontation were continuing to suck in ever-greater munitions and logistical requirements from the USA, as the USAAF geared up for a major air assault on mainland Japan. All the indications were that this would be the biggest bloodbath of the war – for the Japanese, if their homeland were invaded, would fight to the very last man, woman and child. In anticipation of joining the Americans in liberating the occupied countries of South-east Asia, therefore, the British prepared to sail east and join their US cousins.

Chapter 17
A Rain of Ruin

THE JAPANESE had conquered Burma by June 1942 and severed the vital supply route with China along the Burma Road. Elsewhere, the monsoons had brought the Japanese invasion of India to a halt, allowing the British to begin a consolidation of effort to prevent a complete occupation of the Indian subcontinent from where Japanese forces could dominate the Indian Ocean.

The American Volunteer Group (AVG), also known as the Flying Tigers, had been organized by Brig Gen Claire L. Chennault on behalf of China to defend the Burma Road and to assist the Chinese army with air support. Chennault was called back to active duty and promoted to brigadier general, at a time when the AVG had only 30 P-40 Warhawk fighters and seven B-25 Mitchell bombers.

Elsewhere in the region, Gen Brereton had taken over command of the newly formed 10th Air Force in Delhi on 5 March. However, he was ordered out to the Middle East in June when the defences of Egypt came under threat. The number of German forces overwhelming the British in North Africa and marching on India from the west while the Japanese were advancing upon it from the east made 1942 one of the most critical periods of the whole war. What's more, because of that redeployment, for a while the 10th Air Fleet was left without a single combat unit in the region.

The decision was made in Washington DC that resupply for the Chinese forces fighting the Japanese was as important as the US combat missions in the region. This was because the loss of Burma made it vital to supply Chinese forces from India. However, doing so involved flying 'over the Hump' of the Himalayas – through passes 14,000 ft high and over peaks of 16,500 ft. Monsoons brought violent storms throughout the Himalayas and C-47 Skytrain transport aircraft, a militarized version of the DC-3 Dakota, were hard pressed to maintain the air bridge.

After 1 December 1942, with the establishment of the AAF Air Transport Command, the situation gradually began to improve and 2,800 tons of supplies were moved in February 1943 – a figure that was still below the minimum 3,500 tons considered necessary. However, by October that had increased to 7,000 tons and to 12,000 each month during the first six months of 1944, reaching a peak of 71,000 tons in July 1945.

The 14th Air Force was established in China at the specific order of President Roosevelt on 10 March 1943, with Chennault in charge and now promoted to major general. Tasked with harrying the Japanese at every opportunity, the 14th made it possible for the Chinese to receive sustained air support, which they would not have had otherwise. But having the 10th Air Force down in India, the juxtaposition of regional commanders in disagreement, and a highly spirited defence of their own individual units, conflict at an administrative level was a serious impediment to progress. Maj Gen George E. Stratemeyer, commander of all US forces in the theatre between 1943 and 1945, described the situation as an unusual animal, 'all headquarters and no hindquarters!'

It was only with the combined help of these air forces and of the British forces in the Indian border area – along with the aid of more than 20,000 tons of supplies for the 150,000 British soldiers there – that the Japanese were gradually pushed further back from Imphal. In May and June, the British Fourteenth Army drove the Japanese back but had it not been for air support the situation could well have been different; the American air forces had made the critical difference with transports and combat air units in both India and China. To consolidate the pressure on the Japanese, American transport aircraft such as the C-46 Commando and the C-47 Skytrain were brought in, along with a special US air commando unit, famously known as the Chindits. Supplied entirely from the air, these long-range penetration groups struck effectively at Japanese positions, releasing their grip on Burma.

The Chindits weren't alone. A Chinese corps trained by the Americans, known as 'Merrill's Marauders', also advanced through the jungles sustained entirely by accurate air drops of supplies as they advanced on the Japanese, taking the airfield at Myitkyina in Burma in May 1944. With supplies now lifted directly to the airfields, the corps reopened the Burma Road to China in January 1945, beginning the long and tortuous roll-back of Japanese forces. Supported by bombers and fighters from the 10th Air Force, the British drove all before them, the tactical air forces harrying the enemy all the way. This represented a unique 'first' in that all the support for the Fourteenth Army was delivered by air drop alone. By April 1945, the Anglo-American Combat Cargo Task Force had supplied a total of 345,000 advancing troops.

The situation had been rather different in China, where from the spring of 1944 a sustained and heavy Japanese assault drove Chennault's men deep into the interior of China, the enemy steamrolling the tired and demoralized Chinese forces. As the situation got better in Burma, two American-trained Chinese divisions were airlifted from there to China in December 1944 and, supported by the 14th Air Force, they mounted a vigorous counter-offensive in March 1945. With help from the 14th Air Force, flying supply mission over the Himalayas, the Chinese fought back and retook ground, all supported by air power. Had this not happened, a high-ranking Japanese officer claimed after the war that 'we [the Japanese] could have gone anywhere we wished'.

THE BIG PUNCH

While an enormous effort was made to support the ground operations that were essential to stemming Japanese invasion plans and turning them back from further and more ambitious goals, air power was being exploited where it was most needed through transport and logistical supply drops, the movement of men and materiel, and in casualty evacuation by air. When President Roosevelt and Prime Minister Churchill met in Washington during May 1943 for the Trident Conference, they had the historically significant task of deciding the best way to use a single aeroplane type to drive a new strategy that would be pivotal to the defeat of Imperial Japan.

That aircraft was the Boeing B-29 Superfortress, which emerged from a multiplicity of requirements, proposals and design concepts rather than a single all-embracing specification. In March 1938, the AAF had sought a version of the B-17 with pressurized crew compartments and a tricycle undercarriage. While the AAC was at that time heavily committed to buying the B-17, there was little money for a new aeroplane and Boeing, again, put in its own money for the Model 334A proposal of July 1939, with a mock-up completed in the December. The following month, the Army began to define what it really wanted: a 400 mph aircraft with a range of 5,333 miles and a 2,000 lb bomb load delivered at half that distance.

Benefitting from the experience of the European aircraft designers with regard to armament, sealed fuel tanks and armour, the revised Model 345 was proposed on 11 May 1940. It got attention and the Army found some money for wind tunnel tests, contracting two prototypes on 24 August with a third added on 6 September. The Army became so excited by the possibilities that were opened up by this aircraft that in May 1941 it placed an order for 250, increased to 500 in January 1942. With fully pressurized cabins, a great increase in range, unprecedented load-carrying capacity and armament employing remote-controlled power gun turrets, this aircraft was quite unlike anything in the skies at that time. Indeed, it heralded the age of the superbomber – a line of uniquely American bombers that would begin with the B-29 and proceed on through the B-36 and eventually the B-52.

The possibilities opened up by superbombers gripped the imagination of the Army Air Force to the extent that in late 1940, when many felt that Britain was under imminent threat from invasion, it considered that the USA could one day have to fight Nazi Germany from mainland USA. On 11 April 1941, it issued a requirement for an even larger and more capable aircraft, one with a standard bomb load of 10,000 lb, a maximum bomb load of 72,000 lb, a maximum speed of up to 300 mph and a range of 5,000 miles. This was unprecedented and energized a completely new way of thinking about strategic warfare.

From four designs submitted, Consolidated's Model 37 with slightly swept back wings, six pusher engines and twin tail fins and rudders was selected, and two prototypes were ordered as the XB-36. This was highly significant; the only other aircraft to be ordered into production off the drawing board had been the B-26 Marauder, in 1939. Work was slow due to priority being placed on B-24 production but in 1943 activity was speeded up when it appeared that the type would be needed to bomb Japan from existing bases in the Pacific. A contract was awarded for 100 aircraft on 23 July 1943, by which time the design had changed to give the B-36 a single vertical tail and rudder. Which brings us back to the Trident Conference, just before the decision to accelerate B-29 flight test and production.

The imminent availability of the B-29 was assured by a successful first flight on 21 September 1942, with the second aircraft flying seven days later. The aircraft was sufficiently impressive to be imported as a plan-changing asset portending a new generation of technology in bomber capabilities. It was for this reason it was discussed by Roosevelt and Churchill as a means of taking the war directly to the Japanese mainland – an objective that had hitherto been frustratingly difficult to achieve due to the great distance bombers would have to fly to both reach and return from their targets.

Now, with North Africa safely back in Allied hands and the strategic bombing campaign of Germany under way, the two leaders agreed to step up commitment to the war against Japan, having already stemmed the tide of the Japanese eastwards at Midway and southwards at the Solomon Islands and New Guinea. Considered options were along two separate and conflicting tracks: the first was that an end to the war in Europe could be achieved by December 1944, freeing forces at that time for redeployment to the Pacific; the second, that flagging progress in Burma and China was causing the Chongqing government to grow suspicious of American intentions and sue for peace with Japan. However, the latter could not wait, and the B-29 seemed to provide an answer.

While support for the Chinese had been strong, the war could not be won from there. This was because mounting a front against the Japanese involved going over the top of the Himalayas, which was out of the question. That said, the B-29s could attack targets in Japan from bases in China if they were to deploy there and bolster the Chinese effort, reinvigorating the Chongqing government to greater efforts. In the end, the decision was postponed both at the Trident and the Quebec conferences in August and another in Cairo that November, although tacit agreement had been made to deploy the superbomber to bases in China.

The AAF proposed to build a chain of airfields along a 400-mile-long axis north and south of Changsha in the Hunan Province. This was located 1,500 miles from most of Japan's industries, which meant the B-29s could reach them. The expectation was that with groups flying five missions a month at 50 per cent strength, 168 group-months would suffice to destroy the designated targets within a 12-month period. Logistical support for these forward bases would be effected through B-24s released from Europe and converted into transports (C-87s) with 200 per B-29 group, 2,000 by October 1944 and 4,000 by May 1945. Ports were adequately placed to move in a total of 596,000 tons per month. By this date, B-29 groups could fly 500 sorties per month with Calcutta – where the B-29s would be primarily based – handling 58,000 tons a month.

STRATEGIC AIR POWER

The discontinuity in operational control of the China-Burma-India (CBI) theatre of operations reverberated through the Army Air Force command structure. Gen Arnold was well aware of the problem of strategic air power ostensibly being siphoned off to tactical support for ground forces, causing distraction where there should be focus and agreement. With the imminent availability of the B-29, Arnold was determined that this would not be the case with the superbomber, now officially categorized as a Very Heavy Bomber – an aircraft type wholly unsuited to diversified roles other than as a weapon of ultimate strategic power.

In the two years since Pearl Harbor, command procedures for Army air forces had taken on a standardized pattern, where air units were assigned to theatre commanders working under broad directives from the Joint or Combined Chiefs of Staff. These units were organized into a theatre air force, given a number and divided into fighter, fighter-bomber, air service, etc. Although the theatre commander had control of the air as well as of the ground forces, he usually afforded an air force commander wide latitude in how air power might be used.

This system had proved eminently sensible and generally worked well, but with the advent of a strategic offensive from the air – independent of land or sea operations at a tactical level – there could be difficulties. To avoid those, Gen Arnold followed the precedent set when the Combined Bomber Offensive had been agreed with the Royal Air Force on 21 January 1943, and, in reality, set the stage for an independent air force. He wanted a very different structure and it was in support of this that the 20th Air Force was set up on 4 April 1944, with Arnold in command. This was to operate completely autonomously; in all but designation, it operated as a separate Air Force from the Army command structure. It was an indication of what would come three years later with the formation of a completely independent US Air Force, and it was also the precursor to Strategic Air Command, dedicated to strategic warfare. Six days later, on 10 April 1944, the Joint Chiefs agreed to the strategic bombardment of Japan.

As to the employment of the B-29, that proved more difficult than expected as the giant aircraft required considerable conversion training for command, flight and ground crew alike. Substitute aircraft were employed to speed up the process and familiarization training required bespoke tuition and attainment. This was because the level of technical expertise required to man the aircraft was highly specialized when compared to the B-17 and the B-24.

The first B-29 unit, the 58th Bombardment Wing (Very Heavy) was activated on 1 June 1943, and a previous expectation that the aircraft would be used in the European theatre of war was cancelled at the end of 1943. It was to concentrate its use with XX Bomber Command – which had been formed on 19 November 1943 before moving to Kharagpur, India, in early 1944 – and begin bombing operations against the Japanese mainland from forward bases in China.

The 58th Bombardment Wing arrived there on 28 March, under the command of Maj Gen Kenneth B. Wolfe, and after a short period of training, the first mission was flown on 5 June 1944 against the Japanese-held city of Bangkok. Some 98 B-29s flew out from India and 77 dropped 368 tons of bombs on the railroad shops. Five were lost due to technical problems and crew error. The remaining aircraft landed back at the forward staging airfields in China and then returned to India. The aircraft was going to take some time to bed in, and the familiarization programme was modified. The second mission took place on 15 June, when 68 Superfortresses, as the B-29 was named, left by night from their staging field at Chengdu. Only 37 bombed their target, the Imperial Iron and Steel Works at Yawata – the first raid on mainland Japan since the Doolittle Raid of April 1942. One B-29 was shot down, the first combat loss of this type.

Gen Arnold had been dissatisfied with Maj Gen Wolfe's performance and replaced him with Brig Gen LaVerne G. Sanders on 6 July. This was only as a temporary measure, however, until Maj Gen Curtis E. LeMay could arrive from the European theatre, which he did to take command of XX Bomber Command from 29 August 1944. Meanwhile, the second full-scale strike against Japan did not take place until 7 July when 14 B-29s bombed Sasebo, Omura and Tobata. Three other Superfortresses attacked secondary targets. However, the sheer scale of mounting operations in this way was unsustainable in the long term. Several B-29s had to be converted to lift supplies and fuel to the Chengdu base and for each aircraft sent on a bombing mission, six B-29s were required to provide the fuel, the munitions and the supplies to maintain the aircraft. Fortunately for the Allies, a solution had already been found.

On 12 March 1945, the Joint Chiefs of Staff had ordered Adm Chester W. Nimitz, chief of naval operations in the Pacific, to seize the Marianas islands for the use of Boeing B-29 Superfortress bombers by 15 June, so that this mighty aircraft could make its operational debut against targets on mainland Japan from bases hewn out of these atolls. Consisting of Saipan, Tinian and Guam, the Marianas were about 1,500 miles from Tokyo and would operate as an effective base from which to operate, being easily resupplied by sea.

Five great airfields were built there, each occupied by a VHB (Very Heavy Bombardment) wing, with two on Guam, one on Saipan and two on Tinian. Guam also supported an air depot, headquarters for XXI Bomber Command (which merged to become the 20th Air Force) and a forward headquarters. Later, Iwo Jima was converted into a giant airbase for staging B-29s and for the use of long-range fighter aircraft. None of the original schedule held up and only on Saipan was base development even partially met. Runways 8,500 ft long by 150 ft wide had to be laid down in a major engineering exercise that required considerable resources.

The entire operation grew commensurate with the capability of the B-29 force and a new command and control authority was needed. The United States Strategic Air Forces in the Pacific (USASTAF) was duly formed on 6 June 1945, with headquarters on Guam. Commanded by Gen Spaatz, it was the operational equivalent of the USSTAF, which had been formed to govern overall command of US air forces in Europe. Operational deployment of the B-29s to the Marianas built up while operations with XXI Bomber Command continued to fly costly and not altogether successful missions from India to forward bases in China and on to Japan.

The situation in China was complicated: a revolutionary war triggered by Mao Zedong against the imperial government of Chiang Kai-shek had been put on hold when both sides agreed to suspend the brutal conflict in the long-term interests of China. Gen LeMay negotiated with Mao, who offered better bases further north, in the territory the Communist rebels had control over, but the range from that location to the Japanese mainland was too far for the B-29s. Interestingly, immediately after the war, when US government diplomats met with Mao they found his military units more disciplined and effective than those of Chiang Kai-Shek.

TARGETED WARFARE

The first B-29s arrived at the new airfield on Saipan on 12 October 1944. Preparations were made to begin air raids against Japanese industrial and military targets. Becoming operational was a major task, with a lot of infrastructure required to support the long-distance raids – targets were as far from the Marianas as London is from Moscow. Eventually, 20 bomber groups would operate from these islands, though the build-up was slow, over time bringing incredible operational results. The number of personnel alone is indicative of the commitment. In August 1944 there were 51,230 AAF personnel in the theatre, growing to 166,345 by mid-July 1945, many of them in aviation engineer battalions organized by the Engineer Aviation Regiments on Okinawa. The number of aircraft grew from 999 of all types in August 1944 to 2,006 on hand in mid-July 1945. The number of B-29s alone grew from none to 59 by the end of November and 985 in mid-July 1945. Peak delivery had been achieved in April 1945, with 177 flying in, and with 451 P-47N fighters arriving between March and July and 348 by July 1945. The P-38s and P-39s were soon made redundant, while the number of B-17s in theatre remained at the same mediocre levels – evidence of the changing nature of air warfare where a new and infusive technology was making redundant weapons of war that only a few months before had helped to win the fight against Hitler.

Logistical demands on bringing in adequate quantities of bombs reached new heights, in part because the B-29 was capable of carrying more than twice the load of a B-17 or a B-24. Gen Arnold stipulated a four-month supply of bombs, and based on a monthly consumption of 75,000 tons, that meant 300,000 tons needed to be stockpiled for delivery. This was never met, despite Gen LeMay protesting in the most emphatic way possible. Both Arnold and LeMay were counting on a long and protracted build-up towards a war that would last well into 1946 but given that the total tonnage of bombs dropped by the B-29s between November 1944 and August 1945 was 157,502 tons, it is difficult to argue against the logic of limiting that total.

The initial target for the first raid against Japan was Tokyo and the strategy was to hit the manufacturing plants, oil depots and machine shops. Japan had raised aircraft production from 445 warplanes in 1930 to 1,181 in 1936, whereupon the aggressive war against China brought a surge in demand and in 1941 its industry turned out 5,088 aircraft. After Pearl Harbor, production increased rapidly, growing to 8,861 in 1942, to 16,692 in 1943 and to 28,180 in 1944, with high-quality manufacturing and some advanced and highly capable aircraft. These were flown by intensively prepared pilots, committed in a unique way to offer up their own lives rather than live in comfort under an occupation force.

After a series of training raids against Truk and other islands, the first B-29 raid from the Marianas was mounted on 24 November 1944. This force of 111 bombers was led by the 73rd Bombardment Wing, under Commanding General O'Donnell, piloting *Dauntless Dotty*. It was co-piloted by Maj Robert K. Morgan, pilot of the famous B-17F *Memphis Belle* – one of the first B-17s to complete 25 missions in Europe and the subject of several books and films. It was the first in a series of high-altitude, high-precision attacks that aimed to destroy the Japanese aircraft industry. In the event, only 88 of the aircraft were able to drop bombs and results were poor, partly because of bad weather over the target.

For several months, these high-altitude precision raids carried on but the results continued to be poor thanks to appalling bombing accuracy, technical problems, aircraft ditching at sea, pilots frustrated by an initial lack of escort fighters and a flawed strategy. Yet Gen Arnold sought results. In January 1945, he ordered LeMay to succeed Brig Gen Hansell, commander. Angered by the lack of performance, and after analyzing the Japanese industry, on 19 February LeMay issued a new directive calling for the bombing of the myriad small cottage industries that fed the major factories and assembly plants. LeMay chose to use incendiaries, rather than high explosives, to destroy the homes and the workspaces of those little companies, which were often situated in frail buildings around the outskirts of the main industrial cities. In doing this, LeMay was adopting the carpet-bombing strategy that had been used by Sir Arthur Harris, C-in-C of RAF Bomber Command during its critical years.

On the day LeMay issued his directive – which was to make him known as one of the greatest operational air commanders of the war – the US Marines landed on Iwo Jima after the B-24s of the 7th Air Force had pounded the island to rubble in 19 of the previous 20 days. A bloodbath ensued and lasted for four weeks before the island was taken. The landing strips laid down quickly after all Japanese resistance had been eliminated went on to provide emergency landing places for 2,400 B-29s between this date and the end of the war, arguably saving the lives of 25,000 crewmen who would have come down in the sea. Chief of Naval Operations Adm Ernest J. King later estimated that the lives saved were probably greater than the 4,900 lives lost taking the island.

LeMay wanted to protect the bombers and impose the greatest possible damage on the Japanese war machine. To do that, he wanted to bomb at night from lower altitude. By removing the defensive armament – the guns and 8,000 rounds of ammunition – he could add 3,200 lb to the bombload of a B-29. It was a big gamble, made all the more challenging because he did not get permission from Gen Arnold or the staffers in Washington. But it worked. The first attack on the night of 9/10 March had 279 bombers of the 325 that got airborne blast the urban area of Tokyo, burning out 267,000 buildings across almost 16 square miles and killing 83,000 people – the highest death toll of any single raid in history, including that from either of the two atom bombs.

Japanese night defences were almost non-existent and LeMay followed with further raids on Nagoya, Osaka and Kobe, also returning to Tokyo several times. The war was thus taken directly to the heart of Japan. As well as bombs, aircraft also dropped warning leaflets to people in the next target cities, urging them to flee. The effect on morale of even a single raid was immense and the fear engendered through such warnings of an impending attack created panic in some cities. There was a growing dissatisfaction with the war in general and the havoc it had brought upon the Japanese people. Secret negotiations therefore began via neutral countries, and the US State Department was already engaged in discussions preceding total surrender.

While the firestorm raids continued, LeMay maintained precision attacks as he turned towards the destruction of Japanese industry, achieving with the B-29 what had not been possible in Europe. Incendiary attacks had burned out up to 78 per cent of cities on a comprehensive list drawn up to meticulously disconnect the country from sustained economic survival. In addition, the 20th Air Force flew 1,528 mining sorties, sinking 800,000 tons of Japanese shipping and reducing the total remaining afloat to a mere 1.5 million tons. By August, industry was operating at less than 25 per cent efficiency.

The Japanese city of Osaka after a firestorm raid which destroyed large parts of the populated sector and commercial area. USAF

Lessons from the bombing raids on Germany informed decisions regarding the type of explosives and the mix of munitions to use against the Japanese cities and adjacent factories. Unlike German industry, there had been no dispersal of manufacturing and assembly plants. What's more, LeMay chose to significantly expand the US production of napalm, a jelly-based product that stuck to anything it touched and burned with a fierce intensity. Napalm production increased from 500,000 lb in 1943 to almost 4,000 tons a year later and that, high explosives and cluster bombs were the devices of choice when it came to bombing-up the B-29s.

The ferocity and scale of the bombing offensive on Japan was greater than that on German cities and adopted a different policy. The exactitude with which the raids were planned, the detailed selection of explosives, bombs, mines and incendiaries defined by the specific material structures on individual targets, was matched only by the forensic analysis carried out by LeMay's staff – military personnel and civilian scientists, engineers and statisticians. They all worked out in great detail the effects of these various war loads. They also studied the results obtained through photographic reconnaissance and bomb damage assessment studies that continued after the war, when these specialists could get in and do the ground work, piecing together the overall effect of this kind of aerial warfare.

Nothing like this had been done before. New rules for warfare were being written. Among the specialists who provided LeMay with detailed analytical reports was Robert S. McNamara, who was from 1961 until 1968 the US Secretary of Defense. He took his slide rules, statistics and calculations to war again – over Vietnam – during that decade. McNamara came to regret the role he had played in utilizing massive air power on such a colossal scale – so great in fact that the quantity of bomb tonnage dropped on Vietnam – 2 million tons – exceeded the total dropped by all the belligerent powers in both the world wars.

THE ATOM BOMB

There was one final chapter to the story of aerial warfare in the period 1930–45. This was the development of the atomic bomb, which had been made possible by the scientific exploration of the constituents of an atom during the 1930s – a study in which Britain's major universities in Oxford and Cambridge came to play a significant role. It promised a bomb so powerful that it could revolutionize warfare, not only from the air but also on the land and at sea. It came too late to be used against the Germans, but this single device would now open possibilities of unimaginable destruction and death. As a point of interest, the Nazis had also been researching the atom bomb, as had the Japanese, without getting very far.

On 6 August 1945, a single B-29 piloted by Col Paul W. Tibbets, Jr, dropped one atomic bomb on the city of Hiroshima. This device had been developed with the help of British and German scientists, the latter having fled Nazi Germany before the war. It destroyed 4.7 square miles of the city. It was followed three days later by a second bomb, dropped on Nagasaki. On the same day, the Soviet Union invaded Manchuria and began a dash down towards the Kuril Islands and Japanese territory.

On 10 August, the Japanese decided that they could not go on and formally declared acceptance of the surrender terms offered, the formal ceremony coming in Tokyo Bay aboard the USS *Missouri* on 2 September. The contribution of the B-29 was summed up by Japan's Prince Konoye when he said that 'the determination to make peace was the prolonged bombing by the B-29s'. His sentiment was endorsed by Premier Suzuki, who said that 'on the basis of the B-29s alone I was convinced that Japan should sue for peace'. For the first time in history, a war of immense magnitude had been brought to an end by the use of air power.

A temple monument stands alone amid the devastation of Nagasaki after the dropping of the second atomic bomb on 9 August 1945, heralding a new era in aerial warfare from which there was no turning back. USAF

A LESSON FROM HISTORY

Before the two atomic bombs were used against Hiroshima and Nagasaki, the firestorm raids on Japanese cities had killed at least 650,000–900,000 people. Added to those were the estimated 130,000–225,000 killed, or who eventually died, from the effects of the atomic bombs.

The long history of aerial warfare, which arguably began in 1914, had within little more than 30 years developed into the most destructive weapon devised by science. Soon after the war was over, atomic bombs would lead to thermonuclear bombs – any one of which could have the explosive yield of 1,000 Hiroshima bombs, or ten times the explosive yield of all the bombs dropped in history. And from two bombs dropped on the Japanese cities in 1945 would grow an arsenal of more than 60,000 such weapons at the peak years in the 1960s. And we have them today, fewer in number but greater in proliferation.

Nuclear weapons are implausible devices for use in war and can only exist as instruments of retribution, but it is a signal reminder of how we, as humans, justify our actions by re-identifying government departments for 'war' as departments for 'defence', a dangerous slide towards the acceptability of waging conflict just to protect ourselves. For it is from there only a very small step to including the use of nuclear weapons in our arsenals, not as a deterrent but as just another type of bomb. From that assumption, it is very easy to deploy them in our 'defence' – and use them again. It would be ironic if the instrument that so many claimed had ended the greatest and most destructive conflict in history – one in which more than 55 million people perished – was next employed to start another war, one in which the whole of humanity may find itself in a new Stone Age.

TOTAL NUMBER OF MILITARY AIRCRAFT PRODUCED BY EACH COUNTRY 1939–45

Country	1939	1940	1941	1942	1943	1944	1945	TOTAL
UK	7,940	15,049	20,094	23,672	26,263	26,461	12,070	131,549
USA	2,141	6,068	18,466	46,907	84,853	96,270	45,852	300,557
USSR	10,382	10,565	15,737	25,436	34,900	40,300	20,900	158,220
Germany	1,928	7,829	9,422	12,822	20,599	35,076	7,052	94,622
Japan	4,467	4,768	5,088	8,861	16,693	28,180	8,263	76,320
TOTAL	26,858	44,279	68,807	117,698	183,308	226,287	94,137	761,374

Note:

1. All French production was subsumed into the German output since they were an occupied country working for Germany. As for Italy, they had exceptionally low output and used a lot of aircraft procured from Germany.

2. The figures quoted here are approximate and do not include production of civilian aircraft requisitioned for military service for roles such as transport and training.

Index